Dynastic Dee

Hunt scenes in the funerary imagery of the Achaemenid Eastern Mediterranean

Alessandro Poggio

BAR INTERNATIONAL SERIES 2974 | 2020

BAR
PUBLISHING

Published in 2020 by
BAR Publishing, Oxford

BAR International Series 2974

Dynastic Deeds

ISBN 978 1 4073 5638 9 paperback
ISBN 978 1 4073 5466 8 e-format

DOI https://doi.org/10.30861/9781407356389

COVER IMAGE *Detail of the lion hunt on the Alexander Sarcophagus from Sidon. Istanbul, Archaeological Museum 370. Photo: Istanbul, Archaeological Museum.*

BAR
PUBLISHING

BAR titles are available from:

BAR Publishing
122 Banbury Rd, Oxford, OX2 7BP, UK
EMAIL info@barpublishing.com
PHONE +44 (0)1865 310431
FAX +44 (0)1865 316916
www.barpublishing.com

Of Related Interest

Art et archéologie du Proche-Orient hellénistique et romain: les circulations artistiques entre Orient et Occident, volume 2
Actes de la journée d'études du 29 mai 2018, Institut Catholique de Paris
Edited by Caroline Arnould-Béhar and Véronique Vassal

Oxford, BAR Publishing, 2019 BAR International Series **2934**

Art et archéologie du Proche-Orient hellénistique et romain
Les circulations artistiques entre Orient et Occident: Actes de la journée d'études du 11 mai 2017, Institut Catholique de Paris
Edited by Caroline Arnould-Béhar and Véronique Vassal

Oxford, BAR Publishing, 2018 BAR International Series **2897**

Mortuary Practice in Ancient Iran from the Achaemenid to the Sasanian Period
Mahdokht Farjamirad

Oxford, BAR Publishing, 2015 BAR International Series **2747**

Die Funktion und Bedeutung der Reiter-und Pferdeführerdarstellungen auf attischen Grab- und Weihreliefs des 5. und 4. Jhs. v. Chr.
Angelos Tillios

Oxford, BAR Publishing, 2010 BAR International Series **2137**

Acknowledgments

This book grew out of my PhD dissertation which I presented at the Scuola Normale Superiore in 2011. I am much indebted to this institution and its community, which provided the ideal environment both in terms of exchange of ideas and logistic and financial assistance to conduct this research.

My interest in the artistic and cultural dynamics in the Eastern Mediterranean started while I was a graduate student at the Scuola Normale Superiore and the University of Pisa, where I met a number of inspiring mentors.

This book and its methodological approach owes much to Salvatore Settis, who has constantly followed my research interests since the very first year of my university studies and has supported this work throughout with invaluable advice and encouragement. I am deeply indebted to him.

Attending seminars conducted by Paul Zanker was an invaluable help. I am grateful to him for the precious support and the stimuli he provided in looking at the monuments concerned and in addressing new research questions.

I would like to offer my special thanks to Stefania Mazzoni who – first at the University of Pisa, then from the University of Florence – has constantly followed my work with insightful comments and advice that crossed the borders between disciplines.

An important part of this research was nourished by numerous and prolonged stays in Turkey.

Since my very first stay in Turkey the Deutsches Archäologisches Institut – Abteilung Istanbul has been a crucial reference point with its lively community and helpful staff, as well as its precious library and photographic archive. My very great appreciation is extended to the director, Felix Pirson, who has constantly offered the best conditions in which to pursue my research and who has always supported my work with valuable comments.

I am grateful to the Ministry of Foreign Affairs and International Cooperation of the Italian Republic and the Ministry of Foreign Affairs of the Republic of Turkey for a useful studentship in Antalya in 2008.

I am likewise very grateful to the Koç University Research Center for Anatolian Civilizations, its former director Scott Redford, the 2010/11 fellow community and the entire staff for their support while I was the recipient of a Junior Fellowship.

The TÜBİTAK (Türkiye Bilimsel ve Teknolojik Araştirma Kurumu / Scientific and Technological Research Council of Turkey) granted me a post-doctoral fellowship in the period 2011/12, generously supported and supervised by Christine Özgan, director of the Archaeology Department at the Mimar Sinan Fine Arts University, to whom I am very grateful.

I am also grateful to Anna Lucia D'Agata and Giovanni Salmeri for including me in the team of the Cilicia Survey Project and the Misis Höyük Excavation Project active at Misis/Mopsouestia under the auspices of the University of Pisa and the CNR (Consiglio Nazionale delle Ricerche / National Research Council) of Rome. During my visits to Turkey I also benefitted from the warm welcome of many missions that offered their help by showing me their results: I would like to thank the late Thomas Marksteiner and Martin Seyer (Limyra), Jacques des Courtils and Laurence Cavalier (Xanthos and Letoon), Francesco D'Andria (Hierapolis of Phrygia), Françoise and Geoffrey Summers (Kerkenes Dağ), Anacleto D'Agostino and Valentina Orsi (Uşaklı Höyük), Volkmar von Graeve and Philipp Niewöhner (Miletus) and Alessandra Ricci (Küçükyalı, Istanbul).

Moreover, my thanks are due to the Ministry of Culture and Tourism of the Republic of Turkey and the Istanbul Archaeological Museums, in particular the former director Zeynep Sevim Kızıltan and Şehrazat Karagöz, for allowing me to study the collection in Istanbul.

Among the people I met during my stays in Turkey, I mention with gratitude Gianluca Alberini and Elena Schenone, Oya Dinler, Jeffrey Michael Featherstone, Emanuele Fiorilli and Oktavia Brugger, Nicolas Gailhard, Katja Piesker, Bärbel Ruhl, Zsolt Simon, Lucienne Thys-Şenocak, Inge Uytterhoeven and Alexandra Wirsching.

Clemente Marconi's research was very important in defining the theoretical framework of this book, and I am much indebted to him.

I am grateful to Francesco de Angelis for his invaluable and generous suggestions on my research.

During my post-doctoral fellowship at the Scuola Normale Superiore I received useful advice on my work from Gianfranco Adornato, whom I also thank for giving me the opportunity to present some preliminary results in various conferences.

At the Scuola Normale Superiore I benefitted from discussions of certain methodological issues of the present work with Howard Burns, the late Maria Monica Donato and Massimo Ferretti.

More recently, my research has found a fruitful environment at the IMT School for Advanced Studies Lucca: I am grateful to Maria Luisa Catoni for offering her constant support in the final stage of this work and to all my colleagues at "LYNX – Center for the interdisciplinary Analysis of Images".

My collaboration with Lorenzo Lazzarini has stimulated many reflections on the use and circulation of marble: my special thanks are due to him for his inspiring comments and advice. My study on the marbles used in Anatolia has been facilitated by the support of the LAMA (Laboratorio di Analisi dei Materiali Antichi / Laboratory of Ancient Material Analysis) of the IUAV University of Venice; I thank the director Fabrizio Antonelli.

Particular attention towards my research interests has been shown by Massimo Osanna, whom I thank for the stimulating exchanges of ideas.

Among the different institutions that supported my work I would like to mention the École Normale Supérieure in Paris, the Warburg Institute in London and the American Academy in Rome; as to the latter, I am particularly grateful to the former director, Carmela Vircillo Franklin, and the staff of the library. I am indebted to the Getty Research Institute and the Getty Museum at the Villa for having fostered my work on cultural interactions in the Eastern Mediterranean during a residential scholarship within the programme "The Classical World in Context: Persia": in particular I thank Thomas W. Gaehtgens, Timothy Potts, Jeffrey Spiers, A. Alexa Sekyra and the entire staff for their effective support. During my stay in Los Angeles I was also able to attend the stimulating environment at UCLA and UCI: I extend my appreciation to Giorgio Buccellati and Marilyn Kelly-Buccellati, Touraj Daryaee, Sarah Morris, Ali Mousavi and Rahim Shayegan for their warm welcome.

Moreover, my research has benefited from a fruitful exchange of ideas with many scholars: I would like to thank Joan Aruz, Judith M. Barringer, the late Sonia Bellan, Marilina Betrò, Pierre Briant, Domitilla Campanile, Olivier Casabonne, Faya Causey, Stefano de Martino, Maria Luisa Doglio, Catherine Draycott, Jaś Elsner, Margherita Facella, Lucia Faedo, Andreas Furtwängler, Andrea Giardina, Christopher H. Hallett, Ömür Harmanşah, the late Christine Hellmann, Olivier Henry, Antonio Invernizzi, Bruno Jacobs, Kenneth Lapatin, Alice Landskron, Bruce Lincoln, Yannick Lintz, Mario Liverani, John Ma, Consuelo Manetta, Jake Nabel, Olga Palagia, Marinella Pasquinucci, Francis Prost, Robert Rollinger, Ilaria Romeo, David Scahill, Bert Smith, Rolf Strootman, Tasos Tanoulas and Recai Tekoğlu.

For their willingness to facilitate my work I am very grateful to Ian Jenkins and the curatorial staff of the Department of Greece and Rome at the British Museum; to Kurt Gschwantler, Alfred Bernhard-Walcher, Georg Plattner and Karoline Zhuber-Okrog at the Antikensammlung of the Kunsthistorisches Museum of Vienna; to Marielle Pic, Marianne Cotty and Mahmoud Alassi of the Musée du Louvre; to Mathilde Avisseau-Broustet at the Bibliothèque nationale de France; to Sean Hemingway and Joan Mertens at the Metropolitan Museum of Art.

For their kind assistance in providing the images and related permits for publication I thank Sir John Boardman, William A.P. Childs, Mark B. Garrison, Vassos Karageorgis, Kitan Kitanov, Mario Iozzo, Marion Meyer, Bruno Overlaet, Birte Poulsen, Chrysoula Paliadeli, Brian Rose, Joseph Wiesehöfer, the photo archive and the Pergamonarchiv at the DAI Istanbul, the Istanbul Archaeological Museums, the Oriental Institute of the University of Chicago, the National Museum of Denmark and the *Museo Archeologico Nazionale di Napoli*.

I am also grateful to Angela Arnone for her helpful collaboration in the translation of this volume.

Among friends and colleagues I would also like to thank Anna Anguissola, Giorgio Bacci, Marianna Castiglione, Gabriella Cirucci, Floriana Conte, Sevgi Doğan, Federico D'Onofrio, Eva Falaschi, Massimiliano Grava, Fabio Guidetti, Marina Haiduk, Maria Lidova, Monia Manescalchi, Melissa Ricetti, Daniele Rivoletti and Anka Ziefer.

Finally, I would like to thank my family for their enthusiastic support and invaluable encouragement throughout my studies.

This work is dedicated to Federica.

Pisa/Lucca/Firenze, December 2019

Figure 1. (following page) Statue of a panther from the Mausoleum of Halicarnassus, Sculpture 1095. London, British Museum 1857,1220.256. © Trustees of the British Museum.

Table of contents

List of Illustrations

Figure 2. (following page) The main mounted hunter on the long side of the Satrap Sarcophagus. Istanbul, Archaeological Museum 367. D-DAI-IST-78-139 (Photo: W. Schiele 1978).

Introduction

The hunt and power

The hunt and power are an enduring pair that pervades the entire course of history, from antiquity up to our contemporary societies. For instance, in 2009 a debate in the French press arose about the possibility of bringing back the presidential hunts, defining this practice as "the most visible expression of monarchical survival"[1]. Indeed, the political meaning of hunting is as old as the first manifestations of complex societies, as shown by the lion hunt stele from the "first city" of Uruk (fourth millennium BC).[2]

The investigation of the political values of hunting, notably in connection with power, offers the possibility of tracing a long-honoured tradition in antiquity: however, there are cultural contexts that have not been investigated from this perspective yet, i.e. the Eastern Mediterranean between the end of the fifth and the last decades of the fourth centuries BC. Here, indeed, images of the hunt, more precisely, multiple-quarry hunt images, built around the combination of prey of different species, were generally part of the self-representation of power. In this research I identify the multiple-quarry hunt as the main hunt iconography associated with rulers in the Eastern Mediterranean of this period, although it was not the only hunting iconography used at this time (Fig. 2).

A new transregional approach

In this book the wide area of the Eastern Mediterranean between the end of the fifth and the last decades of the fourth centuries BC is considered from a transregional perspective for the first time: here I discuss the "Eastern Mediterranean" to include the southern coast of Anatolia and the Levant, notably ancient Caria and Lycia in present-day Turkey, and ancient Phoenicia in present-day Lebanon (Fig. 3).

The present research thus aims to pinpoint common features across this wide area by considering regional peculiarities. The multiple-quarry hunt images – in my opinion – are one of the key elements to interpreting this cultural area from a unified perspective, as I shall try to demonstrate in this book.

Between the fifth and the fourth centuries BC the area of the Eastern Mediterranean under consideration here was politically part of the Persian Achaemenid Empire, but the Greek world exerted a significant cultural impact on it. For this reason, the regions belonging to this vast area have traditionally been considered a contact zone between the Persian and the Greek worlds.[3] While the present research will certainly consider the impact of the two important protagonists of that time, the Persian and the Greek worlds, the reality is more complex than such a "black and white" picture. In fact, the Eastern Mediterranean between the fifth and the fourth centuries BC developed a well-defined profile that arose out of its "internal" dynamics, and which this book will attempt to outline and consider in itself for the first time. By outlining local specificities it will be possible to overturn the widespread perception of "influence" from the Persian and Greek worlds. Of course the starting point of the present work is the research on the history and art of the single regions concerned here,[4] but the Eastern Mediterranean under Persian Achaemenid rule will be analysed rather as an interconnected area through the analysis of the "circulation of materials, people, and ideas" between the concerned regions.[5] Methodologically speaking, this will provide a wider and more colourful picture by outlining different kinds of contact, connecting stories which have been unconnected up until now, and reconstructing phenomena from a well-rounded perspective.

While this wide outlook uses the Eastern Mediterranean as the geographical reference of the research, the chronological coordinate is offered by a diachronic approach in which multiple-quarry hunt representations are analysed in the Bronze and Iron Ages. The combination of these coordinates that take into account preceding and contemporary cultural horizons will provide a reliable picture of continuity and novelty in the fifth to fourth centuries BC in southern Anatolia and the Levant.

Finally, moving from multiple-quarry hunt representations, this book intends to delineate a more complex picture of the fifth to fourth centuries BC Eastern Mediterranean: by considering a wide range of visual evidence with multiple-quarry hunts, this research will explore the artistic, cultural and social features of the concerned area.

By doing so, this study aims at overcoming the predictable and universalistic statement of the political values of hunting images in order to assess their meanings in this specific cultural and political context.

[1] "Longtemps, les chasses présidentielles furent l'un des plus spectaculaires lieux de pouvoir français. Et sans doute aussi la plus visible traduction de survivances monarchiques" (R. Bacqué, *Scénes de chasses présidentielles*, in «Le Monde», 18.12.2009). The translation from French is mine.

[2] *RAVA* V: 236; Groenewegen-Frankfort 1978: 152–3; Börker-Klähn 1982: 113–4, no. 1. On Uruk see Liverani 2006.

[3] See, for instance, Asheri 1983.

[4] Caria: Henry 2013. Lycia: Hoff 2017; Kolb 2018. Phoenicia: Martin 2017.

[5] Quotation from DaCosta Kaufmann, Dossin and Joyeux-Prunel 2016: 2. For overland mobility in the Persian Achaemenid Empire, see Colburn 2013.

Figure 3. Map of the Persian Achaemenid Empire with the main sites and regions mentioned in the text. The original location of the dynastic monuments considered in the present study: 1 – the Mausoleum of Halicarnassus; 2 – the Nereid Monument of Xanthos; 3 – the Heroon of Trysa; 4 – the Heroon of Limyra; 5 – the Sarcophagi of Sidon. Modified after Wiesehöfer 2001: 6. Courtesy of J. Wiesehöfer.

The visual evidence under examination

Thanks to the tools offered by semiotics and social studies, this book will analyse renowned monuments from the south-western coast of Anatolia, such as the Mausoleum of Halicarnassus and the Nereid Monument of Xanthos, but also the sarcophagi from the Phoenician city of Sidon, which have the hunt as one of the main themes of their lavish decoration.

In support of the transregional perspective proposed here, it is important to consider that against a number of regional peculiarities, these tombs have many common features. They appeared on the coastal regions of the western part of the Persian Achaemenid Empire, mostly dating back to the fourth century BC. On the basis of topographical context, architectural proportions, materials, craftsmanship, and iconography they can be attributed to the local rulers who exerted their power within the wider frame of the Persian Achaemenid Empire, "a range of figures with varying levels of local power" whom scholars normally define as "dynasts", a shorthand that I shall maintain.[6]

A further element shared by these tombs that has drawn my attention is the nearly constant presence of a specific hunting iconography, the aforementioned multiple-quarry hunt. This makes the multiple-quarry hunt iconography well-connected to dynastic power.

Circulation of materials, people, and ideas

My investigation of multiple-quarry hunt images across different regions of the Eastern Mediterranean allows exploration of the mechanisms that made the spread of this iconography possible. In the study of the western part of the Persian Achaemenid Empire between the fifth and the fourth century BC, circulation of materials, people, and ideas appears as the connecting threads across the multiple regional horizons of the Mediterranean.[7]

Current scholarship has been engaged mainly with in-depth stylistic analyses of the above-mentioned dynastic monuments, correctly recognising the role of Greek or Greek-trained artists who worked at meeting the demands of the local dynasts. The present research will take into account these studies but it will additionally focus on connectivity dynamics affecting the regions of the dynastic monuments. Political and cultural processes of interaction will be investigated, and

[6] Draycott 2007: 103–4. The term "dynast" appears as the most inclusive, although the title of "king" or the claim to "kingship" is attested for the majority of the rulers concerned in the present study. For discussion on royal titles, see Hornblower 1982: 55–62 (for Caria); Keen 2002: 273–7 (for Lycia); Woolmer 2017: 57–62 (for Phoenicia).

[7] On the attention to the regional horizons, see Horden and Purcell 2000.

particular attention will be devoted to connectivity issues related to art. My interest here is to highlight the phenomenon of the mobility of artists, patterns, and materials in order to stress issues that are mostly unconsidered.

For instance, the study of the material dimension of the evidence under examination is particularly promising. In the present study I underline that the making of these dynastic tombs – as shown by macroscopic observations and archaeometric analyses of the materials – marked a growing use of white marble, a costly and prestigious material from the Aegean basin that allowed high quality works: this fact implied a long-distance movement of this material eastwards, along the coasts of southern Anatolia and the Levant, alongside with the mobility of artists and artistic patterns. The presence of such a long-distance movement of marble has not received enough attention, although it was already rooted in previous phases, as shown by recent archaeometric analyses.[8]

The approach adopted here is also inspired by the current interest in ecology and the growing role of geography in providing spatial dimension to human history: routes, modes of circulation, and the use of natural resources such as marble are part of a complex discourse aimed at a better understanding of artistic and cultural phenomena.

The multiple-quarry hunt: *status quaestionis*

Hunting representations from the coastal areas of Anatolia and Phoenicia have been investigated *per se* only with reference to a particular kind of hunt, the boar hunt.[9] Eastern Mediterranean images of multiple-quarry hunts and their values, instead, have never been at the centre of specific research.

B. Tripodi was the first to elaborate a specific definition of the multiple-quarry hunt iconography in his 1991 article.[10] Tripodi focuses his study on the hunting frieze of the Macedonian royal tomb in Vergina. Tracing back similarities to the hunting representations on our dynastic monuments, he considers the Macedonian frieze as a result of the use of "eastern" iconographic patterns.

M.C. Miller, instead, investigated the multiple-quarry hunt further in 2003 by moving from a different artefact, the decorated squat lekythos found in modern Kerch (Crimea) and signed by the Athenian artist Xenophantos. The scholar reaffirmed that such iconography belonged to the Persian Achaemenid context, in particular to the western part of this empire.[11]

These two articles are the most extensive pieces of research on multiple-quarry hunts, but they focus on visual sources from Macedonia and the Black Sea. This book, instead, focuses on the area that according to these scholars provided the model for the Vergina frieze and the lekythos from Kerch by moving from the observation – as already underlined – that the multiple-quarry hunt was a widely shared iconography among the dynastic tombs of the Eastern Mediterranean under Persian Achaemenid rule.

In this book the multiple-quarry hunt iconography is understood to be the combination of prey of different species in a single scene, or within hunting episodes occupying portions of the same figurative field or at least parts of the same figurative programme. This definition takes Tripodi and Miller's studies as a starting point, but enlarges their definitions in two directions: first, the temporality of the scenes is wider, since it is considered that the various hunts are not necessarily contemporary; second, since the fragmentation of the figurative programmes of these tombs should be avoided, these are interpreted as a whole, therefore different hunting scenes on different parts of the monuments are here considered together.

In this book I address a number of questions: Why was this iconography so popular among the dynasts of the Eastern Mediterranean? Is it possible to assign more specific meanings to this iconography? What kind of artistic and social implications can be inferred by the widespread use of this iconography along the shores of the Eastern Mediterranean? These questions have never been substantially addressed within this context.

Visual evidence: transmediality

Although I am aware that a study of the hunt in antiquity can be carried out using different methodologies and tools such as visual and literary representations, philosophical approaches, juridical perspectives or zooarchaeological analyses, I am interested here mostly in visual evidence.[12] I will explore how multiple-quarry hunting representations – within a rich set of images – conveyed a specific message of power in a corpus of tombs that can be attributed to Eastern Mediterranean dynastic figures ruling under Persian Achaemenid rule.

However, in order to better understand the contexts in which the figurative programmes under examination were produced, I will take into account a wide range of evidence, mainly figurative and textual: different categories of artefacts bearing multiple-quarry hunt images, from monumental decoration to portable objects such as seals, are rigorously considered within their contexts of production in order to interpret the imagery they convey.[13]

Sculpture, in particular those of marble and limestone reliefs, emerge as the main medium of the multiple-quarry

[8] Lazzarini and Marconi 2014; Poggio 2018c.

[9] Nollé 2001; Borchhardt and Bleibtreu 2008.

[10] "[...] la rappresentazione di una caccia condotta contemporaneamente da più cacciatori a più animali di specie diverse" (Tripodi 1991: 153).

[11] Miller 2003: 30.

[12] For a broad range of issues related to the hunt in different contexts, see Sidéra 2006; Trinquier and Vendries 2009.

[13] I use the term "seal" instead of "gem" following J.E. Gates' observations (Gates 2002: 109–10).

hunts of the Eastern Mediterranean: primarily, the images on the dynastic tombs of the Eastern Mediterranean, and also those on western Anatolian funerary evidence of smaller scale such as the sarcophagi in Lycia, the so-called Graeco-Persian stelae and the Çan Sarcophagus, all dating from the fifth and fourth centuries BC. The depiction of different prey can be traced back to an even smaller scale in Graeco-Persian tabloid glyptic. This means that the iconography of the multiple-quarry hunt was shared not only across different geographical areas but also various media in the same period. In addition, other pieces of evidence that do not belong to the Eastern Mediterranean attest to the use of this iconography elsewhere and in other media. The fourth-century BC lekythos by Xenophantos is the most striking depiction of multiple-quarry hunt on decorated pottery. Wall painting is not excluded since the famous Macedonian Tomb II of the royal tumulus in Vergina and the Thracian tomb of Alexandrovo confirm the role of this iconography in funerary contexts.

From the present research thus it emerges that one of the features of the multiple-quarry hunt is its transmediality.[14] Political and social values, in other words, are conveyed by different media, thus this research will take into account a translational dynamic in order to investigate the multimedial reception of the multiple-quarry hunt iconography and its meaning.

Literary sources

The literary sources used in this book are a medium that requires a specific caveat. Notably, this study makes use of mostly Greek literary sources, which – as underlined by P. Briant – emerge both as crucial and problematic with reference to the Persian Achaemenid Empire.[15] Although they provide precious information that would not be available otherwise, these sources are blamed for offering an external perspective of this topic.[16] This argument was emphasised after the 1970s, when postcolonialism determined criticism of the hellenocentric perspective on the Achaemenid Empire.[17] In parallel, increasing attention to Persian administrative documents, such as monumental inscriptions and archival records, emerged.[18] A further critical element is that many contemporary Greek sources have been transmitted by later authors such as Plutarch.[19] However, a careful use of Greek literary sources is still preferable to their aprioristic rejection.[20] In addition, in the context of this research the label "Greek" appears vague: undoubtedly, Greeks from Ionia and Caria, regions belonging to western Anatolia and therefore parts of the Persian Achaemenid Empire, had a different perspective of the situation. Scholarly debate on fourth-century BC writers has emphasised the importance of authors of *Persica* such as Ctesias of Cnidus, who served also as a physician at the Persian court, Deinon (perhaps from Colophon) and Heracleides of Cyme.[21] Secondly, considerations on personal experience also play an important role. The Athenian Xenophon, living between the second half of the fifth century BC and the first half of the fourth, wrote the *Cyropaedia* with moralistic intents, but he had first-hand contacts with the Persian world: he travelled through Anatolia and the Near East to Cunaxa, about 80 km away from Babylon, taking part in the Spartan expedition organised by the satrap of western Anatolia, Cyrus the Younger, against the Great King. Finally, this set of observations on Greek authors writing about the Persian world reveals that their idea of the Persian Achaemenid Empire might have been shaped by the Eastern Mediterranean itself, since the dynastic societies described in the present research had to be the most immediate interface of the Persian world from the Greek perspective. Therefore, Greek literary sources are another fundamental medium to investigate the role of multiple-quarry hunt in the discourse of power in the Eastern Mediterranean.

Methodological reference studies

The rich reflection on hunting in the Greek and Roman worlds developed from the second half of the nineteenth century onwards.[22] The success of this theme might be explained through a wide range of reasons: the development of a reflection on this activity in different periods of the Graeco-Roman world thanks to the literary genre of *Cynegetica*; the possibility of a fruitful interplay between literary and archaeological sources; the study of representations and actual techniques and the political value of this activity. The hunting theme was affected by the renovation of classical studies promoted since 1970s by French scholars, who applied the study of imagery in the Greek *polis* – especially on Greek vases – and the tools of historical anthropology through semiotic approaches. A. Schnapp, in particular, investigated social aspects in the world of hunting through Greek imagery, a research culminated in the volume entitled *Le chasseur et la cité*.[23] In his wake it is worth mentioning J.M. Barringer's work, which considers hunting images in Greek vase painting as a source of detecting social values.[24] All these studies will be taken into account since the methods they developed will be useful to explore the socio-historical dimension of the dynastic multiple-quarry hunts. Already J. Fornasier has explored hunting representations in our

---

[14] "Transmedial phenomena here refer to those artistic forms or contents that are shared by or spread across various media [...]. Transmediality does not presuppose a source medium from which certain patterns are transferred to another" (Wolf 2016: 104–5).

[15] For the sources of Persian history, see Briant 1996: 14–19.

[16] Lenfant 2011; Morgan 2016. For information conveyed by literary sources and archaeological evidence, see the case of Sardis (Dusinberre 1999).

[17] See also Briant 1996: 632–3; Sancisi-Weerdenburg 1987.

[18] Lenfant 2011: 6–7; Poggio 2018b. See also Jacobs, Henkelman and Stolper 2017.

[19] On Plutarch and the sources on Persia, see Almagor 2018.

[20] See also Briant 1982: 491–506.

[21] On *Persica*, see Stevenson 1997. On these authors, see also Lenfant 2009 and Waters 2017.

[22] See the bibliographical list in Buchholz, Jöhrens and Maull 1973: 191–5. See now Santillo Frizell 2004; Kalof 2007; Fögen and Thomas 2017.

[23] Schnapp 1979a; 1979b; Schmitt Pantel and Schnapp 1982; Schnapp 1997. For the banquet see Schmitt Pantel 1992.

[24] Barringer 2001.

contexts between the sixth and the fourth centuries BC, moving from the Greek world and considering Anatolia and the Levant as contact zones.[25] As already stated, the present research intends to go further: recognising the multiple-quarry hunt as the preferred iconography for dynastic self-representation, this book aims at exploring artistic and social dynamics moving precisely from those societies and adopting – as much as possible – an "Eastern Mediterranean perspective".

Socio-political issues

The political values of hunting have been investigated also for Persia and Macedonia, the two major monarchical powers of that time.[26] Of particular importance for visual studies has been the study of the hunting frieze of Vergina as a visual expression of the Macedonian kingship and Macedonian social values.[27] Court studies, which have developed extensively in recent years both on the ancient and the modern sides, have provided useful methodological tools for the present research.[28] Representations of the court in all its components – dynast and family, officials and servants – had a precise function in the celebratory imagery of funerary monuments from our area: a compact family nucleus, linked to aspects of succession, dignitaries respecting dynastic authority and efficient servants contributed to the creation of positive images of the courts, the core for the different local potentates of the Eastern Mediterranean.

N. Elias's sociological research based on the court of the Sun King, Louis XIV of France, interpreted court etiquette as an instrument of domination: complex rules for ceremonial protocol regulated the tensions and rivalries within the court.[29] This model was well received but it also attracted criticism, notably for the image of an elite, powerless against an omnipotent sovereign.[30] Nevertheless, bearing in mind the necessary caveats, at a methodological level the Elias model is still fundamental for approaching those ancient societies characterised by a strongly hierarchical structure, as was the Persian case and, on a smaller scale, the Eastern Mediterranean dynastic societies.[31] Hunting images offer an effective tool to investigate court dynamics, as recent studies on the political meaning of the hunt in the European courts of the modern age have demonstrated.[32] Eastern Mediterranean representations with crowded hunting teams are not an exception. In the present research whether the visual organisation of the participants can reveal details of the organisation of the dynastic courts and the management of power will be investigated.

Moreover, the emergence of a favoured theme for the dynastic tombs – the multiple-quarry hunt – is investigated for the first time from a socio-historical perspective not only within the single courts but also within a wider dynamic of the Eastern Mediterranean in the Persian Achaemenid period. In particular, this research will outline how – in combination with connectivity issues – a dynamic of competition and emulation among rulers favoured shared artistic processes across different regions of the Eastern Mediterranean.[33]

The present work addresses a wide range of issues from different disciplines, such as Persian and Classical studies, but also Anatolian and Levantine art and history. It encompasses themes related to art and archaeology, but also social and political history, notably in connection with hunting. By doing so, the present research underscores the importance of the dynastic Eastern Mediterranean in the creation of an enduring visual language of power, contributing to shed light on a still underestimated chapter of the hunt in antiquity.

Outline of chapters

The first two chapters are focused on the historical, cultural and artistic context of the present research. Chapter One analyses the Eastern Mediterranean under Persian rule from different perspectives. After introducing the role played by this area in the Persian Achaemenid Empire, this chapter sheds light on those political and cultural dynamics – usually not considered – that interconnected this broad area. Finally, the concept of Graeco-Persian art is explored and reassessed in order to elucidate advantages and limitations of such a label.

Chapter Two introduces on a regional basis the corpus of materials at the core of this work, which are the dynastic funerary monuments from the fifth- and fourth-century BC Eastern Mediterranean. I consider each monument as a whole and – when possible – its role as a landmark. The multiple-quarry hunt depictions I analyse are reliefs that are part of wider figurative programmes and must be considered within them. In addition, this chapter proposes a comparison among these tombs by taking into account different aspects – architecture, topography, display and imagery – in order to outline similarities and differences. Finally, issues such as materials, artists and workshop practices will be taken into account.

The results of this first part of the research provide new observations on the artistic and cultural processes in the Eastern Mediterranean under Persian rule. These data constitute the necessary background for the in-depth analysis of multiple-quarry iconography in the following three chapters.

[25] Fornasier 2001: 231–57.
[26] Seyer 2007.
[27] Cohen 2010; Franks 2012.
[28] For antiquity, see Spawforth 2007a (with a mention of the lesser courts in the Persian Achaemenid Empire in Spawforth 2007b: 92); Strootman 2014; Erskine, Llewellyn-Jones and Wallace 2017. More focused on the Persian court are Jacobs and Rollinger 2010; Llewellyn-Jones 2013. For modern age, see Duindam, Artan and Kunt 2011.
[29] Elias 1983.
[30] Duindam 2011: 5–9.
[31] See Brosius 2007: 17–9.
[32] Merlotti 2017; Barberi Squarotti, Colturato and Goria 2018.
[33] On the role of competition see also Zanker 1988: ch. 1.

Chapter Three intends to explore the artistic roots of the single regional horizons within the wide area under research here. It surveys the presence and the role of earlier multiple-quarry hunting representations in order to detect the previous traditions in this area and in the ancient Near East. Moreover, it investigates the contemporary hunting iconography in Persian and Greek contexts, since these provide reference horizons for Eastern Mediterranean art of the fifth and fourth centuries BC.

Chapter Four considers in detail the iconographic and iconological features of multiple-quarry hunts on dynastic tombs, including also other typologies of monuments and classes of materials such as Graeco-Persian stelae and seals. In order to reassess the multiple-quarry hunt definition and interpretation, this chapter focuses on the most frequently represented prey and the hunting techniques. Moreover, recurrent orders in the sequences of hunting scenes are explored to find a possible criterion for reading them and interpreting their meaning. For this purpose, the interaction between visual details and other sources such as literary is very useful. Finally, this research intends to offer a new interpretation of the multiple-quarry hunts in the area under analysis with reflections on the temporal dimension of these images.

Chapter Five deals with the social values of dynastic multiple-quarry hunts, by focusing on the representation of the actors in the multiple-quarry hunts; in other words, the chapter is centred on what these images can say about the societies that produced them.

Chapter Six draws conclusions from the earlier chapters by offering a new interpretation of cultural and political dynamics within the Eastern Mediterranean under Persian Achaemenid rule. Moreover, this chapter considers case studies of multiple-quarry hunts beyond the chronological or geographical horizons analysed by this study, underscoring the importance of the dynastic Eastern Mediterranean in the creation of an enduring new language of power.

Figure 4. (following page) Silver coin with the head of Athena on the obverse and the bearded head of the Lycian dynast Kherẽi on the reverse. London, British Museum 1930,0802.2. © Trustees of the British Museum.

1

Historical and Artistic Background

This analysis will focus on the coastal strip from Caria to Phoenicia, in which local dynasts developed a distinctive and innovative language of power, in particular during the fourth century BC. This chapter aims to introduce the historical framework and the political, cultural and artistic dynamics that developed at this time.

1.1. The Eastern Mediterranean under Persian rule

After the conquest of the Median kingdom, between 553 and 550 BC, the Persians, led by Cyrus the Great (*ca.* 600-530 BC), became the new protagonists of the Near East. Moreover, they managed to unify the eastern basin of the Mediterranean. In the middle of the 540s BC Cyrus conquered Sardis, the capital of the Lydian kingdom, which hitherto had dominated western Anatolia. As Herodotus recounted in the so-called *logos* of Croesus (Hdt. 1.6–94), the Lydian king, planning to attack the Persians, consulted several oracles, finally acknowledging the accuracy of those of Delphi and Amphiaraus. The king equipped some Lydian ambassadors with expensive gifts and sent them to consult these oracles, who replied that Croesus would destroy a great empire if he were to attack the Persians. Interpreting these responses as approval, Croesus began hostilities, but he was defeated in the end by Cyrus.[1]

This event paved the way for the inclusion of western Anatolia in Cyrus' domain, a crucial moment in the construction of the Persian Achaemenid Empire. Starting in central-western Anatolia, the Persian army marched to Ionia, then southwards and eastwards in order to conquer areas along the Mediterranean coast, such as Caria, Lycia and Cilicia. After the conquest of Babylon in 539 BC, Cyrus the Great eliminated the neo-Babylonian Empire, his most formidable neighbour. Its former territories, including the eastern shore of the Mediterranean, were absorbed into a Persian satrapy. Effective Persian control over this area, however, took place after the expedition of Cambyses – Cyrus' successor – in Egypt between 525 and 522 BC. The Phoenician cities became an essential part of the western area of the empire due to their economic strength and crucial contribution to the Persian fleet.

This situation, which was unstable throughout the following decades, resulted in an unprecedented picture. Persian hegemony, indeed, stretched over the largest empire yet seen, the boundaries of which were the Caucasus, the Aegean Sea, Egypt and the Indus (Fig. 3). By the end of the sixth century BC the entire eastern basin of the Mediterranean was under the same power. As scholarly debate, since the late twentieth century has shown, it is no longer possible to regard the Persian Empire as "invisible". Rather, the variety of political and administrative solutions it adopted enabled different levels of autonomy and cultural identity to coexist (Fig. 5).[2] The empire's main administrative units were the satrapies, where the representative of the central power was established.[3] Sardis, for instance, was the capital of the satrapy in western Anatolia; occasionally, as under Cyrus the Younger (*ca.* 423-401 BC) at the end of the fifth century BC, the satrap was also head of the army (*karanos*).

This system, however, did not supplant the local dynastic governments. The first picture of the coexistence of different dynasts in the Eastern Mediterranean under Persian rule is provided by Herodotus, who recorded that they participated directly in the Second Persian War (480-479 BC) as commanders of naval contingents, under the orders of Persian officers (Hdt. 7.98–99). A wide body of material and literary evidence witnesses the existence of these dynasts along the eastern shores of the Mediterranean. In Lycia, for instance, funerary monuments, coinage and epigraphic documents reveal the elaboration of a precise language of power related to the local rulers (Figs. 4 and 6). In Cilicia, it seems that the local dynasty, under the name or title of Syennesis, survived until at least Cyrus the Younger's expedition at the end of the fifth century BC.[4] Phoenicia became part of the Persian Empire yet enjoyed considerable independence, organised as a cluster of city-states governed by monarchs. In addition, in the fifth century BC the district of Trans-Euphrates was separated from Babylonia; Sidon thus became the capital of Phoenicia and the seat of the imperial representative.

1.2. The Eastern Mediterranean as an interconnected area

Although the main outlines of the historical and cultural background of the Eastern Mediterranean during the fifth and fourth centuries BC are well-known, the network of direct and indirect contacts among these regions has not yet been sufficiently explored.[5] Investigating contacts is crucial in order to understand routes and modes of circulation of people, objects, materials and ideas, elements that had an important impact on artistic and cultural phenomena. Evidence related to this region is scattered, therefore in this section relevant information

[1] Poggio 2018a: 499–50, with bibliography. On a new chronology of Croesus' reign, see Wallace 2016.

[2] On Persian visibility, see Root 1991.

[3] Briant 1987; Tuplin 1987; Petit 1990; Klinkott 2005. See also Marek 2016: 139–79.

[4] For the debate on Syennesis, see now Simon 2019.

[5] For an extensive record of relations of these areas – in particular western Anatolia – with Hellenic and Persian cultures, refer to Starr 1975; 1977; Lewis 1977; Asheri 1983: 15–82.

Figure 5. The personifications of subject people lifting up the platform with the Great King on Darius I's tomb relief at Naqsh-i Rustam. Courtesy of the Oriental Institute of the University of Chicago.

Figure 6. The dynast of the Nereid Monument, Sculpture 879. London, British Museum 1848,1020.62. © Trustees of the British Museum.

will be collated, on four categories of contact: treaties and alliances; variations of dynasts' domains; matrimonial politics; mobility of people.

The Persian Wars constituted an exceptional opportunity for the rulers governing within the framework of the western empire to communicate directly with each other. As mentioned above, Herodotus recounts that, during the expedition of the Second Persian War, the dynasts of the Eastern Mediterranean participated directly in the conflict as leaders of several fleet contingents under the orders of Persian commanders (Hdt. 7.98–99).[6]

In the following decades rulers of this area established relations among themselves. An important role was played by treaties and alliances. For example, at the beginning of the fourth century BC Acoris, king of Egypt, had contact not only with the Cypriot ruler Evagoras of Salamis, who visited Acoris to join the common cause of the war against the Persians, and brought money to Cyprus from the Egyptian king. He also made a pact with the Pisidians, a people of southern Anatolia.[7] Scholars have tried to identify links between these types of contacts and the mobility of individuals. For example, this argument has been used to explain the presence at the Lycian court of the Peloponnesian seer Symmachus of Pellana, who wrote the commemorative text for Arbinas found in the Letoon, the sanctuary near Xanthos dedicated to the triad of Leto, Apollo and Artemis. Gergis, father of Arbinas, was possibly the arbitrator of the third agreement between Sparta and the satrap of Sardis Tissaphernes, which was drawn up in Caunus, on the Lycia–Caria border, in 412 BC.[8] Likewise, it has been stressed that the participation of Theodectes, a native of the Lycian city of Phaselis who was active in Athens, in the funerary contest for the Carian ruler Mausolus should be connected with the agreement between Mausolus and Phaselis (Fig. 7).[9]

An additional factor that might have promoted contacts was the variation in the individual spheres of influence of the dynasts, although there is often a tendency to consider these areas immune to changes. Violent conflicts characterised the Eastern Mediterranean in the fifth and fourth centuries BC. First, rivalries between rulers of the western part of the empire played an important role in determining local balances of power. For instance, it is known that Lycia was affected by domestic struggles during this period, as testified by dynastic inscriptions.[10]

The fourth-century BC Letoon Trilingual Stele attests to the direct control of Pixodarus of Caria over Lycia.[11] Evagoras of Salamis conquered Tyre and sacked other Phoenician cities, while Evagoras II, stripped of his rule of Salamis in Cyprus, became king of Sidon for a short period, between 344/3 and 342/1 BC.[12]

Nor should one overlook the matrimonial politics of dynastic families, which undoubtedly favoured the interweaving of relations between regions near and far.[13] As early as the beginning of the fifth century BC, the daughter of Syennesis of Cilicia was married with a Carian named Pixodarus, son of Mausolus of Cindya, possibly an ancestor of the Hecatomnids and certainly a prominent figure in the Carian community (Hdt. 5.118).[14] Relations between the two regions continued after the death of Syennesis at the battle of Salamis in 480 BC, since the Great King assigned Cilicia to Xenagoras of Halicarnassus.[15] Unlike his brothers Mausolus and Idrieus, who married their sisters Artemisia and Ada, in the fourth century BC Pixodarus, son of Hecatomnus and satrap of Caria, had taken a Cappadocian woman, Aphneis, for his bride. It would be difficult not to presume she was of high rank. Pixodarus moreover suggested to Philip II of Macedonia that they arrange a marriage between his daughter, Ada II, and Philip Arrhidaeus – a plan thwarted by Alexander, who claimed the bride for himself – before marrying her to the Persian Orontobates (Plut. *Alex*. 10.1–3).[16] These examples suggest that a network of matrimonial alliances developed across the Eastern Mediterranean throughout the Persian period.

The mobility of monarchs must also have facilitated contacts among the various courts. At the end of the fifth century BC, for instance, Evagoras of Cyprus took refuge in Soloi, in Cilicia, before taking power in Salamis (Isoc. 9.27). A little later Epyaxa, wife of Syennesis, left Cilicia for a long journey to inner Anatolia, to reach Cyrus the Younger (Xen. *An*. 1.2.12).

However, the dynastic courts of the Eastern Mediterranean were real poles of attraction for different figures, who created interregional contacts. Athenaeus – on the basis of fourth-century BC sources – recalled that two kings of that time, Straton of Sidon and Nicocles of Salamis in Cyprus, were able to discuss what their guests had observed at the rival court:[17]

[6] For the command structure of the Persian fleet in 480 BC, see Hauben 1973.
[7] Diod. Sic. 15.4.3; 15.8.1; Phot. *Bibl*. 176.120b.4–5 = *FGrH* 115 F 103 (§ 13). Kuhrt 2007: 394–5, no. 61; Briant (1996: 670) has doubts about the alliance between the king of Egypt and the Pisidians.
[8] Briant 1996: 626–7. On Symmachus, see also Asheri 1983: 101 and 103–4; Petrovic 2009: 196–200. On the Xanthos inscription, see Kuhrt 2007: 339–41, no. 29.
[9] Hornblower 1982: 122–3 and 333–5; Ruzicka 1992: 198 note 15; Ottone 2009: 142–5. Hornblower (1982: 123) suggests that a policy of conciliation had been favoured by the poet himself. In any case, it cannot be ruled out that the agreement facilitated Theodectes' relationship with the Carian environment.
[10] Domingo Gygax 2001: 68–92; see also Robert 1978.
[11] Hornblower 1982: 119–22. On the Letoon Trilingual Stele, see *infra*.
[12] Isoc. 9.62; Diod. Sic. 15.2.4. Hill 1940: 147 and note 3.
[13] Casabonne 1996: 114–5.
[14] Hornblower 1982: 26 and 141–2.
[15] Aesch. *Pers*. 329-331; Hdt. 9.107. On the text of Herodotus' passage, see Masaracchia 1978, *ad loc.* Furthermore, Cornelius Nepos (Nep. 14.1) informs us that Datames' Carian father was given power over a part of the Cilician province probably at the beginning of the reign of Artaxerxes II (405/4–359 BC). For further considerations see Sekunda 1988.
[16] For this episode, see Hatzopoulos 1982; Hornblower 1982: 49–50 and 220–2; Ruzicka 1992: 130–2.
[17] Ath. 12.531a–e = *FGrH* 115 F 114. The sources for Athenaeus are Theopompus of Chios and Anaximenes of Lampsacus, both from the fourth century BC. See also Aelian's version (*VH* 7.2). On this passage see also Briant 1996: 215.

Figure 7. "Mausolus" (right) and "Artemisia" (left) from the Mausoleum of Halicarnassus, Sculptures 1000 and 1001. London, British Museum 1857,1220.232 and 1857,1220.233. © Trustees of the British Museum.

Theopompus says in Book XV of his *History of Philip* that Straton, the king of Sidon, outdid everyone else in the world in the extravagant style in which he lived and his addiction to luxury. Because the life that Homer in his stories represents the Phaeacians as leading – having festivals, drinking, and listening to citharodes and rhapsodes – is how Straton behaved for a long time. He was even more excited about pleasure than they were, to the extent that the Phaeacians, according to Homer, used to drink in the company of their own wives and daughters, whereas Straton arranged for his parties to include girls who played the pipes, the harp, and the lyre. He imported large numbers of prostitutes from the Peloponnese, and many female musicians from Ionia, and other young women from all over Greece, some of whom were singers, while others danced. He made it a practice to have contests with his friends that involved these women, and he spent all his time with them, both because he enjoyed living this way, since his personality made him a slave to pleasure, and even more important, because he was engaged in a competition with Nicocles. For they were extremely competitive with one another, and each of them was concerned to make his own life the more pleasurable and easier. Their rivalry became so extreme, I hear, that they questioned their visitors about furnishings in the other man's house, and about how expensive the sacrifices he made were, and made aggressive efforts to outdo one another in these areas. They were eager to appear to be wealthy and fortunate; but their luck certainly did not continue where the end of their lives was concerned, and instead they both died a violent death. Anaximenes in his work entitled *Royal Ups and Downs* offers similar information about Straton, saying that he was a rival of Nicocles, the king of Cyprian Salamis, who was devoted to luxury and lewd behavior, and that both men died violently.[18]

The mobility of people in the Eastern Mediterranean thus fuelled the long-distance rivalry between the two rulers. Ambassadors, merchants, artists, and intellectuals travelled across the Eastern Mediterranean moving from court to court. The Athenians, for example, honoured Straton for the help offered during their expedition to the Great King, a trip that may have involved several stops other than that at Sidon.[19] In fact, journeys of a diplomatic nature were undertaken in the same way as those along trade routes connected to coastal navigation: Thucydides testifies to the presence of a trade route between the coasts of Anatolia and Phoenicia (Thuc. 2.69.1).[20] Trade itself favoured relations among the Eastern Mediterranean areas. Dynastic centres like Halicarnassus and Amathus in Cyprus, for example, testify to an extensive trade in pottery from distant places in the fourth century BC.[21]

In particular, the mobility of intellectuals and artists was a well-established phenomenon in the Eastern Mediterranean during the fourth century BC.[22] Here the role played by the dynastic courts in the western part of the Persian Empire was decisive, striving to attract the best talents in circulation – poets, rhetoricians, thinkers and artists – in accordance with the principle pronounced by the famous Athenian rhetorician Isocrates to Nicocles, king of Salamis in Cyprus (Isoc. 2.12–13):[23]

On the contrary, be convinced that education and diligence are in the highest degree potent to improve our nature, and associate yourself with the wisest of those who are about you and send for the wisest men from abroad whenever this is possible. And do not imagine that you can afford to be ignorant of any one either of the famous poets or of the sages; rather you should listen to the poets and learn from the sages and so equip your mind to judge those who are inferior and to emulate those who are superior to yourself [...].[24]

Isocrates himself composed an encomium in honour of Nicocles' father, Evagoras, in approximately 370 BC.[25] The production of this encomium – a real turning point in Greek literature – must be seen in the context of the programme of competitions that Nicocles organised in honour of his late father (Isoc. 9.1).[26] The practice of organising literary competitions was widespread in the fourth-century BC Eastern Mediterranean, and it stimulated mobility. Artemisia, widow of Mausolus of Halicarnassus, promoted a literary competition in honour of her deceased husband.[27] Among the participants was Theopompus of Chios, who settled at the court of Philip II of Macedonia.[28] Moreover, artists travelled from outside to take part in the construction of the Mausoleum itself, as will be shown below. As mentioned above, intellectuals of Greek origin were active at the court of Arbinas, ruler of Xanthos at the beginning of the fourth century BC. They included the seer Symmachus of Pellana and the *paidotribes* who composed poems in Greek for the dynast. The attractiveness exerted by the Lycian and Carian capitals on artists and intellectuals is emblematic.[29]

All this information, which does not claim to be exhaustive, reinforces the idea that in the fifth and, above all, the fourth century BC the complex "supraregional network" developed in the Eastern Mediterranean meant the different rulers could not ignore one another.[30]

1.3. "Graeco-Persian" art and culture

From an artistic point of view, the perspective of the Eastern Mediterranean as an interconnected world is not new. Scholars have used the much-debated concept of "international style" for the Late Bronze Age (notably *ca.* 1400-1200 BC), which was a period characterised by a supraregional network of commercial contacts and diplomatic exchanges.[31] As for the period under analysis here, some scholars have instead used the category of "pre-Hellenistic *koinè*".[32] In such a climate, "Graeco-

[18] Translation from Olson 2010.
[19] *IG* II² 141.
[20] Elayi 1988: 322; Briant 1996: 600.
[21] Halicarnassus: Vaag, Nørskov and Lund 2002: 75–6. Amathus: Marangou and Petit 1992; Petit 1996: 220.
[22] Ryle 1966: 40–41 and 59; Hornblower 1982: 333 note 6. On wandering in ancient Greek culture, see Montiglio 2005; Hunter and Rutherford 2009.
[23] Poliakoff (2001: 56–7) underscores that competitiveness intensified in Athens exactly from the fifth to the fourth century BC, through contests of various kinds.
[24] Translation from Norlin 1966.
[25] Momigliano 1993a: 49; Alexiou 2010: 39.
[26] Alexiou 2010: 66–7.
[27] Gell. *NA* 10.18 = *FGrH* 115 T 6b; Euseb. *Praep. evang.* 10.3.5 = *FGrH* 115 F 345. See Ruzicka 1992: 102–3.
[28] On his participation in the Carian contest, see Ottone 2009, 142–5. See also *infra*, § 6.2. On the participation of Isocrates, see Hornblower 1982: 334.
[29] See also Le Roy 1996: 352.
[30] Petit 2007: 12.
[31] On the supraregional network and the formation of an "international style" discussed by Feldman 2006, see Harmanşah 2008.
[32] Stucky 1993. See also the observations in Weinberg 1976.

Persian" is the most important category used by scholars to designate the artistic language of the contexts analysed in this research.

The "Graeco-Persian" formula refers to very different phenomena: on the one hand, scholars define as Graeco-Persian the two series of conflicts that took place in the first quarter of the fifth century BC between the Greeks and Persians. On the other hand, this formula is applied to different classes of evidence – glyptic, sculpture, painting, metalwork – characterised by an artistic language peculiar of the contact areas between the Greek and Persian worlds, such as western Anatolia[33]. In the first case it embodies an opposition, in the latter it implies a constructive contact. Such an ambiguity reveals a variety of contacts between the Greek and Persian worlds that it is necessary to reconsider on the basis of a wide range of evidence from an interdisciplinary perspective.

A. Furtwängler first raised this issue in 1900 when he identified the class of "Graeco-Persian gems", a corpus of unprovenanced objects with artistic features attributable both to Greek and Persian contexts (Fig. 8). He divided the glyptic production of the Persian Empire into two phases, the "Persian" (sixth to fifth centuries BC) and the "Graeco-Persian" (fifth to fourth centuries BC). He considered that both these tendencies were produced by Greek artists but the Greek artistic character – present in Persian art from the beginning – manifested itself progressively; he thought that it remained unexpressed due to the demands of patrons and markedly emerged in the Graeco-Persian phase. He dated this phase to the period between the second half of the fifth century BC and the mid-fourth. He attributed it to the western regions of the Persian Empire where interchanges between the two cultures would have been easier.[34] Furtwängler, however, did not make systematic comparisons with other types of monuments, such as dynastic tombs, and did not define the phenomenon more precisely. The term "Graeco-Persian art", therefore, stood for Greek art outside Greece, patronised by Persians.

G.M.A. Richter and J. Boardman were among those in favour of Furtwängler's theory. According to Richter, the originality of Persian art was determined by the work of foreign artists – mainly Greeks – in the service of the Persian kings.[35] Boardman investigated another important category, that of pyramidal seals, and concluded that they belonged to a formative phase of Graeco-Persian seals. In this study an undertone connected with the issue of the artists' ethnic origins is present.[36] M.E. Maximova, followed by H. Seyrig, imitated Furtwängler in tracking down the ethnic origins of the artists, but identified them as Persians, thus moving the markers of the problem.[37]

The issue could not advance simply by swinging from one extreme to the other, with Greece and Persia almost in opposition. It was necessary to focus on the areas that Furtwängler had correctly identified as a meeting point between the different cultural trends. Although he supported Furtwängler's identification of Anatolia as the origin of the so-called tabloid seals, A. Procopé-Walter preferred the geographic label "kleinasiatisch" ("of Asia Minor", therefore "Anatolian") rather than the ethnic "persisch-griechisch" ("Persian-Greek").[38] Returning to the debate, Boardman underscored the validity of the "Graeco-Persian" label and suggested Anatolian origin.[39]

One of the most fruitful developments lay in the comparison of seals with figurative artworks – painting or more specifically sculpture – that definitely came from Anatolia. Focusing on Anatolian reliefs, J. Borchhardt highlighted the local elements in the artistic production of this area.[40] Discoveries such as the so-called Karaburun II Tomb (*ca.* 470 BC; Fig. 9), a painted tomb in inland Lycia, led to fresh reflection on the Graeco-Persian category as a product of a specific cultural context: "we can speak indeed of Anatolia as a link between Orient and Occident, and of Graeco-Persian art as an important entity instead of a provincial offshoot of Greek art".[41] In N.M. Nikulina's research, comparisons with the monumental evidence from the Eastern Mediterranean provided further support for locating the source of Graeco-Persian glyptic in "peripheral regions", which stimulated the mixture of figurative languages.[42] M. Nollé included in the Graeco-Persian category the sculpted stelae from Dascylium (modern-day Ergili; Fig. 10), satrapic capital of Hellespontine Phrygia in north-west Anatolia.[43] The extension of the label to other types of evidence is now well-established, and its importance is demonstrated by Ş. Karagöz's examination of different classes of objects from Anatolia now in the Istanbul Archaeological Museum.[44]

Several factors determined a new development in the topic, especially from the second half of the 1980s: on the one hand, historiographical trends, stimulated by initiatives like the "Achaemenid History Workshops" and on the other, increasing archaeological knowledge of Anatolia.[45] This phase focused on the centre–periphery dialectic. B. Jacobs emphasised the importance of indigenous elements in Lycian art rather than Persian influence, and reiterated subsequently that imperial political affiliation did not necessarily involve the transmission of artistic models from the centre to the periphery.[46] W.A.P. Childs, however,

[33] Gates 2002; Draycott 2010; Karagöz 2013: 1–6.
[34] Furtwängler 1900: III, 116–7.
[35] Richter 1946: 30.
[36] Boardman 1970a; 1970b.
[37] Maximova 1928; Seyrig 1952.

[38] Procopé-Walter 1937: 26 note 1.
[39] Boardman 2000: 168–71.
[40] Borchhardt 1968.
[41] Mellink 1971: 254. See also Mellink 1972.
[42] Nikoulina 1971. See also Starr 1977: 73–4. Zazoff (1970: 16) emphasised that in the case of the Graeco-Persian scaraboid seals in blue chalcedony, it is the material itself that suggests a provenance in Anatolia.
[43] Nollé 1992. See also Kubala 2003.
[44] Karagöz 2013.
[45] Briant 2000; Briant and Boucharlat 2005; Poggio 2018b.
[46] Jacobs 1987: 64; 2002: 345–52.

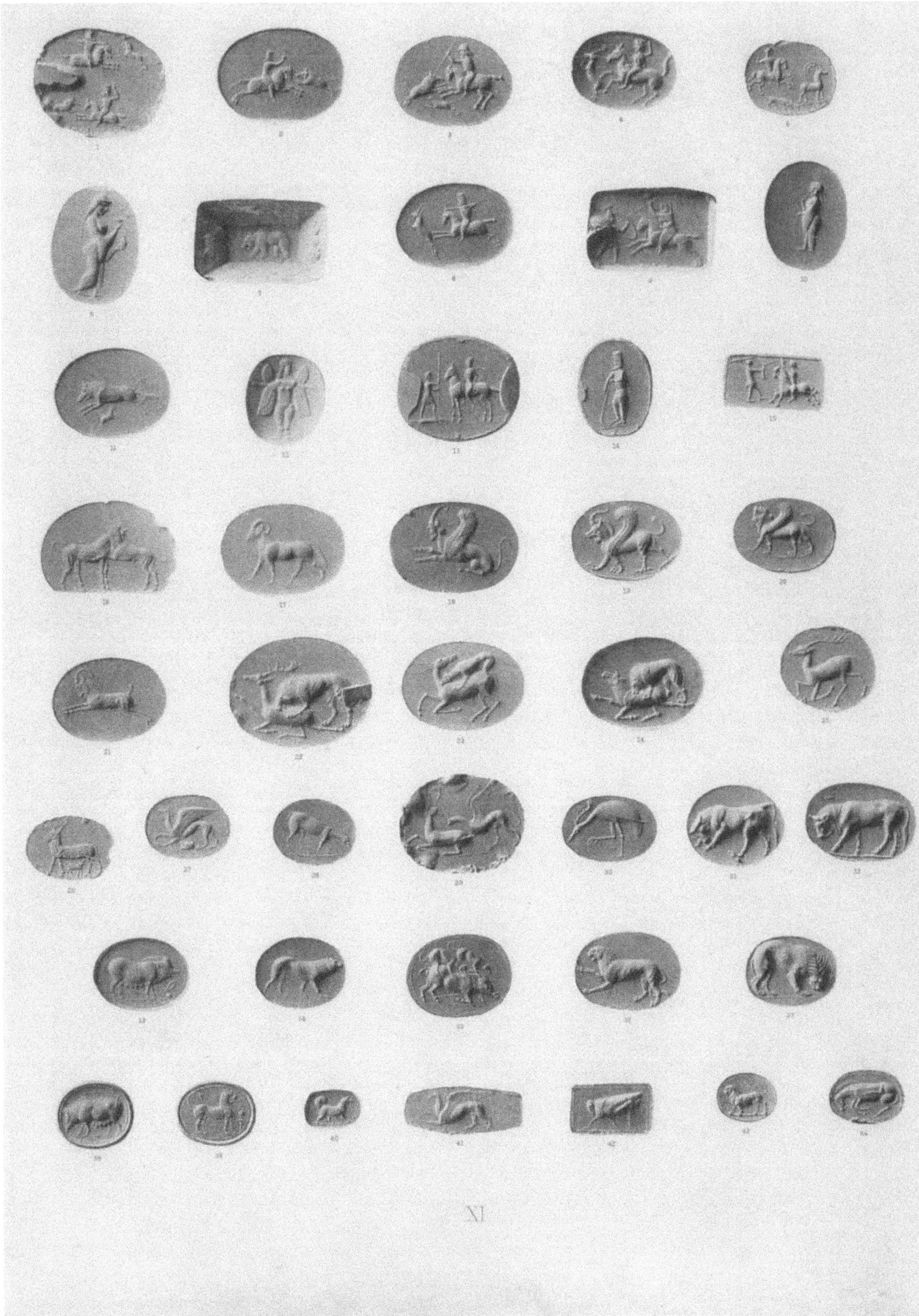

Figure 8. "Graeco-Persian gems". After Furtwängler 1900: I, pl. XI.

Figure 9. Karaburun II Tomb, main wall (stolen in 2011). © Bryn Mawr College (Photo: Machteld J. Mellink). https://library.artstor.org/asset/BRYN_MAWR_955__955_1680978.

a supporter of the presence in Lycian art of neo-Assyrian elements, stressed that the imperial system facilitated the transmission of models among the potentates it comprised.[47] At the same time M.C. Root published a paper that proposed setting aside the ethnicity mechanism of artists and audiences, and challenged the notion of an evanescent Persian Empire without cultural impact on its subject territories, particularly those in the West.[48] This trend culminated in E.R.M. Dusinberre's research into the Achaemenid phase of Sardis. She identified a polyethnic imperial elite composed of locals and Persians, and theorised the birth of an imperial ideology that manifested itself in various aspects, including art objects for public and private use, burial customs and cults.[49]

The focus of debate in recent years, therefore, has been on the imperial dynamics in spreading a figurative language from the centre of power to the "peripheral" regions. It is increasingly clear, however, that relations between the outskirts and the heart of the empire were multi-faceted: the different regions not only responded to impulses from the central power – which is undeniable, if one considers the Meydancıkkale reliefs in Rough Cilicia[50] – but assumed, in turn, an active role in developing a local language that also incorporated characteristics of imperial ideology and imagery.[51] The result is the abandonment of the classicist vision that the Graeco-Persian formula gave supremacy to Greek civilisation, which was always identified with the "Greek miracle" of the fifth century BC,[52] while neglecting the different contexts in which the encounter between Greek and Persian art occurred. Consistently, in current formulas like "Perso-Anatolian" and "Anatolo-Persian" the Greek component has disappeared and the focus shifted to Anatolia as part of the Persian Empire, from where there were interactions between Persian elements and various local cultures.[53]

In 2013 E.R.M. Dusinberre wrote that the centre–periphery model was likely to prove too dualistic, since it ignored the interaction among the different peripheries. She proposed a new "authority-autonomy" model, which focused both on the role of the Persian central power and on the different areas subject to it, which is interpreted as an interconnected system.[54]

[47] Childs 1991. For neo-Assyrian elements in Lycian art, see Childs 1978.
[48] Root 1991.
[49] Dusinberre 2003: esp. 5–7. For further observations, see also Baughan 2002–4.
[50] Davesne 1998; Gates 2005: 62–3.

[51] Miller 2007.
[52] For considerations on the nineteenth-century classicist imprint in the study of "centre" and "periphery" in the Greek world, see Frisone and Lombardo 2007: 180–2.
[53] Polat 1994; Boffo 2008: 66; Draycott 2010; Miller 2011. See also Greaves 2007 and Şare 2013: 72.
[54] Dusinberre 2013: 3–8. On this study, see Draycott 2014 and Boucharlat 2015.

Figure 10. Stele from Dascylium, detail. Istanbul, Archaeological Museum 5763. D-DAI-IST-68/89 (Photo: W. Schiele).

This brief history focuses on the increasing demand for flexibility in formulating models, reflecting not only the evolution of studies in the field but also the fluidity of the geopolitical situation between the twentieth and twenty-first centuries. The case of the Eastern Mediterranean in the fourth century BC indicates the complexity of this context. As demonstrated, a network of contacts developed among the different regional contexts that helped to develop common features in the language of power. In this context, "supraregional" factors, such as the growing role of Greek cultural elements, especially along the coast, and belonging to the same political entity – the Persian Empire – were crucial. Nevertheless, the regional dimension, in which the various local identities maintained their distinctive character, should not be forgotten.[55]

For a full understanding of the artistic processes in these areas one must consider other specific phenomena, such as bilingualism – meaning the use of two or more languages by individuals or within a community with various levels of skill.[56] For the areas of the Eastern Mediterranean, suffice it to say that Thucydides defined the Carian Gaulites as *diglottos* (Thuc. 8.85.2). He was sent to Sparta by the satrap Tissaphernes because of his knowledge of Greek and Aramaic, two "international" languages of the time. Gaulites, however, may have been at least trilingual, since it may be assumed that he also spoke a native language.[57] Diglossia, which is defined as the use of multiple languages in specific domains, should be considered part of the phenomenon of bilingualism. Aramaic, for example, was used as an administrative language spoken in the western regions of the Persian Empire: it appeared as such in the fourth century BC on the Letoon Trilingual Stele which combines Greek, Lycian and Aramaic.[58] As has been highlighted, behaviours play a significant role in the phenomenon of bilingualism – in other words, intentional or unintentional processes that create osmosis between the language skills of an individual.[59]

This provides the wider context for reinterpreting the Graeco-Persian art label. Furtwängler's classification is still significant today, though conventional: his division into phases certainly needs to be revised and updated, but the chronology of A. Furtwängler's Graeco-Persian label (between the second half of the fifth century BC and the mid-fourth century BC) presents a correct distinction of the cultural dynamics of the Eastern Mediterranean. In the light of recent research, the generic expression of these two cultural trends active in the Eastern Mediterranean must be analysed at a regional level so as to highlight the local variants that interacted with the supraregional context. Moreover, it is useful to consider the many regional horizons of Anatolia as some of the actors in this dynamic, since the Graeco-Persian phenomenon seems to extend along the Eastern Mediterranean shores.[60] Among more recent voices, Th. Petit has interpreted this category as an artistic expression of the ruling dynasties of the Eastern Mediterranean.[61]

Graeco-Persian art, in other words, should be considered a macro-category designating a general and far from homogeneous figurative trend – and not just a class of evidence – within a cultural climate favouring complex and multi-faceted processes of osmosis. The ruling classes of the Eastern Mediterranean during the fifth and fourth centuries BC adopted this artistic language in order to convey specific messages connected with their status. Rulers' patronage, in particular, as already stated, was at the centre of such processes by creating poles of attraction for intellectuals and artists from the Greek world. Any analysis of this artistic phenomenon should comprise the various horizons of this broad area, such as the local, the Persian and the heterogeneous Greek.

[55] See also Kubala 2003: 116.
[56] There are numerous recent studies on the phenomenon of bilingualism in the ancient world: Adams, Janse and Swain 2002; Adams 2003; Mullen and James 2012; Mairs 2013.
[57] Lewis 1977: 14 and 110. For the interpretation of the term *diglottos* referring to Gaulites and the phenomenon of bilingualism and trilingualism in Anatolia, see Asheri 1983: 20–2; Salmeri 1994: 92–3.
[58] On the Trilingual Stele from the Letoon, see Metzger *et al.* 1979; Briant 1998; Rutherford 2002; Maddoli 2006, with further bibliography. On the linguistic phenomena in Cilicia, see Salmeri 2004.
[59] Mairs 2013. See also the useful observations in Wallace-Hadrill 2008: ch. 1. On the use of linguistic phenomena providing models for cultural dynamics, see Osborne 2012.
[60] Carstens (2006:126) however, reiterated the Anatolian confines of the Graeco-Persian phenomenon: "The Graeco-Persian style [. . .] was confined to Anatolia".
[61] Petit 2007: 12.

Figure 11. (following page) The Nereid Monument of Xanthos, eastern façade. London, British Museum. © Trustees of the British Museum.

2

Dynastic Tombs and Artistic Phenomena

Dynastic tombs with figurative decoration are the best expressions of artistic phenomena in the Eastern Mediterranean during the fifth and fourth centuries BC. These tombs were the privileged expression for the self-representation of deceased local dynasts of the Persian Achaemenid Empire, who wanted to assert their political power with increasingly monumental and often original solutions.

One of the aims of this chapter is to outline a well-defined corpus of dynastic tombs in the Eastern Mediterranean that show shared artistic features. The following chapters will be focused on the hunting representations of these tombs, and therefore it would be useful to outline by region – from West to East, and in a chronological arrangement within the same site – the main features of each tomb in order to put the hunting representations into the broader context of each figurative programme. Therefore, a fragmentation of the figurative programmes of these tombs and their separation from the architectural frameworks should be avoided, as C. Marconi emphasised in regard to architectural decoration in the Greek world.[1]

As this chapter will make clear, the artistic language of these tombs was the result of a movement of people, ideas, and technologies across political and cultural boundaries. From a stylistic point of view, the dynastic tombs being researched are generally considered as "Greek artworks" outside the Greek world. They were created by Greek artists or sculptors trained by Greek artists, showing stylistic features that are characteristic of the Greek world.[2] However, they have been found in regions politically belonging to the Persian Achaemenid Empire. The idea of Greek artists working in the service of the dynasts ruling under the Persian power was implied by the "Graeco-Persian" label as soon as it was applied to glyptic, and then it was extended to other media, including sculpture, as mentioned in Chapter One. However, the picture is more complex and far from homogenous, since the concept of "Greek art" is not monolithic and encompasses regional schools and different backgrounds according to each region. The styles of the tombs have been extensively discussed in scholarship as evidence of a relationship with the Greek world. Therefore, particular attention will be paid here to circulation of iconographies and materials.

The most tangible element of this connectivity was the material used for these tombs. Almost the entire corpus of dynastic tombs discussed here are characterised by the use of white marble. Keeping aside the western Mediterranean, in this period white marble was a resource typical of the Aegean world comprising the Greek mainland, Greek islands, and the Aegean part of Anatolia. Thus the marble used for the dynastic tombs researched here was imported from the Aegean basin. Caria was the only region with easier access to quarries, due to its geographic position at the edge of the Aegean world.[3] The location of these dynastic tombs along the coasts of the Eastern Mediterranean – southern Anatolia and Phoenicia – is not a coincidence: on one hand, the dynastic centres along the coast underwent a greater openness towards the coast, while on the other hand white marble could be transported here with ease and artists could travel alongside this material.[4] Therefore, the coastal strip from Caria to Phoenicia played an important artistic and political role.

2.1. A regional survey

2.1.1. Caria

Caria is an important case study since it was ruled during the fourth century BC by the Hecatomnid dynasty.[5] Their architectural achievements demonstrate their deep awareness of the ideology of power.

The corpus of Hecatomnid dynastic tombs has been enlarged in recent years.[6] In particular, since 2010 a monumental tomb has been investigated in Milas, the ancient Mylasa, which was the capital of Caria before Mausolus moved it to Halicarnassus. Initially, based on architectural style, this monumental tomb was considered to be that which Mausolus began for himself and left unfinished after the capital was moved. However, with the discovery of the lavishly decorated funerary chamber and its marble sarcophagus, the tomb has since been assigned to Hecatomnus (d. 377/6 BC), Mausolus' father: it is known thus as "Hekatomneion". Among the themes represented on the "Hecatomnus Sarcophagus" there is a mounted lion hunt of the dynast and a banquet, themes that are relevant to the funerary iconography of the area.[7]

---

1 Marconi 2007: xiii.

2 As to the Alexander Sarcophagus, for instance, see discussion in von Graeve 1970: ch. 5; Frel 1971. For the sarcophagi from Sidon, however, Elayi (1988: 320) has argued that sculptors were of Phoenician origin.

3 See Freccero 2015.

4 For a caveat on the circulation of commodities in the Eastern Mediterranean, see Martin 2017: 133–5.

5 Also see Marek 2015, with bibliography.

6 On the Hecatomnid tombs, see Henry 2009: 135–55; 2010; 2014.

7 Rumscheid 2010; Papini 2012: 46 note 1; Hoepfner 2013: 121–2; Konuk 2013: 111 note 65; Marek and Zingg 2018; Işık 2019. This tomb is only briefly described in the present research since it is under publication; therefore, it will be not included into the corpus under analysis, but it will be mentioned when necessary. For the specific value of the lion hunt associated with kingship, see Cassin 1981; McMahon 2009: 121–3, with bibliography.

Other architectural activities in Caria should be considered that refer directly to dynastic patronage. For instance, the fourth-century BC expansion on a monumental scale of the Labraunda sanctuary included an important innovation in the history of architecture: the practice of explicitly stating the patronage on the architraves with inscriptions bearing the name of the rulers.[8]

The Mausoleum of Halicarnassus

Among the Hecatomnid dynastic tombs, the Mausoleum of Halicarnassus is a particularly interesting case study. The term "mausoleum" means "tomb of Mausolus", who was the patron of this structure alongside his wife and sister Artemisia according to ancient sources. Indeed, it was built at the urban centre of Halicarnassus, which was re-founded when Mausolus moved the capital here from Mylasa (Vitr. *De arch.* 2.8.11).[9] The Mausoleum was situated in an open space accessible through a propylon.[10]

The reconstruction of the architectural layout itself has been possible due to the records of Vitruvius and Pliny the Elder. Moreover excavations have increased our knowledge of the site. The complex architecture of the Mausoleum consisted of a two- or three-stepped podium above which stood an Ionic colonnade surmounted by a stepped pyramidal roof (Fig. 12).[11] The size of the monument made it visible from the sea.

Archaeometric analysis has ascertained that marble from different sources was used: Pentelic, insular and possibly Proconnesian.[12] As S. Hornblower pointed out, the effort and economic cost to transport this prestigious material was far from insignificant.[13] These data are consistent with the literary sources that testify that covering slabs of Proconnesian marble were used for the first time in the decoration of the Palace of Mausolus (Plin. *HN* 36.47; see also Vitr. *De arch.* 2.8.10).

The tomb was also adorned with marble sculptures. The battles of the Greeks and Amazons (Amazonomachy; Fig. 13) and of Lapiths and Centaurs (Centauromachy) were represented in friezes, while one coffer bearing an exploit of Theseus has also been preserved. Free-standing sculptures from the intercolumniation of the Ionian colonnade represented the ancestors of the Hecatomnid family, and a marble quadriga crowned the pyramidal roof. The presence of fragments of free-standing sculptures of wild beasts, such as boar and panthers, and dogs, which scholars have attributed to hunting scenes, makes the Mausoleum pertinent to this study (Fig. 1). It is possible that the sixth-century AD author Gregory of Tours, describing the Carian tomb, indicates the hunting representations.[14] Scholars located the sculptures of animals on the western and southern sides of the podium's lower step, a multiple-quarry hunt was thus represented in a visible position.[15]

The ancient authors additionally transmitted the identity of the architects and the artists who worked on this monument. Vitruvius mentions the architects Satyrus and Pytheus, who also wrote a treaty on the monument, and he lists the artists involved in the work of each side of the Mausoleum. These include artists of the calibre of Leochares, Bryaxis, Scopas and Praxiteles, and Vitruvius notes that some of his sources included Timotheus (*De arch.* 7 *praef.* 12–13). Pliny the Elder assigned to each sculptor one specific side of the monument, mentioning Timotheus instead of Praxiteles (Plin. *HN* 36.30–31).[16]

The exceptional layout and decoration of the Mausoleum made it a cornerstone of ancient architecture and art, and it was included in the Hellenistic canon of the Seven Wonders of the Ancient World, becoming influential in the modern period. The term "mausoleum", therefore, began to be used to refer to any grand funerary monument, and its use became widespread, even after antiquity.[17]

2.1.2. Lycia

Lycia – a well-defined region both from a geographic and a cultural perspective – was characterised by a specific typology of funerary monuments, the so-called pillar tombs, identified from the sixth century BC. They were tall monolithic blocks crowned by a burial chamber. The exterior of the burial chamber was often decorated with reliefs, which allow scholars to define the chronology.[18] Their monumental size, materials and decoration have led to these tombs being assigned to local rulers. However changes occurred at the end of the fifth century BC and the beginning of the fourth, both in architectural typology and the iconography of the decoration.

The Nereid Monument of Xanthos

This tomb, today in the British Museum, embodies these changes. Marking a significant departure from the tradition of pillar tombs, it is considered to be the first of a new series of funerary monuments in Lycia (390–380 BC).[19] It is generally attributed to the dynast Erbbina/Arbinas.

[8] See Umholtz 2002: 262, 273–6.
[9] Pedersen 1991: 95; Jenkins 2006: 206–9; Caliò and Interdonato 2005: 53–9. On the phases of occupation of the Mausoleum site and the foundations of the monument, see Jeppesen 2000; Zahle and Kjeldsen 2004.
[10] Fedak 1990: 73; Jeppesen 1992: 59–63; Lippolis and Caliò 2016: 151–2.
[11] On the architecture and decoration of the Mausoleum, see Waywell 1978; Jeppesen 2002; Cook 2005; Jenkins 2006: 209–27; Lucchese 2009; Hoepfner 2013: 71–133; Tanner 2013.
[12] Walker and Matthews 1997; Cook 2005: 29; Matthews 2005; Lucchese 2009: 29; Higgs 2006: 179; Prost 2013: 183.
[13] Hornblower 1982: 264–6.
[14] Gregory of Tours *De cursu stellarum ratio* 12.
[15] Jeppesen 1958: 51–2; Waywell 1978: 45–6, 110–2, no. 34; Lucchese 2009: 33.
[16] Jex-Blake and Sellers 1982: *ad loc.*; Ferri 2000: *ad loc.* On the sculptors, see Corso 2019.
[17] See Leick 2013: 17–9.
[18] On this type, see Deltour-Levie 1982; Draycott 2007.
[19] Coupel and Demargne 1969; Childs 1973a (in particular on the dating); Childs and Demargne 1989; Keen 1992: 59; Ridgway 1997: 79–88; Prost 2012a; Poggio 2016b; Hoff 2017: 68–71, 518–522, cat. S88; Kolb 2018: 658–64. See Bruns-Özgan (1987: 35–52 and 259–60, cat. M 9) for an earlier dating.

Figure 12. Model of the Mausoleum of Halicarnassus by Kristian Jeppesen and Axel Sønderborg (old display). Museum of Ancient Art and Archaeology, Aarhus University. Courtesy of the Halikarnassos Project.

The Nereid Monument stood on a terrace located at the southern edge of the settlement, so that it dominated the Xanthos Valley.[20] The monument was possibly enclosed by a precinct.[21]

[20] Keen 1998: 147. On the history of the area south of Xanthos, see Des Courtils 2007: 160; 2012: 155–7. On the Xanthos Valley, see Zimmermann 2020.

[21] Roux 1975; Fedak 1990: 66; on the terrace of the monument, see also Coupel and Demargne 1969: 27–30.

The Nereid Monument was an Ionic temple-like tomb standing on a high podium (Fig. 11).[22] Of the Lycian dynastic monuments, it was the only one to use marble extensively, with only the lower courses of the podium in local limestone.[23] Earlier, marble, if used at all, was

[22] As for the problem of interpreting this monument according to the conventions of a Greek temple, see Ridgway 1997: 84–5.

[23] Poggio 2016b: 211–2.

Figure 13. The Amazonomachy from the Mausoleum of Halicarnassus, Sculpture 1014. London, British Museum 1857,1220.269. © Trustees of the British Museum.

limited to single elements of monumental buildings, such as the decorated frieze of the Harpy Tomb and the peplophoroi statues of the "Building G", from the Lycian Acropolis of Xanthos.[24] A further noteworthy feature is the combination of different white marbles according to their specific properties: analysis seems to confirm the use of Parian marble for most of the free-standing sculptures, while Anatolian marble was employed for other parts of the structure.[25] As discussed above, this practice also applied to the Mausoleum of Halicarnassus.

From the architectural point of view, in spite of the smaller proportions, a parallel with the Carian tomb can be suggested by the Ionian colonnade on the podium. Scholars usually consider the tomb at Halicarnassus to be influenced by the Nereid Monument, although different opinions have recently been expressed.[26] If the Mausoleum of Halicarnassus now appears to descend from the monumental tomb in Mylasa, an-intra regional development in Caria is thus highly probable, nevertheless the issue of the relationship with Lycia in creating new models for dynastic tombs remains open.

Another feature that can associate the two monuments is the lavish decoration. On the basis of the generally accepted reconstruction, the podium of the Nereid Monument had two superimposed friezes. Two continuous friezes ringed the upper part of the monument, on the architrave and the external wall of the cella. Finally, the two pediments were decorated with reliefs.

The figurative programme included non-mythological representations referring to the life of the deceased: battle scenes including city sieges and an audience scene (Fig. 6); a multiple-quarry hunting scene focused on a bear and a boar; offering-bearers; a symposium-style gathering; a sacrifice; the family of the dynast; and a battle scene on horseback. The generic battle theme of the larger podium frieze followed an Amazonomachy pattern.

The free-standing sculptures represented mythological subjects, arranged as intercolumnar statues – the "Nereids" that gave the tomb its name – or as acroteria, for example the group interpreted as Peleus and Thetis.[27]

The Heroon of Trysa

The Heroon of Trysa was a dynastic funerary monument from the first half of the fourth century BC (*ca.* 380-370 BC), occupying a dominant position on a terrace near the acropolis of the settlement.[28] It was a polygonal temenos, richly decorated with superimposed friezes addressing a number of themes: battle, hunting and feasting are the most significant, shown both in mythological and non-

[24] On the peplophoroi statues see now Poggio 2018c.

[25] Childs and Demargne 1989: 16–7; Walker and Hughes 2010: 447–51; Higgs 2006: 165–6.

[26] For the reliance of the Mausoleum on the Nereid Monument, see Lucchese 2009: 78. New readings on the relationship between the two tombs have been put forward by Pedersen 2013: 132–40 (the Nereid Monument depending on Carian architectural solutions) and Prost 2013 (complex interaction between different cultural horizons).

[27] Robinson 1995; Barringer 1995: 59–66; Jenkins 2006: 196–8. See also Reinhardt 2018: 224–8.

[28] On Trysa, see Marksteiner 2002; 2010: 143–8. On the Heroon, see Benndorf and Niemann 1889; Eichler 1950; Bruns-Özgan 1987: 56–81 and 256–7, cat. M 3; Bérard 1988; Oberleitner 1994; Ridgway 1997: 88–94; Poggio 2007; Landskron 2011; 2015; 2017; Hoff 2017: 78–79, 491–496, cat. S70; Kolb 2018: 664–90; Poggio forthcoming. Childs (1973b and 1976) dates the monument to *ca.* 370 BC; for a new earlier dating, see Landskron 2015: 347–9. On the modern history of the Heroon, see Szemethy 2005.

mythological contexts (Figs. 14 and 15).[29] At present, it is the only tomb that does not use white marble for its structure and architectural decoration, although marble fragments were found inside the temenos; the orography of the territory of Trysa did not favour the extensive use of this material.

On the exterior, only the outer southern wall was adorned by a sculpted band, which depicted battle themes derived both from mythological and non-mythological sources. Access to the precinct was through a double door, decorated by a sculpted architrave. Accordingly, there was a hierarchy of access: some viewers were able to view only the outer southern wall, while others were allowed inside the enclosure. It was likely that this distinction impacted on the distribution of the themes.[30]

At the centre of the precinct was a Lycian house-shaped tomb, and possibly a marble statue and other sarcophagi.[31] In the south-east corner, immediately to the right of the entrance, there may have been a wooden structure – corresponding to symposiastic decorations – used for funerary rites.[32] A continuous band consisting of two superimposed friezes ran along the four interior walls, presenting a greater variety of subjects than the exterior. Here the visual itinerary was more flexible.[33]

Although some portions of the programme, notably the eastern wall, are poorly preserved, it is interesting to underline some general considerations on the entire programme. Scenes of a warlike character maintained a dominant role within the entire figurative programme. As on the façade, the depictions of war are divided between historical themes (the siege of a city on the western wall) and mythological content (Amazonomachy on the western wall, Centauromachy on the northern and eastern walls). The banquet and the hunt were also depicted in both historical and mythological scenes and offered flexible reading paths. For instance, the inner southern and northern walls are linked by a hunting theme, respectively the Calydonian Boar Hunt and a multiple-quarry hunt composed by a sequence of nine hunt scenes,[34] while the banquet theme is dominant on the two halves of the inner southern wall, with the representation of a symposium-like gathering and the slaughter of Penelope's suitors in the banquet hall of Odysseus' palace. The banquet theme may also be evoked by the preparation of a feast in the scene of the abduction of Leucippus' daughters on the northern wall.[35]

From this brief analysis it can be seen that the figurative cycle decorating the Heroon was carefully planned and had flexible reading paths, thanks to the different strategies that linked the narrative segments. In addition, the main themes – battle, banquet, and hunt – unfolded as both historical and mythological representations, a combination suited to the heroic exaltation of the dynast.[36]

The Heroon of Limyra

The Heroon of Limyra (*ca.* 370–360 BC), in eastern Lycia, is generally attributed to the dynast Perikle, who ruled over the city and extended his power over most of Lycia between 380 and 362 BC.[37] This monumental tomb was located halfway up a steep hill, at 230 m above sea level, on the road leading from the necropolis to the fortified acropolis. Delimited by an enclosure, it was situated on a terrace where rites for the deceased were held until the end of the Hellenistic period.[38] In such an elevated position, the Heroon dominated the coast and was visible from the sea.[39]

It was a temple-like tomb, with a high podium, similar to the Nereid Monument (Fig. 16). The staircase on the axis of the main façade did not have a practical function, but enhanced the solemnity of the complex. Above the podium there was a tetrastyle amphiprostyle structure which was provided with Caryatids instead of columns and contained a burial chamber.

Other free-standing sculptures decorated the monument, including the central acroteria representing Perseus holding the head of Medusa, and Bellerophon riding Pegasus and slaying the Chimaera, with related sculptures at the corners of the gables.[40] The use of white marble was limited to these sculptures and it is no coincidence that the marble sculptures of this monument are associated with Scopasian stylistic features.[41]

The mythological subjects of the acroteria fit very well with the figurative programmes of other contemporary Lycian dynastic tombs. Conversely, the lack of standard iconography on the Heroon of Limyra, such as battle, hunting and banquet scenes, should be emphasised. Two friezes decorated the outer eastern and western walls of the cella, and the southern outer wall was also possibly decorated.[42] Both the west and east friezes, which are both slightly different, depict a procession marching

[29] Dimension of the temenos: 21.65 x 26.54 x 22.70 x 25.50 m (Barringer 2008: 173).
[30] Poggio 2007; 2015.
[31] Marksteiner 2002: 160–76; Barringer 2008: 173–4; Landskron 2008: 219–22. For the architectural typology, see Fedak 1990: 88–91; Marksteiner 2002: 177–89.
[32] Eichler 1950: 36; Oberleitner 1994: 19. For a possible continuity of the heroic cult in the Hellenistic period, see Kolb 2018: 666 note 229.
[33] Poggio forthcoming.
[34] Benndorf and Niemann 1889: 106–15; 168–70.
[35] Bérard 1988: 189.

[36] Barringer 2001: 190; 2008: 196–7.
[37] On the monument, see Borchhardt 1976; Ridgway 1997: 94–9; Şare 2013; Kolb 2018: 690–4. On the attribution to Perikle, see Keen 1998: 158–9; Şare 2013: 57. See also Bruns-Özgan 1987: 81–91 and 255–6, cat. M 1, with a different interpretation and dating. On the sculpture of the Heroon and its dating, see lastly Hoff 2017: 71–73, 459–461, cat. S27.
[38] Fedak 1990: 70; Şare 2013: 59.
[39] *Götter, Heroen, Herrscher* 1990: 170; Şare 2013: 58.
[40] For the sculptural decoration of the tomb, see Borchhardt 1976; 1993; Boardman 1995: 191 and Figs 21.1-2; Benda-Weber 2005: 141–3.
[41] Borchhardt 1976: 92–3; Ridgway 1997: 97.
[42] Borchhardt 1976: 49; Şare 2013: 60.

Figure 14. Model of the Heroon of Trysa. Vienna, Ephesos Museum, Kunsthistorisches Museum, ANSA XIV Z 265. © KHM-Museumsverband.

from north to south, converging towards the main façade. J. Borchhardt interpreted the eastern frieze as a departure scene for a royal hunt with the dynast and the Great King Artaxerxes III, and he identified the western frieze as a military procession.[43] T. Şare, instead, considered both reliefs to represent military processions.[44]

Beyond the specific hypotheses, it is worth noting that no action, neither battles nor hunts – associated to dynastic rank on the other Lycian funerary monuments – is depicted here in its acme. This is a significant departure of this tomb from the Nereid Monument and the Heroon of Trysa, a difference that may reveal precise strategies of self-representation within a concurrence horizon.[45]

2.1.3. Phoenicia

This section will consider the royal architectural sarcophagi from Sidon, a well-defined cluster of four tombs that were produced in white Greek marble between the end of the fifth century BC and the end of the fourth. These marble sarcophagi were excavated in the hypogaeum of the Royal Necropolis of Sidon by Osman Hamdi in 1887, an event that started Ottoman archaeological activity, and then transported to Istanbul, an act that marked a new phase for Ottoman museum history.[46] The hypogaeum housed the anthropoid sarcophagus of Tabnit, king of Sidon: the long-standing use of this hypogaeum with its lavishly decorated marble sarcophagi points to the royal identity of the deceased. As mentioned, in the fifth century BC Sidon became the capital of Phoenicia and the seat of the imperial representative after the separation of the district of Trans-Euphrates from Babylonia.

The Phoenician tradition of royal burials in decorated sarcophagi should be dated back to the Sarcophagus of Ahiram, king of Byblos (*ca.* 1000 BC).[47] Here, the identification of the deceased is established by an inscription – the first in the Phoenician alphabet – mentioning the king, who is possibly represented as an enthroned figure on the bas-relief on the long side. The development of the architectural marble sarcophagi from the Royal Necropolis demonstrates the contribution of Egyptian and Hellenic elements, in addition to contacts with Cyprus.[48]

The Satrap Sarcophagus

This sarcophagus seems to mark the transition from the preceding anthropoid form, whose shape is retained inside the coffin only, to the sarcophagi with an architectural structure and rich figurative decoration (Fig. 17). Its material is generally identified as Parian marble.[49] It is generally dated to the last quarter of the fifth century BC, which makes it not only the oldest example among the sarcophagi of Sidon concerned here, but is earlier than the Anatolian rulers' tombs already mentioned.[50]

[43] Borchhardt 1976: 75.
[44] Şare 2013: 65–70.
[45] Pirson 2014: 153.
[46] Osman Hamdy Bey and Reinach 1892. On the hypogaeum, see also Assmann 1963 and Gabelmann 1979, with different hypotheses for the dating of the sarcophagi. On the archaeology of the Ottoman Empire, Bahrani, Çelik and Eldem 2011.

[47] Rehm 2004; Lehmann 2005.
[48] On the Phoenician sarcophagi, see Ferron 1993. See also Martin 2017: 143–4.
[49] Istanbul, Archaeological Museum 367. Kleemann 1958: esp. 35–50 on the typology; Ferron 1993: 107–16. For the *theke* sarcophagi in the Mediterranean, see Hitzl 1991: 24–131. For the start of production of marble anthropoid sarcophagi, see Lembke 2001: 84.
[50] Schmidt-Dounas (1985: 117) proposes to date the sarcophagus to 400 BC, Gabelmann (1979: 177) to 380–370 BC. On issues of dating, see Hitzl 1991: 76–7.

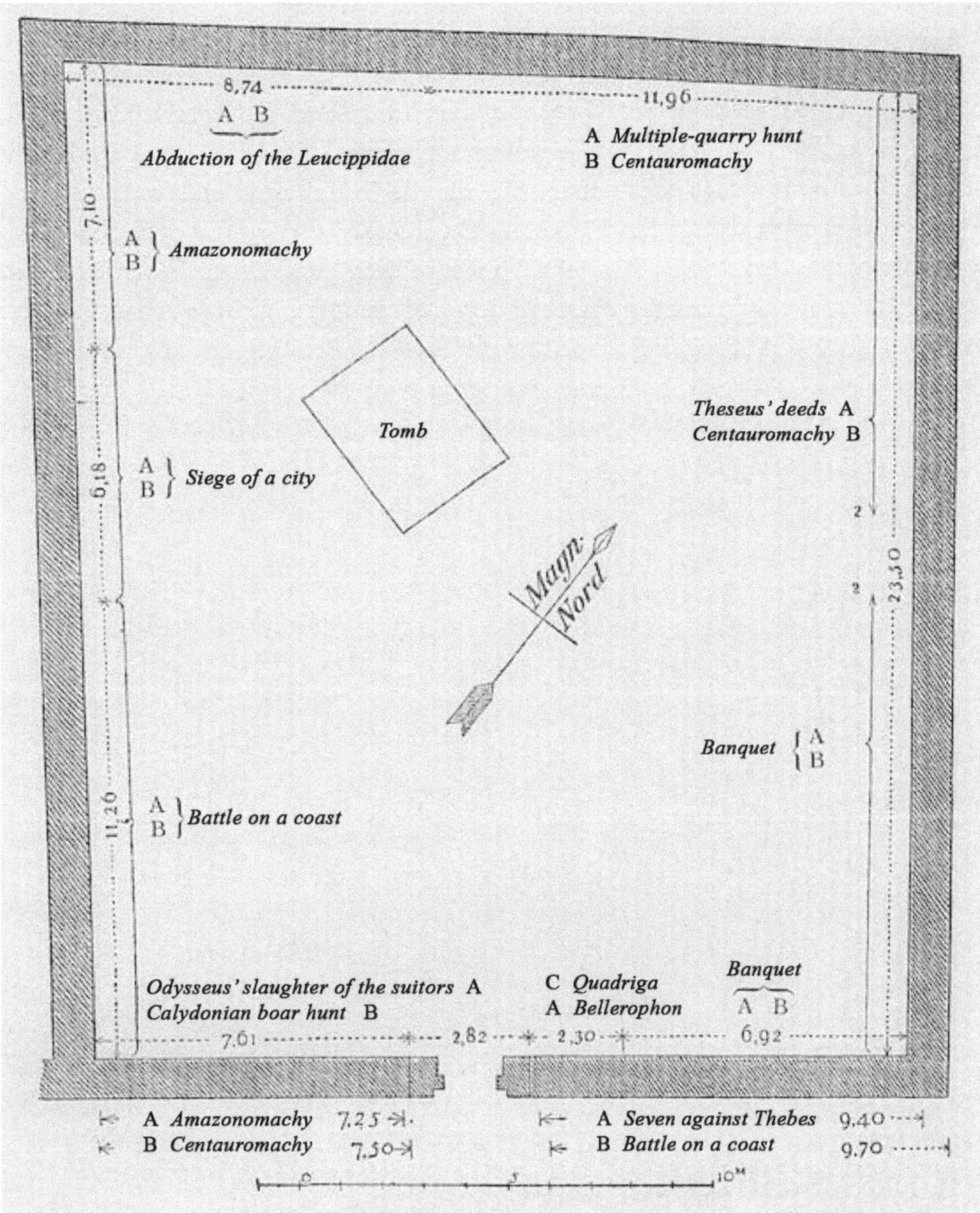

Figure 15. The themes of the friezes of the Heroon of Trysa. Modified after Benndorf and Niemann 1889: 55, fig. 37.

The name of the sarcophagus comes from the personage who is represented on three of the four sides. On one of the longer sides, which was the most visible in the hypogaeum, three figures hunt a deer and a panther (Fig. 56). The dynast is clearly recognisable due to his attire, his headdress and his majestic gesture while spearing the panther (Fig. 2). A fourth rider on the right is shown being dragged by a startled horse, running from the core of the scene.[51] On the opposite long side the main character is enthroned

[51] Poggio 2011: 485–7.

Figure 16. Model of the Heroon of Limyra. Reconstruction of Jürgen Borchhardt. Archaeological Collection, Institute for Classical Archaeology, University of Vienna. Courtesy of the Archäologische Sammlung, Institut für Klassische Archäologie, Universität Wien.

Figure 17. Scene of departure on the long side of the Satrap Sarcophagus. Istanbul, Archaeological Museum 367. D-DAI-IST-70-043 (Photo: W. Schiele 1970).

according to the usual "audience scene" theme (Fig. 17): he is looking at a scene that has been interpreted as the preparation of the royal chariot or as a departure.[52] Some servants are standing behind him. This representation should be included in the category of the "departure of the warrior"; the gesture of the figure on the throne, now lost, may have been a solemn salute to the person mounting the chariot, perhaps his young heir.[53] On one of the short sides four standing men in Persian garb holding spears are represented in relaxed poses. On the opposite short side the dynast is banqueting in a lavish environment with valuable accoutrements such as the drinking horn (Fig. 18). Alongside the main character are the dynast's wife in the attitude of a mourner and two servants.[54]

The Lycian Sarcophagus

This sarcophagus is probably of Parian marble and is datable to the first quarter of the fourth century BC.[55] Its name derives from its particular shape – a coffin with a gabled lid – which is unique in the Sidonian context (Figs. 19–20). Close similarities to the fourth-century BC sarcophagi of the Lycian elite, such as the Payava and Merehi sarcophagi from Xanthos, have led to the hypothesis that this sarcophagus was intended for outdoor use in Lycia, but then was plundered and brought to Sidon as war booty.[56] However, the proportions, material and artistic quality fit very well with the Sidonian context. The Lycian Sarcophagus shows differences from Lycian examples such as the material: there is scanty evidence for the production of marble Lycian sarcophagi.[57] Therefore, it is probable that the Lycian Sarcophagus was created for a Sidonian ruler according to a Lycian model, being a good example of imitation and movement of artistic patterns along the coastal areas of the Eastern Mediterranean.[58]

Compared to the Satrap Sarcophagus, the themes depicted are fewer. On the long sides, two hunting scenes, on horseback and from chariots, are represented (Figs. 19

[52] Kleemann 1958: 152.

[53] The theme of the departure of the warrior dates to the sixth century BC in Lycia, on the western wall of the painted tomb of Kızılbel (Mellink 1998: 59).

[54] Kleemann 1958: 120–5; Dentzer 1982: 243–5.

[55] Istanbul, Archaeological Museum 369. Schmidt-Dounas 1985; Ferron 1993: 117–25; Langer-Karrenbrock 2000; Fischer-Bossert 2003. For the chronology, see Schmidt-Dounas 1985: 100–17.

[56] Langer-Karrenbrock 2000: 200–1.

[57] See also Elayi 1988: 305. For a fragmentary marble lid of a typical Lycian sarcophagus, for which different chronologies have been suggested, see Demargne and Laroche 1974: 110–1; Prost 2015: 220; Hoff 2017: 522, cat. S89.

[58] See also Poggio 2017a.

Figure 18. The banquet scene on the Satrap Sarcophagus from Sidon. Istanbul, Archaeological Museum 367. D-DAI-IST-70-040 (Photo: W. Schiele 1970).

Figure 19. The feline hunt on the Lycian Sarcophagus from Sidon. Istanbul, Archaeological Museum 369. D-DAI-IST-71-58 (Photo: W. Schiele 1971).

and 57). In one of them five horsemen – one bearded and four clean-shaven – surround a boar, whereas in the opposite, hunters in chariots, interpreted as young princes or Amazons, pursue a lion.[59] The reliefs on the short sides represent Centaurs: on one side the episode of Caeneus according to the usual iconographical scheme is represented; on the other side, two Centaurs struggle over the body of a deer, the prey of a hunt (Fig. 20). On the short sides of the lid, seated sphinxes are depicted.

The Mourning Women Sarcophagus

The Mourning Women Sarcophagus, in Pentelic or Parian marble, is generally dated to the second quarter of the fourth century BC, and is attributed to King Straton I (ʻAbdʻašhtart in Phoenician), who was honoured by Athens when he welcomed an Athenian embassy on its way to Persia (Fig. 21).[60]

The sarcophagus derives its name from the majestic representation of female mourners standing or sitting between Ionic columns on the sides of the coffin (Fig. 22). These female figures have been interpreted as members of the deceased's family, the deceased's concubines or Muses.[61] Further elements of the sarcophagus are decorated. On the long sides of the "balustrade" of the lid are two processions with human figures, horses, chariots and carts.[62] These processions follow the pattern of the so-called Graeco-Persian convoy scheme, to be found on the Graeco-Persian stelae and in other funerary contexts, generally interpreted as funeral pomp with the transportation of the deceased's coffin. The theme of the "balustrade" thus would reinforce the mourning characteristics of the sarcophagus, already expressed by the women.[63] On the short sides of the "balustrade" pairs of male figures are represented on the raking cornices of two pediments (one of the pairs is not well preserved). The seated, bearded figures appear to be in mourning; the unbearded figures on side C address the older men, whereas the younger man on side D is also seated and turns towards the older one.[64] Each of the pediments, instead, are decorated by female figures: at the centre a seated mourning female is framed by two reclining figures. Each pediment is completed by two lateral acroteria, in

[59] For a debate on the identity of the hunters on chariots, see Fischer-Bossert 2003: 191. Non-mythological interpretation: § 5.2.2.

[60] Istanbul, Archaeological Museum 368. Fleischer 1983: 7, 61–3; Apicella 2010: 69–70. See also Ferron 1993: 125–44.

[61] See Fleischer (1983: 40–4) for a bibliographical overview on the subject; see also Elayi 1988: 314 (interpretation as Muses).

[62] Weller 1970.

[63] For a different interpretation of the convoy scheme, see Draycott 2011.

[64] This younger figure would be a female with cut hair, according to Osman Hamdy Bey and Reinach 1892: 248-9. The indication of the sides of this sarcophagus with letters follows Fleischer 1983.

Figure 20. Struggling Centaurs on the Lycian Sarcophagus from Sidon. Istanbul, Archaeological Museum 369. D-DAI-IST-71/57 (Photo: W. Schiele).

the shape of sphinxes, and one central floral acroterion. Another important theme occupies the socle of the tomb: a long frieze encircling the lower part of the sarcophagus is crowded with hunting scenes on the long sides and scenes of the return from the hunt on the short sides.

The relationship of the mourning women with the Ionic architectural structure of the coffin has fuelled diverse hypotheses on possible models. In this regard the Sidonian sarcophagus is mostly compared with contemporary dynastic tombs from southern Anatolia, the Nereid Monument and the Mausoleum of Halicarnassus, which had statues in their intercolumniation.[65] However, the theme of mourning figures seems to be a local feature: it recalls the royal sarcophagus of Ahiram from Byblos, and it was also on a relief near Byblos, in addition to some of the sarcophagi considered here.[66]

[65] Hellmann 2002: 217.

[66] Seyrig 1940: 113–4.

The Alexander Sarcophagus

The so-called Alexander Sarcophagus, whose material has been identified as Pentelic marble, is the latest of the four large sarcophagi in the Sidon Royal Necropolis, and is generally dated to the last quarter of the fourth century BC (Fig. 23).[67] It is thus attributed to Abdalonymus, who was appointed by Alexander the Great in late 333 or early 332 BC, and died perhaps in 312 BC.[68] Alexander and members of his entourage have been identified as the figures on the long sides.

The sarcophagus stands out among those previously analysed, showing innovative features. On one of the long sides a complex battle scene between Greeks and Persians is characterised by an unusual dramatic quality and vividness, which marked the beginning of a new figurative tendency in the Hellenistic period.[69] On the opposite long side a lively lion hunt with horsemen, men on foot and dogs is represented alongside a deer hunt on the right, forming a multiple-quarry hunt (Fig. 61). The two short sides are thematically consistent with the long sides. On one a panther hunt is depicted with a startled horse (Fig. 62), whereas on the second short side three pairs of warriors are represented, each pair composed of one Persian and one Greek. Hence this sarcophagus is the only one in Sidon to show a perfectly balanced combination of non-mythological hunts and battle scenes on the coffin.

The pediments depict two battle scenes: on one side it represents a battle between Greeks, on the other one a battle between Persians and Greeks. This implies that the overall programme shows a predominance of the battle theme, which is unique among the figurated sarcophagi from Sidon.

2.2. A comparative analysis of dynastic tombs

2.2.1. Topography and display

On the basis of the above analysis it is clear that the southern Anatolian dynastic monuments occupied prominent positions within cityscapes and landscapes.[70] Crucial factors were the architectural layout and the scenic position of these tombs, which were visible to those who sailed along the coast or approached the settlement from the sea. This visibility accords with new settlement patterns in Lycia and Caria, characterised by greater openness towards the coast.[71] The most significant example was the move of the Carian capital from inland

[67] Istanbul, Archaeological Museum 370. On the Alexander Sarcophagus: Osman Hamdy Bey and Reinach 1892: 272–342; Mendel 1912: 171–200; Winter 1912; Hiller 1961: 34–9; Schefold 1968; von Graeve 1970; Frel 1971; Hölscher 1973: 189–96; Messerschmidt 1989; Ferron 1993: 144–58; Houser 1998; Heckel 2006; Queyrel 2011; Martin 2017: 137–52.

[68] See lastly Martin 2017: 144. For the identification of the owner of the sarcophagus as Mazaeus, see Heckel 2006.

[69] Hölscher 2007: 27.

[70] For landmarks in fourth-century BC Caria, see Williamson 2014.

[71] For Lycia, see Zimmermann 2003: 270–2. For Caria, see Caliò and Interdonato 2005: 51–3; Caliò 2006: 596; 2007–8: 497; Prost 2013: 175.

Figure 21. The Mourning Women Sarcophagus from Sidon. Istanbul, Archaeological Museum 368. D-DAI-IST-71-98 (Photo: W. Schiele 1971).

Mylasa to coastal Halicarnassus, where Mausolus built his residence overlooking the sea.[72]

Other elements marked the reference to sea, which played an important role in the geopolitical context at that time. The "Nereids" of the Nereid Monument in Xanthos – whatever their interpretation – are undoubtedly entities of marine nature: at their feet elements such as a fish, a crab and a sea-shell are represented.[73] As for the Heroon of Trysa, the only outer wall that was monumentalised was the southern one: it overlooked the sea and one of its friezes showed a coastal battle, perhaps the representation of the defensive action coordinated by the local ruler against an invasion from the sea.

Another feature of these monuments, which must be analysed in close correlation with their visual prominence, was the presence of a temenos, implying an area with controlled access: the case of the Heroon of Trysa shows a monumentalisation of the enclosure itself. It follows that the function of landscape markers, visible to all, went hand in hand with restricted, or at least regulated access to the monument. This restriction set apart members of the dynastic families and local elites from the wider audience: it was not only linked to the approach to the building itself, conditioning the visibility of the tomb decoration, but also related to participation in rituals in honour of the deceased, documented at the Mausoleum of Halicarnassus and the Heroon of Limyra for long periods long after the time of burial.[74]

From the architectonic point of view one of the most striking elements of these tombs was the quest for increasing monumentality. The use of composite architectural typologies – often based on the temple pattern used in a funerary context, as in the Nereid Monument, the Heroon of Limyra and the Mausoleum of Halicarnassus – implied increasingly monumental structures, which offered the space to richer decorative displays. Nonetheless, it cannot be ruled out that to some extent the need to have more surface to decorate led to greater monumentalisation of the structures.

The case of Lycia is significant because developments in the typology of dynastic tombs can be traced on a regional

[72] For the residence of Mausolus, see Pedersen 2009.
[73] See for instance Sappho fr. 5: here the Nereids are invoked as divinities protecting sea-travels (Lidov 2016: 68). For an overview of the interpretation of these statues see Barringer 1995: 59–66 and Robinson 1995. For the Nereids in the Hekatomneion, Işık 2019: 29–31.

[74] For Halicarnassus, see Jeppesen, Højlund and Aaris-Sørensen 1981; Caliò 2007–8: 523. For the Heroon of Limyra, see Şare 2013: 59. In Caria see also the monumental tomb at Labraunda (Karlsson, Blid and Henry 2012: 76–80; Henry 2014).

Figure 22. Detail of one of the mourners on the Mourning Women Sarcophagus from Sidon. Istanbul, Archaeological Museum 368. D-DAI-IST-78/124 (Photo: W. Schiele 1978).

and transregional scale. Here on a regional basis, a pillar tomb typology of a monolithic block topped by stone slabs, often decorated on the exterior, which defined the burial chamber, underwent a marked development towards greater monumentality both in size and lavishness of material.[75] This is shown by the sequence of the Xanthian pillar tombs: the Lion Tomb, which at the moment is considered to be the oldest example (*ca.* 540 BC), the Harpy Tomb (second quarter of the fifth century BC) and the Inscribed Pillar (end of the fifth century BC).[76] In the first half of the fourth century BC – a time when significant rivalries are documented in the region – different funerary typologies emerged, partly new, partly based on the reinterpretation of traditional patterns.[77] The local adaptations of Hellenic architectural and iconographic elements suggest some awareness of the Greek world and artistic language, since artists and craftsmen active in Lycia must have been familiar with at least the major Ionic sanctuaries.[78] Further, the need to convey specific messages combined with Lycian traditions implied an original elaboration of the models.

Beyond these intra-regional dynamics, it is also possible to investigate transregional interactions. Contacts between Caria and Lycia were fundamental to create the cultural milieu that favoured the increasing monumentality of dynastic tombs here.[79] In addition, although scholars tend to consider the decorated sarcophagi from the Royal Necropolis of Sidon separately, they may contribute to a full understanding of the trends of that period.[80] These sarcophagi were smaller in size than the monumental tombs of the southern Anatolian coast. Moreover, this use of the dynastic hypogaeum differed from the practice of fourth-century BC dynasts in southern Anatolia, since there was no impact on the surrounding cityscape and landscape and the visibility of these sarcophagi was limited.[81] Nevertheless, royal burials at Sidon underwent a monumentalisation that could be compared with that just described for southern Anatolia in the same decades. Within this broader analysis of the Eastern Mediterranean royal burials from the sixth to the fourth century BC, it is interesting to note that the typological change occurred in Sidon at the end of the fifth century BC from an anthropoid to an architectonic sarcophagus slightly predated the analogous departure from the traditional local funerary shape – the pillar tombs – in Lycia. The Satrap Sarcophagus indeed can be dated to the period when the Lycian pillar tomb typology achieved its most monumental form in the Inscribed Pillar at Xanthos, before the turning point represented by the Nereid Monument.[82]

This transition, marked by increased monumentality and the presence (or appearance, in Caria and Phoenicia) of figural reliefs on tombs of dynastic rank, was common to distant coastal regions of the Eastern Mediterranean, and may be attributed to the interconnected character of this broad area, as already noted in Chapter One. A more marked openness towards the sea in the fourth century BC, demonstrated by the moving of the Carian capital from Mylasa to Halicarnassus and the visibility of the dynastic tombs from the coast, certainly facilitated that supraregional network. The use of a typically Lycian shape in the Lycian Sarcophagus from Sidon may testify to the effectiveness of overseas connections in the Eastern Mediterranean.

[75] For the increasing size of these monuments, see Draycott 2007.

[76] See Akurgal 1941: 3–51; Demargne 1958: 29–33, 37–47, 79–105; Marksteiner 2002: 278–85; Rudolph 2003; Draycott 2007; Seyer 2016; Rondholz 2020.

[77] For the ideology of dynastic power in Lycia, see Domingo Gygax 2001: 72–4. See also Poggio 2012: 231.

[78] See Poggio 2010; Fedak (1990: 66), instead, says that "the true nature of Greek sacred buildings was not quite clear to them [the Lycians]".

[79] See § 2.1.2.

[80] For monumental tombs in Anatolia see Fedak 1990: ch. 3; Israel 2016: chs. 3 and 4. Guimier-Sorbets (2008) pinpoints Macedonia as the driving force for the diffusion of monumental funerary models eastwards, excluding some pre-Hellenistic dynastic tombs, such as the Phoenician.

[81] See, in this regard, Apicella 2010: 71; Queyrel 2011: 39.

[82] On the proportions of the Inscribed Pillar at Xanthos, see Draycott 2007: 121, fig. 10. On the monument and its inscriptions, see *TAM* I: 38–48, no. 44; Demargne 1958: 79–105; Shahbazi 1975: 51–74; Asheri 1983: 85–97; Savalli 1988; Ceccarelli 1996; Cau 1999; 2003; Domingo Gygax and Tietz 2005; Schürr 2009; Burgin 2011; Dönmez and Schürr 2015; Schürr 2016; Müseler and Schürr 2018; Facella 2018.

Figure 23. The battle representation on the long side of the Alexander Sarcophagus from Sidon. Istanbul, Archaeological Museum 370. D-DAI-IST-8122 (Photo: Sébah & Joaillier about 1900).

2.2.2. The figurative programmes

The rich sculptural decoration of these monuments celebrated the dynasts, their families and their retinues. The programmes included similar and recurring themes, both mythological and non-mythological. In particular, hunting and battle scenes, banquets and representations of court life were depicted and combined to form a *leitmotiv* of the dynastic language in the Persian-period Eastern Mediterranean.[83] On the basis of the extant evidence, one can state that the aforementioned changes in funerary typologies at the end of the fifth century BC and the beginning of the fourth corresponded to a change in visual language as well. Lycia is the best case study to detect such phenomena, since it is possible to trace development over two centuries for the main figurative themes.

Material evidence and visual art testify to the marked importance of the social practice of the banquet in Persian-period western Anatolia.[84] The sixth-century BC relief of the Tüse Pillar from Lycia represented two banqueters on their own *klinai* with a servant, perhaps a fan-bearer. This image follows western Anatolian conventions, redoubling the "monoposiast" scheme, characterised by a man reclining alone on a *kline* and surrounded by other figures, such as on the Graeco-Persian stelae.[85] In these representations particular attention was paid to the social status of the deceased, shown through the presence of furniture and servants.[86] A change occurred at the beginning of the fourth century BC, when in Lycia – in Cadyanda, Xanthos and Trysa – multiple banquet scenes became popular, with attendants arranged in pairs on *klinai*.[87] The reliefs of the Heroon of Trysa, on the two halves of the inner south wall, stressed the importance of the collective banquet both in the historical

[83] See Jacobs 2014.

[84] Fehr 1971: 125; Baughan 2011 and 2013; Dusinberre 1999; 2013: 114–40; Draycott 2016; Poggio 2017b.

[85] For the Tüse Tomb, see Geppert 1998; Marksteiner 2002: 271; Draycott 2007: 113–4.

[86] Fabricius 1999: 33–8; Poggio 2017b. For banquet scenes in the Syro-Hittite context, see examples in Bonatz 2000. However, it should be noted that the banquet in the ancient Near East, apart from the relief of the North Palace of Ashurbanipal at Nineveh (London, British Museum 124920; Barnett 1976: pl. LXIV), was characterised by seated, not recumbent diners.

[87] The single banquet continues, however, for reasons related to the availability of surfaces to be decorated but undoubtedly also for aspects related to status; on banquet iconography in Lycia, see Dentzer 1982: 394–427. For the classification of the Lycian banquet and some clarification on the term "banquet", see Tofi 2006: 830; Lockwood 2016: 301.

(the dynast's banquet) and the mythical contexts (slaughter of the suitors).[88] In this new phenomenon the contribution of Greek art was undoubtedly important, as suggested by the appearance of a crater on the Nereid Monument frieze, absent in earlier Lycian images of banquets. The adoption of symposium iconography, however, was not devoid of local reinterpretation: on the Nereid Monument the egalitarianism of the Greek symposium – a principle embodied by the crater as a shared mixing vessel – is broken by the majestic solitude of the dynast (Sculpture 903; Fig. 24), depicted with proportions and attributes that set him apart from the other participants: here the coexistence of the crater and the precious rhyta of the banqueters in a homogenous style perfectly embodies the Graeco-Persian art.[89] Similarly, on the tomb of Salas in Cadyanda, on the border between Lycia and Caria, a single symposiast – possibly the wife of Salas – is surrounded by figures arranged in pairs.[90] This local version of the symposium, in which Greek iconography with adjustments provides a visual model for the dynastic ideology of that area, fits with the hierarchic arrangement of couches in the fourth-century BC *andrones* in Labraunda, which were patronised by the Hecatomnid dynasty.[91] The importance of banquet as a mirror of the court hierarchy in these regions recalls what is known about royal meals at the Persian Achaemenid court.[92]

Military themes played a prominent role in the imagery of dynastic Lycia.[93] In the sixth century BC strongly iconic scenes appear, such as the typical holding of the enemy's shield, as in the Lion Tomb of Xanthos and the Isinda Tomb, and the act of trampling the enemy, as in a relief from Xanthos, now in the Istanbul Archaeological Museum.[94] In the first half of the fifth century BC the war theme appeared in Xanthos on the Harpy Tomb, in a scene of helmet entrusting, but as dynastic legitimation rather than in association with the defeat of an enemy. In the last decades of the century, the Inscribed Pillar of Xanthos, whose inscriptions celebrate the dynast's military endeavours, once more bears a dominant war theme in an iconic form that appears directly linked to the monuments of the sixth century BC.[95] In the fourth century BC there was again a significant change, thanks to the broad development of narrative images. In the Heroon of Trysa the figures that can be identified as dynasts never fight in the front line. For example, on the battle frieze on the exterior façade the figure of the dynast remains to the rear. Similarly, in the magnificent siege scene on the western wall, the ruler is on the ramparts, coordinating the defence of the city. Consistently, in the narrative sequence of sieges on the small frieze of the podium of the Nereid Monument, the dynast appears in an audience scene, engaged in receiving ambassadors (Sculpture 879; Fig. 6). He is in military attire, but he is not represented as fighting.[96] In the Heroon of Limyra at least one of the two friezes (west) depicts the dynast's departure for war with his army, and once again the ruler's role as commander rather than that as frontline fighter is highlighted.[97]

Similarly, hunting scenes can be analysed throughout the two centuries of Lycian art with a discernible turning point in the fourth century BC. In the Archaic age there are three iconographic hunting schemes. The first consists of the protagonist, presumably the patron or the latter's heroic model, intent on a solitary struggle with the prey, as depicted on the west side of the Lion Tomb from Xanthos (Fig. 25).[98] The second pattern, present on the Isinda Tomb (520s BC; Fig. 26), is characterised by a chase with numerous participants moving in one direction, the core of which was inspired by East Greek models.[99] Finally, the paintings of the Kızılbel Tomb (*ca.* 525 BC) show a hunt by encirclement.[100] Absent on the Harpy Tomb and apparently on the Inscribed Pillar, hunting reappears strongly in the fourth century BC on dynastic tombs, such as the Nereid Monument (Fig. 58) and the Heroon of Trysa (Fig. 59), but also on sarcophagi like the Payava Tomb of Xanthos (Fig. 27). On these monuments, the hunts are apparently devoid of mythological features and follow the multiple-quarry hunt model, where a sequence of hunting episodes is assembled in the same continuous field. Each episode focuses on one or more prey from the same species and appears independent and self-enclosed. This hunt iconography was unknown in this region earlier.

In this analysis the Lycian case is dominant as it offers the unique possibility of a diachronic survey across two centuries of visual images. In Lycia, innovations in the dynastic images of banquets, battles and hunts emerged in the first half of the fourth century BC. Narrative aspects are enhanced and privileged in these figurative programmes. While the fourth-century BC change in Lycia emerges from a comparison with preceding local traditions, in

[88] For the identification of the dynast in the banquet scene on the southern wall, see Landskron 2017: 214–6.

[89] For Graeco-Persian art, § 1.3. Against the interpretation of the isolated banqueter as the dynast, see Borchhardt 1983: 218; 1985: 359. For an analysis of rhyta and the self-representation of the dynast in this banquet scene, see Ebbinghaus 2000; on these vessels in general, see Manassero 2008; Ebbinghaus 2018. For Greek symposium, see Catoni 2010.

[90] Dentzer 1982: 398–401 and Figs. 214–217.

[91] Poggio 2017b: 72–4. However, on the Hecatomnus Sarcophagus the "monoposiast" pattern is represented.

[92] Simpson 2005: 110; Lenfant 2009: 283; Henkelman 2010: 712. See also Ath. 4.145b–c = *FGrH* 689 F 2.

[93] Pirson 2006; 2014: 130–1.

[94] On the Lion Tomb, see Demargne 1958: 30; Marksteiner 2002: 234–8; Rudolph 2003: 35–41; Draycott 2007: 107. The tomb is dated to about 540 BC (Akurgal 1941: 100; see also Demargne 1958: 32 and Rudolph 2003: 41). For the relief, Poggio 2010: 235–6.

[95] For the Inscribed Pillar and its inscriptions, see *supra*. See also the scaraboid seal from Trysa dating back to the end of the fifth century BC (Knauss and Franke 2001).

[96] On the Nereid Monument the ruler was probably depicted as a warrior in the west pediment (Sculpture 925), but an iconic rather than narrative scheme was adopted here.

[97] Borchhardt 1976: 49-80. On the east frieze and different interpretations, see Borchhardt 1993; Şare 2013: 68–9.

[98] London, British Museum 1848,1020.31 (Sculpture B286). Akurgal 1941: 19–29; Demargne 1958: 30; Marksteiner 2002: 234–8; Rudolph 2003: 37.

[99] Istanbul, Archaeological Museum 763 T. Akurgal 1941: 73–92; Deltour-Levie 1982: 171–3; Özhanlı 2001–2; Rudolph 2003: 53; Draycott 2007: 109–10; Colas-Rannou 2009; Poggio 2010: 236; Hoff 2017: 449–50, cat. S17.

[100] Mellink 1998: 61.

Figure 24. The dynast as banqueter on the cella frieze of the Nereid Monument, Sculpture 903. London, British Museum 1848,1020.97. © Trustees of the British Museum.

Caria and Phoenicia it is hard to trace the development of imagery through the centuries.

In Caria, however, the Hecatomnus Sarcophagus and the Mausoleum of Halicarnassus marked the appearance of figurative programmes in dynastic funerary contexts. The royal sarcophagi of Sidon had already developed a neat tendency towards combination of narrative scenes at the end of the fifth century BC, and maintained this aspect in the fourth century BC. However, different choices as to the depicted themes are detectable in Phoenicia. Whereas in Lycia the coexistence of fixed themes on the same monuments appears as an established trend both on monumental tombs – the Nereid Monument and the Heroon of Trysa, and on smaller ones, like the Payava and Merehi sarcophagi of Xanthos,[101] the situation in Sidon appears uneven. Among pre-Hellenistic Sidonian sarcophagi, the Satrap Sarcophagus – the first of the series – bears a multiple-quarry hunt in which the direct participation of the deceased as the main hunter is undeniable, as well as a banquet scene according to the "monoposiast" pattern, in which the reclining dynast is accompanied by his wife and servants (Fig. 18).[102] Moreover, although the military sphere is not completely absent, if the long side with the sitting dynast is a scene of departure to battle, there is no battle representation.

Interestingly, the banquet representation on the Satrap Sarcophagus is the only occurrence of banqueting iconography on the Sidon sarcophagi. Moreover, these

[101] On these sarcophagi, see § 4.2.2.1.

[102] Kleemann 1958: 120–25; Dentzer 1982: 243–5.

Figure 25. Combat of a lion and a man on the Lion Tomb of Xanthos. Drawing. After Boardman 1995: fig. 208.2. Courtesy of Sir John Boardman.

sarcophagi had been devoid of battle scenes before the conquest of Alexander the Great, which took place in 333 or 332 BC. The representation of Centauromachy on the Lycian Sarcophagus can certainly be associated with a war theme, but on a different semantic level.[103] This can be explained by the role of the Phoenician kings, since they had priestly, diplomatic, warrior and judicial functions, but from a military point of view the local ruler's authority was limited both by the Great King and by political bodies such as councils and assemblies.[104]The Phoenician

[103] Schmidt-Dounas 1985: 25–6; Langer-Karrenbrock 2000: 49–53, 99.

[104] Stockwell (2010: 129) states: "It is clear from this historic arc that the Phoenician cities commenced as strong monarchies and ended with relatively weak kings. It is also clear that all along the way, from the fifteenth century BC to the fourth, the leaders were advised by councils or assemblies which gradually took greater power". Woolmer (2017: 62–3), who associates the Phoenician kingship to Near Eastern practices, is more cautious in considering the weight of these institutions throughout the centuries.

Figure 26. Hunt and triumph scenes on the Isinda Tomb. Istanbul, Archaeological Museum 763 T. D-DAI-IST-67-21 (Photo: W. Schiele 1967).

Figure 27. Hunt scenes on the crest beam of the Payava Sarcophagus. Drawing by Sir G. Scharf. London, British Museum 2012,5034.90. © Trustees of the British Museum.

inscriptions lack the exaltation of royal military skills in terms comparable to the Assyrian and neo-Babylonian traditions.[105]

Consistently, on most of the coins minted in Sidon before the arrival of Alexander the Great, the elements related to military activities were devoid of references to the local dynast. This is seen, for example, in the most frequent type, which bears a vessel equipped for war, sometimes in front of city walls. As would be expected Phoenician ships formed the core of the Persian fleet (Fig. 28).[106] On the other hand, organisation into autonomous city-states must have been well-established, and war was probably not perceived as an instrument of assertion among neighbouring centres in the way that it was in Lycia. Hunting depictions, on the contrary, were constantly present on the Sidonian sarcophagi, evidently playing a preponderant role in royal ideology. The preferred iconography is the multiple-quarry hunt in a continuous field, except on the Lycian Sarcophagus, which shows two hunting scenes on two distinct sides of the coffin. As already stated, the Alexander Sarcophagus is marked by a difference in the programme: while on the earlier Sidon sarcophagi the hunt represented the dominant activity, here hunting and war are balanced in terms of the decorated surface of the coffin; indeed, taking into account the pediments too, war scenes outnumber hunt images.[107] On the basis of its dating, this difference could be connected with the rupture from the preceding dynastic phase and a possible change in royal prerogatives implied by the arrival of Alexander the Great, in spite of the continuity of use of the Royal hypogaeum.

The multiple-quarry hunt scheme emerges both in Phoenicia and in southern Anatolia during the same decades as the dominant hunting iconography. It could be inferred that in the Persian period the Phoenician rulers could show their virtues only in hunting depictions. In Lycia, at the same time, the presence of hunting scenes alongside battles in figurative funerary programmes, as well as being linked to a more ancient Anatolian tradition, seems to balance the role of dynasts as strategists in the battle narratives.[108] Other possible meanings in these contexts will be explored in Chapter Five. In other words, the presence of multiple-quarry hunt is shared by the most important dynastic funerary tombs in the Eastern Mediterranean during the fifth and fourth centuries BC as part of complex figurative programmes.

2.3. Artistic phenomena under the dynasts

The preceding section presented the corpus of dynastic tombs at the centre of this research, and the comparative analysis revealed both local peculiarities and features shared across the Eastern Mediterranean. In this section further aspects connected with the artistic phenomena that at the same time contributed to and were the consequence of a supraregional connectivity will be discussed.

2.3.1. Circulation and mobility

In addition to intellectuals and diplomats, artists also circulated throughout in the Eastern Mediterranean, thanks to works commissioned by rich patrons such as the dynasts. The best-documented case is that of the Hecatomnids. Greek artists involved in the construction of the Mausoleum of Halicarnassus (Vitr. *De arch.* 7 *praef.* 12–13; Plin. *HN* 36.30–31) also worked within a wider horizon.[109] For instance, Scopas of Paros worked in Ionia and Caria, where he participated in the construction of the Mausoleum and, according to Pausanias, was the architect of the Temple of Athena Alea at Tegea, in the Peloponnese.[110] Scopas' movement demonstrates that even before Alexander the Great's time intellectuals and artists travelled across the Aegean in several directions, not only from Greece to Anatolia, but also in the opposite direction, with varying degrees of impact. Scopas' presence in western Anatolia, for instance, affected the sculptural production of Lycia – probably through the formation of a workshop – as identifiable from the style of the acroterial statue of Perseus from the Heroon of Limyra.[111]

The mobility of sculptors was connected to the movement of white marble. The circulation of this material along the Eastern Mediterranean shores appears more pronounced from the second quarter of the fifth century BC, with the completion of the Harpy Tomb and the peplophoroi of the "Building G" at Xanthos, as well as the early Phoenician anthropoid sarcophagi.[112] In the fourth century BC patrons made greater effort, and ancient sources and material evidence seem to testify to a marked interest in marble decorations in western Anatolia and Phoenicia during that period. Beyond the cases of the Nereid Monument and the Mausoleum of Halicarnassus, Mausolus himself may have used Proconnesian marble slabs for cladding in the decoration of his palace (Vitr. *De arch.* 2.8.10; Plin. *HN* 36.47).[113] In addition, a fourth-century BC marble fragment with an inscription in Aramaic from Hemite, on the inland Cilician Plain, may be interpreted as the dedication by a local ruler of a columned building with a religious function.[114] Recent archaeometric research on marble findings from Phoenicia has confirmed this

[105] Elayi 1987: 21–37; Woolmer 2017: 57. See also Anderson 1985: 75.
[106] For instance, Betlyon 1982: 6, nos. 7–8.
[107] Poggio 2012: 232 note 33.
[108] For the link with the Anatolian tradition, see Poggio 2012: 231 and Chapter Three.

[109] Corso 2019.
[110] This relationship between Tegea and Caria is further supported by the fact that Idrieus and Ada, the Carian dynastic couple who succeeded Mausolus and Artemisia, dedicated a relief of Zeus Labraundos at the sanctuary of Athena Alea (Waywell 1993; Carstens 2009: 35, 93–4). See Poggio 2019a.
[111] Borchhardt 1976: 92–3; Ridgway 1997: 97.
[112] Poggio 2010; 2018c.
[113] For the use of white marble in Labraunda under the Hecatomnids, see Freccero 2015.
[114] Bossert 1950: 124–5; Dupont-Sommer 1950: 45–7; Lemaire 1991: 205; Casabonne 1999: 59–60; 2000: 96–8; Lemaire 2000b. Held and Kaplan (2015: 180, no. 1) date a base, perhaps of marble, from Meydancıkkale in Rough Cilicia back to the Persian Achaemenid period.

Figure 28. Silver double shekel of 'Abd'eshmun, Sidon (obverse and reverse). New York, American Numismatic Society 1967.152.571. Courtesy of the American Numismatic Society.

tendency in this region as well.[115] This cluster of evidence suggests that in the fourth century BC – to varying degrees according to regional contexts – marble was largely chosen by Eastern Mediterranean patrons who favoured the circulation of people and ideas.[116] This is supported by the fact that seven out eight tombs researched here have been constructed with the use of white marble.[117]

The importance of marble was also due to its quality and durability when compared to soft limestone. Marble required specific skills in order to get the best result possible. For this reason its use implied the work of experienced artists. The Heroon of Limyra was built in local limestone, and this material was used for the friezes and the Caryatids. It is not a coincidence that the only parts to be sculpted in marble were the acroteria, which show a distinctive Greek style, as the Scopasian rendering of the head of Perseus suggests. The Scopasian language is not the only artistic impact from the Greek world that can be detected in these tombs. The reliefs of the Lycian Sarcophagus from Sidon, for instance, shows a marked connection with the Parthenonic art:[118] this can be detected in the rendering of the profile of the hunter with petasos in the boar hunt, comparable with the Parthenon frieze, and in the metopal representation of the Caeneus scene. This is not surprising if one considers that Sidon was in direct connection with Athens: in Chapter One it has already been mentioned that Athenians honoured the King of Sidon Straton.[119]

R. Fleischer has recognised Attic or Attic-trained artists for the Mourning Women Sarcophagus, which is generally assigned – as already seen – to Straton himself.[120] However, the case of the Mourning Women Sarcophagus reminds us that the artistic phenomena is far from being simple and homogenous: in fact, the theme of the balustrade is tightly connected with Anatolian imagery. Here, on the two long sides of the sarcophagus, two cortèges of open and covered carriages with people on foot are represented according to the so-called Graeco-Persian convoy scheme. This theme was mainly used in Anatolian funerary contexts: in the painted tomb of Karaburun II in Lycia, on some Dascylium stelae, and painted in the wooden chamber from Tatarlı. These scenes have been generally interpreted as funerary processions. C.M. Draycott, instead, has suggested a military interpretation of these convoys.[121] Regardless of the interpretation, it is noteworthy that a fifth-century BC Anatolian iconography was adopted around the middle of the fourth century BC on the balustrade of the Sidonian Sarcophagus, here with an unmistakable funerary meaning conveyed by the gestures of some figures.

This means that artistic relationships in the Eastern Mediterranean were complex and multi-faceted: in the case just analysed, what is recognised as the artistic language from mainland Greece is not the only one; rather there were other options, such as the Anatolian horizon, that

[115] Stucky 2012; 2016. See also Stucky 2009.

[116] For a comparative perspective on marble circulation, see Marconi 2010 (on marble sculpture in southern Italy and Sicily) and Ferretti 2007 (on the Italian Renaissance).

[117] For the use of white marble in Trysa, see the section on the Heroon (§ 2.1.2.). Marble was used also in the Hekatomneion.

[118] Ridgway 1997: 173.

[119] *Supra*, § 1.2.

[120] Fleischer 1983: 61–3.

[121] Draycott 2011.

played a relevant role in filtering stylistic and iconographic tendencies eastwards. To exemplify the presence of tendencies peculiar to the Eastern Mediterranean, the occurrences of an amphora used as a weapon by a Centaur in the scene with Caeneus should be considered. This occurs only twice in the art of the Classical period, on the Heroon of Trysa and the Lycian Sarcophagus from Sidon. This fact seems to confirm the direct connection between southern Anatolia and Phoenicia through the circulation of artistic patterns alongside artists and materials.[122]

These circulation patterns are noteworthy for other iconographies. Amazonomachies were represented on the Mausoleum of Halicarnassus and the Heroon of Trysa, and the larger podium frieze of the Nereid Monument was also drawn from this model.[123] Another interesting example is the representation of the deed of Theseus against Sciron, which is found both on the Trysa reliefs and on a coffer from the Mausoleum of Halicarnassus.[124] Centauromachies were depicted on the Mausoleum of Halicarnassus, in Trysa and on the Caeneus Sarcophagus of Limyra.[125] Therefore, it is worth noting that the only explicit mythological images on Sidonian sarcophagi are the Centaurs and – according to some scholars – the Amazons represented on the Lycian Sarcophagus, two themes that are well known from southern Anatolian tombs. Moreover, this Sidonian sarcophagus also shows typological links to southern Anatolia, as already hilghlighted above.[126]

From an architectural point of view, the most impressive example of Greek impact is the Heroon of Limyra, a temple-like building with Caryatids, a pattern that, once more, points to Athens, recalling the famous Caryatid porch of the Erechtheum. This monument, alongside the name of its supposed patron, Perikle, once again raises the question of the role of Athenian models during the fifth and fourth centuries BC in the Eastern Mediterranean.

This list of examples, which is not exhaustive, shows common features in the artistic language of the fourth century BC along the coastal regions of the Eastern Mediterranean in a very restricted timeframe. Moreover, a particular role in this phenomenon should be attributed to the extraordinary expansion of the Greek artistic language along the southern coast of Anatolia in this period, as it will be shown in the following section on workshop practices.

2.3.2. Workshop practices

As for the dynastic tombs under research here, the use of pattern books – here, meaning workshop drawings of an archetype on a reduced scale – has been identified by scholars.[127] The importance of workshop practices and pattern books as part of sculptural activity in antiquity has been acknowledged by F. Chamoux.[128] As outlined by S. Settis, in ancient workshops different steps determined the artistic process, in which drawing was a well-established practice: the definition of the work from the artist's intentions, the interaction with the patron, the composition of the work on a small scale, the production of models on a 1:1 scale, and in the possible use of squaring for transfer.[129]

The fourth-century BC Mediterranean offers different case studies of workshop practices, and Macedonian wall paintings are noteworthy in this respect. According to some scholars, squaring in the *Abduction of Persephone* in Vergina points to a technique for transferring and enlarging drawings.[130] In addition, it has been suggested that the silhouettes of Hades and Persephone correspond to those of Darius and the charioteer fleeing from the assault of Alexander the Great on the mosaic of the House of the Faun in Pompeii, which was probably inspired by a painting by Philoxenus of Eretria, pupil of Nicomachus, who was active at the court of Cassander (Fig. 29).[131] This technique involved the use of cartoons, silhouettes that facilitated the duplication of the outline onto other media.[132] The principle of a basic template of the outline that could be "filled" with the required elements recalls R. Bianchi Bandinelli's theory of reversible schemes (*schemi reversibili*). Regarding the figure of a boxer in the Tomb of the Monkey in Chiusi this scholar explored the possibility of using a single silhouette for two figures with the same outline, one represented from the front and the other from the back, by applying different lines for the body parts within the silhouette.[133] Studies of medieval cartoons have shown extensive flexibility in painting, even in mirror image.[134]

Etruria provides further examples of the serial production of images in the fourth century BC, in particular in Tarquinia, where it seems that in the second half of the century artistic workshops specialising in the decoration of alabaster and marble sarcophagi were active, choosing mainly subjects from Greek mythology and making extensive use of models and cartoons. For instance, according to recent research, a well-defined procedure was used for the decoration of the Amazon Sarcophagus from

[122] Poggio 2017a.

[123] See also the eastern, southern and northern painted friezes of the burial chamber of the Hekatomneion (Işık 2019: 27–46).

[124] For the Trysa relief, see Eichler 1950: 72; for the Mausoleum of Halicarnassus coffer, see Cook 2005: 71, no. 230.

[125] See also the western painted frieze of the burial chamber of the Hekatomneion (Işık 2019: 47–54).

[126] On the role of mythological representations in these dynastic tombs, see Papini 2012: 48–9.

[127] For instance, Bruns-Özgan 1987: 70–1; Ridgway 1997: 88.

[128] Chamoux 1958: 40–1.

[129] Settis 2006: 35–42.

[130] Settis 2006: 42.

[131] Moreno (1979: 713–4) connects this serial production to the *pictura compendiaria*, invented by Philoxenus (Plin. *HN* 35.110); see Ferri 2000: *ad loc.*, and Settis 1970 for a different interpretation of the *pictura compendiaria*.

[132] However, scholars do not agree on this issue concerning workshop practices in Macedonian painting: see, for instance, Brecoulaki's doubts (2006: 86–7; 93, no. 1).

[133] Bianchi Bandinelli 1939: 23–6; *EAA* III: 139.

[134] By their nature, allowing greater ease of transport, in the medieval period these cartoons could enjoy a wide circulation and they were also subject to theft. See Zanardi 1999; 2002: 63; Crivello 2004: 585. On the different types of models, see Nimmo and Olivetti 1985–6.

Figure 29. The Alexander Mosaic from Pompeii. Naples, National Archaeological Museum 10020. Courtesy of the *Ministero per i Beni e le Attività Culturali e per il Turismo – Museo Archeologico Nazionale di Napoli.*

Tarquinia, now in the National Archaeological Museum of Florence. The design was incised onto a white preparatory layer, then retraced in grey paint using a brush. Since no *pentimenti* are noticeable, it has been suggested that models were used to outline the figures (Fig. 30).[135] Another example relevant to Tarquinia is the so-called Sarcophagus of the Priest, in Parian marble, now in the National Archaeological Museum of Tarquinia. On one of the long sides the sacrifice of Trojan prisoners is depicted. This theme was a popular subject in the Tyrrhenian area in different media, with a significant cluster of evidence from the fourth century BC.[136] For instance, despite their larger scale, in the frescoes of the François Tomb of Vulci the representation of the sacrifice of Trojan prisoners in the presence of the shadow of Patroclus derives from the same model, with some variations, as the Tarquinia sarcophagus.[137]

The observations related to Etruscan art are useful for the study of the Eastern Mediterranean from a methodological point of view. The medium of sculpted friezes, which belongs to the plastic arts while sharing an affinity with pictorial practice, offers important insights into workshop practices. Scholars working on the funerary monuments of the fourth-century BC Eastern Mediterranean have explored the notion of "genre style" (*Gattungsstil*).[138] P. Demargne described the architrave with depictions of hunting on the Nereid Monument as "schématique, quantitative, répétitive", adjectives that suggest the use of a few basic elements, often varied, which were clearly legible from afar for these characteristics.[139] B.S. Ridgway indeed refers to the style of the architrave and cella frieze of the Nereid Monument as "almost cartoonlike appearance".[140]

The Nereid Monument is considered one of the most important examples of this "ornamental style".[141] On the hunting scenes of the architrave frieze, the silhouettes of the horses and riders hurling themselves towards wild beasts are similar, with minor variations, as if the individual figures were prepared from the same scheme (Figs. 58b-c). Similarly, on block 888, a single model, with the necessary changes, must have been used as the basis for three figures: two advancing characters looking back with an arm thrust forward, in an animated pose, and the wind instrument player (Fig. 58d).[142] Likewise, in the symposium scene on the cella frieze, most of the figures of servants in motion come from a single model, used in mirror image.

135 Setari 2007: 62.

136 Zevi 1996: 122–3. For the sarcophagus, see Blanck 1982; Martelli 1975: 12–4.

137 Maggiani 1985: 208–12. For the François Tomb of Vulci, see Buranelli 1987; Moretti Sgubini 2004; Paltineri 2012; Podda 2012; Bardelli 2012; Letta 2013.

138 For a discussion with bibliography, see Bruns–Özgan 1987: 191–7. See also Hiller 1960 and 1961; Wiegartz 1968: 55–64.

139 Childs and Demargne 1989: 354. The series of characters on blocks 895, for example, came from the repeated use of the same model in a paratactic way, with variation seen in the figure with the horse, in the hand grabbing the reins.

140 Ridgway 1997: 87.

141 Bruns–Özgan 1987: 193–5.

142 The end of the block probably showed a fourth figure made from the same model.

Figure 30. Sarcophagus of the Amazons. Florence, National Archeological Museum 5811. Courtesy of the *Museo Archeologico Nazionale di Firenze* (*Direzione regionale Musei della Toscana*).

The use of cartoons in producing the decoration of this monument is supported by analysis of the unfinished block 908 of the cella frieze, which allows a reconstruction of the various working phases. The figures, simply outlined, emerge solidly from the background, without any definition of details (Fig. 31).[143] For the Parthenon frieze, scholars have speculated that once the blocks were *in situ* the artists made an initial outline of the subjects to be sculpted on the marble, using small cartoons for the details. Subsequently, they drilled out the contours and carried out the final sculptural work.[144] As in the great Athenian building, the Nereid Monument required preliminary planning to define the layout of the figured friezes and the proportions of individual figures. Block 908 attests to an intermediate stage in relief production, perhaps through drawing. Cartoons may have been used to sketch the silhouettes of the figures, and the sculptor initially outlined the volume and defined the background. Subsequently, details were added using appropriate tools for more refined work, to characterise the figures and differentiate the basic layout provided by the patterns.[145] The possible models used by artists in outlining silhouettes may have been light and easy to handle such as papyrus, leather or clay. It is also known that wood and wax were used in Athens for models or architectural elements.[146]

Indeed, one can hypothesise that models, namely on a scale of 1:1, were used on the Nereid Monument. The use of models in fourth-century BC Xanthos is supported by the analysis of the contemporary sarcophagi from the same site. On the Payava Sarcophagus crest beam the figure of the mounted hunter is replicated three times and the scenes differ only in the prey. The same model was probably also used in mirror image for the two riders on the opposite side of the beam (Fig. 27). A similar technique can be seen in the battle scenes on the beam of the Merehi Sarcophagus: some figures of soldiers seem to be repeated in different directions, with changes in weapons and equipment (Fig. 64a). A further use of patterns in Lycia is seen on the hunting scenes from the slabs of the Heroon of Trysa, in particular with the riders in A11 and A14 (Fig. 59).

One of the main consequences of the use of models is the effect of serial reproduction of the image.[147] This is well demonstrated by another paradigmatic case of *Gattungsstil*, the socle of the Mourning Women Sarcophagus in Sidon (Fig. 32). On the two long sides the figures are distributed in regular intervals, as noted by F. Hiller: each character, in fact, occupies a precise position in relation to the Lesbian kymation below.[148] The lower part of the body of many of the figures comes from a repeated pattern, with the left leg stretched out and the right bent due to the weight of the body, combined with various upper body positions depending on the scene. R. Fleischer even speaks of recurrent and repeated schemes.[149] The measurement of distances between the feet of the individual figures confirms the presence of a constant: A19 and A21, for example, with the mirror-image figure A20, have an inner distance between their feet of 4 cm; B2, B3 and B8 have the same internal distance between their feet. The horse at A10 and between A20 and A21 reflects a mirror image of the same model. The overall effect is that of a tablet on which a cylinder seal has been rolled, impressing a number of repeated figures – an administrative practice that came back into use in the Persian age during the reign of Darius I (522–486 BC).[150] Repeated and varied use of a limited number of patterns along the entire frieze is

[143] Ridgway 1997: 88; Higgs (2006: 176) observes that the tomb was finished quickly, perhaps for lack of money, so the sculptors had no chance to finish their work.
[144] Younger 1991: 295; Neils 2001: 80. Designers and sculptors could be different people, as scholars affirm, but this is not necessarily true.
[145] For an analysis of tools used by sculptors, see Blümel 1969: 73.
[146] Hellmann 2002: 39; for use of clay in serial productions, see Heilmeyer 2009: 652–4.
[147] On seriality in antiquity, see Settis 2015. For a "phenomenology of repetition" in medieval art, and in particular for serial production, see Crivello 2004: 578–80 and 583–6. See also Zanardi 1999; Nimmo and Olivetti 1985–6.
[148] Hiller 1960: 1.
[149] Fleischer 1983: 32.
[150] On seals used in the Achaemenid era, see Meadows 2005: 189.

Figure 31. Unfinished block of the Nereid Monument of Xanthos, Sculpture 908. London, British Museum 1848,1020.104. © Trustees of the British Museum.

B1 B2 B3 B4 B5 B6 B7

Figure 32. Detail of the socle of the Mourning Women Sarcophagus from Sidon. Istanbul, Archaeological Museum 368. D-DAI-IST-R1772 (Photo: W. Schiele 1968).

confirmed by other details: the stag hunting scene with B15 and B16 is the result of a combination of segment A19 and the stag (here reversed), and of that consisting of A15, A16 and A20, with suitable variations, given that A16 and B17 do not overlap completely. On the other hand, the pattern of the hunter leaning forward is repeated with many variations: it is used primarily for the figures looking after the dogs (A7 and A16, and B1 in mirror image), but also for a character leaning down to pick up a stone from the ground (B14), in addition to B17. These figures, by changes in the gestures, create a lively image of the crowded hunt team. Such an analysis leads to reflection on the complex activities required of a workshop dealing with such a commission. It may be assumed that first of all the Lesbian kymation was obtained by reiterating the same pattern. Then, the kymation was used to mark the rhythm of the figuration of the socle frieze.[151] In Phoenicia the presence of workshop practices related to decorative patterns in relief art is also attested.[152]

This aspect of repeated image reproduction has multiple implications. From a social and economic perspective, it implies the organisation of work among various components of the workshop to enable rapid completion, perhaps with time and financial restrictions, and to create complex figurative cycles.[153] From the art-historical perspective, on the other hand, one should not overlook the potential circulation and dissemination of models, a mechanism that justifies common features in the artistic language of the Eastern Mediterranean. Moreover, these artistic processes may also explain the evolution of original iconographies thanks to derivation mechanisms inspired by formal elements from other cultural contexts, such as the Hellenic world.[154]

The fact that artists from the Greek world, or at least trained in Greek artistic language and active in the Eastern Mediterranean, used workshop practice provides a concrete element to reflect on the flexibility and the success of Greek art beyond the Greek world *stricto sensu*. These considerations enable one to include the great dynastic funerary monuments in the context of a form of artistic market. M. Baxandall stated in reference to the Renaissance, that art markets express the orientations of the societies that artists may follow or ignore, responding variously thus to the patron's demands.[155] This was also a widespread trend in the fourth century BC, as the Macedonian and Etruscan examples have shown.

2.4. Conclusion

The dynastic funerary monuments of the fifth and fourth centuries BC form the most important evidence of the artistic language of the Eastern Mediterranean. The comparative analysis has shown both differences and similarities. Among the common features hunt theme seems to be the most recurrent: seven out of the eight dynastic funerary monuments from the late fifth and fourth centuries BC concerned here are characterised by the presence of this theme in their figurative programmes. Only the Heroon of Limyra is devoid of this imagery, although J. Borchhardt, mentioned above, has hypothesised that one of the friezes represented a departure for the royal hunt.[156] If the popularity of the hunt can be traced back to its generic importance within aristocratic societies, there is a striking record that should be considered: the multiple-quarry hunt is the most popular hunting iconography for dynastic tombs.[157] In other words, the great majority of the representation of dynastic hunts follows the same iconographic pattern. This iconography thus conveyed precise values and its investigation may be a privileged field for identifying common elements within the ruling ideology in the Eastern Mediterranean regions during the Persian period.

The presence of shared trends may be explained through internal factors, such as patronage, which played a role in the process of adopting and developing different cultural horizons (local, Hellenic and Persian), and which triggered the circulation of materials such as white marble and the artists themselves, rather than only external reasons, such as the enhanced "reputation of the mainland Greeks".[158] These observations assign to the single local contexts – the Anatolian regions and other Eastern Mediterranean coastal areas such as Phoenicia – an active role in shaping new languages, such as Graeco-Persian.[159]

On the other hand, the wide area concerned in this study is characterised by different roots, on a regional level thus it is important to underscore local peculiarities and traditions. Therefore, in order to investigate the success of the multiple-quarry hunt iconography in this area and detect a possible origin of the iconography, it is important to explore iconographic and iconological aspects in connection with the single cultural horizons.

[151] It is possible that different artists worked on the two phases, as other contexts can demonstrate: in thirteenth-century AD and later painting cycles, for instance, some artists specialised in producing decoration and others in figures (Crivello 2004: 584).
[152] A relief from ancient Antarados has been interpreted as a repertoire of patterns of vegetal motifs to be used by artists in the decoration of monuments (Gubel 2002: 36–7, no. 15). For an overview of Phoenician sculpture, see Fontan 2007 and now Martin 2017. It is worth mentioning that Phoenician relief art enjoyed a long-standing tradition, in particular through the use of ivory (see Di Paolo 2009).
[153] For economic aspects of serial production, see Crivello 2004: 584–5.
[154] On the eastern pediment of the Nereid Monument, see Poggio 2016b: 212–6. By derivation is meant the repetition of an image with new content and a new function compared to the archetype (Crivello 2004: 588).
[155] Baxandall 1980: 95. For the interaction between artists and patrons in the modern age, see Settis 2010.
[156] Borchhardt 1976: 75.
[157] An exception seems to be the Hecatomnus Sarcophagus in Mylasa, with a single-prey hunt; however, it would be interesting to see if a multiple-quarry hunt was intended for the decoration of the exterior of the tomb.
[158] The quote is from Fedak 1990: 65.
[159] On the role of patrons in Lycia and Phoenicia see Ridgway 1997: 102; Martin 2017: 152.

Figure 33. (following page) Hunting scenes on a gilded silver disc belonging to the Oxus Treasure. London, British Museum 123925. © Trustees of the British Museum.

3

The Multiple-Quarry Hunt: History of an Iconography

Hunting has played a crucial role in world history since the appearance of hunter-gatherer societies in the Palaeolithic. Such societies have been much debated by anthropologists, archaeologists and ethnologists, and have been the focus of different perspectives and points of view.[1]

It is indisputable that hunting was an important means of subsistence in these societies, based on pursuing the meat of wild animals through predation. The capacity of humans to carry on this activity in different ecosystems required adaptation to a variety of contexts. Although the introduction of domestication during the Neolithic may have undermined the importance of hunting, it still maintained a complementary role among other activities aimed at subsistence. In particular, in the ancient Near East hunting assumed an important symbolic value in connection with the display of power.

As will be explained, the regions concerned here, which were characterised by dynastic government also took part in the use of this iconography.[2] What this study will underscore is that not only was hunting largely present on the dynastic funerary monuments of the Persian-period Eastern Mediterranean as a sign of social status, but that a specific iconography, the multiple-quarry hunt, conveyed precise socio-political messages, valid for most of the strongly hierarchical societies that developed along the Mediterranean coasts in the shadow of central Persian power.

The remarkable adoption of the multiple-quarry hunt on dynastic monuments of the Persian-period Eastern Mediterranean raises many questions about this iconography. Although hunting as the activity of ruling classes is a constant *leitmotiv* from antiquity to the modern age, the emergence of the multiple-quarry hunt in the context concerned here stimulates research into its origins and meanings. In this chapter the analysis, therefore, will focus on the cultural horizons – preceding and contemporary – that have contributed to the artistic language of the regions concerned here.

3.1. The Eastern Mediterranean and the Near East before the Persian Empire

In order to investigate the endurance and originality of the themes and figurative strategies on monuments during the fifth and fourth centuries BC it is useful to provide a historical framework of the iconography of the earlier multiple-quarry hunt. This analysis will be carried out for the Eastern Mediterranean and other civilisations that may have impacted on the artistic representations researched here.

3.1.1. The Syro-Anatolian area

From an iconographic point of view, in the Hittite and Syro-Hittite contexts representations of hunts combining different species of prey appear to be widespread, but a dominant compositional device cannot be traced. Generally, two strategies can be identified: distinct animal species for each figurative field and the coexistence of multiple prey in a single hunt episode.

3.1.1.1. The Hittites

Hunt scenes are not as common from the Hittite civilisation (seventeenth-twelfth centuries BC), even though this activity was part of their ideology.[3] Since the dynamics between predators and prey impacted on the natural balance, hunting was connected to the sacred values of society and was legitimised through ritualistic ceremonies.[4] In particular, the deer hunt had an important religious role. The association between hunting and cult appears to be a frequent element in Hittite visual arts, from monumental sculpture to portable artefacts. This is shown by a silver stag-shaped drinking vessel, perhaps of the fourteenth century BC, an object used for libations, which is decorated with a figured frieze with an offering to Kuruntiya, the Stag-God, and other elements referring to hunting.[5] In addition, the fact that red deer is the main wild mammal among the remains from the *Unterstadt* of present-day Boğazköy, ancient Hattusha, capital of the Hittite Empire, is connected with the Great Temple.[6]

On the West Tower of the Sphinx Gate of Alaca Höyük, a procession and two hunting scenes were represented on blocks in two rows (Figs. 34a-b).[7] In the upper row, a block

[1] Barnard 2004.

[2] See also Barringer 2001: 182.

[3] Hawkins 2006. See also Klengel 2007: 168–70. For the rareness of hunting scenes, see Orthmann 1971: 426.

[4] Archi 1988. On the connection between the hunt and the sacred, see Güterbock 1956: 55; Crepon 1981: 146–8; De Mérode and Damblon-Willemaers 1983; von der Osten-Sacken 1988: 69–71.

[5] New York, Metropolitan Museum of Art 1989.281.10. Muscarella 1974: no. 123; Güterbock 1989: 113–8; Archi 1988: 31; Hawkins 2006: 50, no. 2; Blanchard 2019a: 58, no. 1 (V. Blanchard). On the artists, see Matthiae 1997: 78.

[6] Berthon 2017: 177. For archaeo-zoological analysis at Hattusha, von den Driesch and Pöllath 2004.

[7] Ankara, Museum of Anatolian Civilisations 13 A.B.C. and 14 A.B.C. Schachner 2012: 137–9. See also Garstang 1929: 124–44 (with doubts on the proposed reconstruction); Güterbock 1956: 54–6; Mellink 1970; Archi 1988: 30–1; Emre 2002: 220; Taracha 2011. Scholars suggest various dates; Schachner (2012: 139; 2013: 537–8) recently proposed the sixteenth to fifteenth century BC.

Figure 34. Orthostats from the West Tower of the Sphinx Gate of Alaca Höyük. (a) Ankara, Museum of Anatolian Civilisations 13 A.B.C. D-DAI-IST-4681. (b) Ankara, Museum of Anatolian Civilisations 14 A.B.C. D-DAI-IST-4669.

hosted two different hunting scenes, organised in two registers. At the far right of each register, a hunter – who Th. Macridy suggested should be identified as one person, the king – is kneeling, ready to shoot an arrow to the left.[8] The quarry in the upper register is a boar that seems to be charging towards the man; below, a deer grazes, tied with a rope, and used as a decoy to attract the animals of the same species represented on the adjacent block.[9] Thus, in the two Alaca Höyük hunt scenes, the separation of the registers is intended to differentiate the species of prey.[10]

The bronze bowl from the Kınık hoard, usually dated to the thirteenth century BC, shows a composition that resembles the Alaca Höyük reliefs.[11] Its repoussé decoration is organised in two superimposed bands. A hunt is represented in the upper register, with numerous specimens including stags, does and ibexes, some of which have already been killed. Only one archer leads the hunt and, as at Alaca Höyük, has a tethered deer as a decoy. On the lower register, two scenes, interspersed with lions attacking bulls, represent a boar and a stag hunt, led by two characters that R.M. Czichon also deems to be the same character. This bowl confirms the importance of the compositional device that keeps the different quarry clearly separated, although the two hunting scenes on the lower register are represented in the same figurative field.[12]

Hittite glyptic art, however, shows a different phenomenon. The partly preserved hunting scene on a seal reconstructed from two partial impressions from Boğazköy represents a kneeling hunter armed with a bow, shooting arrows at a deer and a lion in flight in the outermost figurative field.[13] Here, therefore, two different species of prey are hunted by a single archer within one scene. This arrangement is repeated on the lower register of a small cylinder seal, dated to the mid-second millennium BC, in which one scene shows lions and a number of deer chased by a single hunter in a chariot.[14]

3.1.1.2. The Syro-Hittites

After the fall of the Hittite Empire in the twelfth century BC, a number of states were formed in south-eastern Anatolia and northern Syria, the Syro-Hittite states (twelfth-eighth centuries BC) known also as neo-Hittite or Syro-Anatolian. Their culture was related to the Hittite tradition, although the ethno-linguistic composition of this area was far from homogeneous.[15] Between the eleventh and ninth centuries BC, which was a period of independence before they entered the Assyrian orbit, these states developed an official art linked to royal power, which was expressed mainly in relief-carved orthostats decorating the monumental gates to cities and citadels.[16] As S. Mazzoni has emphasised, these places symbolised the transition from order (city), of which the ruler was guardian and protector, to chaos (outside the city).[17] The presence of a hunt theme at the border area of a settlement may be connected to its ritual value. For this reason, predation activity taking place outside the urban perimeter was represented outside the gates, often accompanied by scenes of ritual purification.[18]

The site of Arslantepe, ancient Melid, has produced two reliefs of the Syro-Hittite context, dating back to the twelfth to tenth century BC and later reused in the Lion Gate.[19] Two blocks carved with bas-reliefs, one with a chariot lion hunt and the other also showing a deer hunt from a chariot (Fig. 35),[20] were probably created for the same cycle: thus, hunts with two different quarry appeared in distinct figurative fields.[21]

At Zincirli, hunting scenes developed on more than one orthostat, both in the Southern City Gate (dating from the late tenth century BC) and in the Outer Citadel Gate (dated to the early ninth century BC).[22] In particular, three reliefs from the Southern City Gate may be considered part of the same narrative segment.[23] A hunter on foot – with a dead hare behind – is armed with a bow and is aiming rightwards (Fig. 36a).[24] On the second relief a stag is already pierced by an arrow and pursued by a dog (Fig. 36b). Finally, it follows a relief with a lion and a stag moving in the same direction. These three reliefs are often interpreted together as a multiple-quarry hunt, but this theory is not unanimous, since it has been proposed that the third orthostat with the lion and stag is an element

8 Macridy 1908: 18–9.

9 Mellink 1970: 19–20. See also Wiesner 1942: 426. More doubtful is the presence of the tethered deer as evidence of this animal being domesticated (De Mérode and Damblon-Willemaers 1983: 177).

10 On another Alaca Höyük relief is a lion hunt (Bittel 1976; Bryce 2002: 193, fig. 6).

11 Kastamonu Museum 946. Emre and Çınaroğlu 1993; Hawkins 1993; Czichon 1995; Matthiae 1997: 78–9; Schachner 2012: 137 and note 16 on dating.

12 For considerations on the composition of the registers, see Czichon 1995: 9–12.

13 Ba 209/a. Güterbock 1942: no. 220; 1956: 55; 1957: 63; 1989: 119.

14 Paris, Musée du Louvre AO 20138. As noted by A. Parrot, four chariots are represented but only one carries a figure armed with a bow, the hunter, while the other figures on chariots seem to simply belong to the hunt team. He also suggests that the presence of deer heads in the lower frame of the figurative field indicates the success of the hunt (Parrot 1951: 185 and 190). See also Güterbock 1957: 63.

15 On the Syro-Hittite states, Liverani 2011: 631–43; Giusfredi 2010; Bryce 2012. See also Novák 2019, with caveats on the different labels used to define these entities.

16 Blanchard 2019b.

17 Mazzoni 1997.

18 Mazzoni 1997: 315. On hunting as part of ritual performances to be held at the gate, as in the Hittite model, see Gilibert 2011: 60–1, 118.

19 Mazzoni 1997: 310–1. For the archaeological context, see Frangipane and Liverani 2013.

20 For the history of the archaeological research, see Delaporte 1940: 5–10; Frangipane 2004: 15–6.

21 Orthmann 1971: 93, 418. According to Delaporte (1940: 55), the two hunt reliefs are not completely contemporary. The Lion Gate's figurative cycle featured ritual, mythological and hunting scenes (Pecorella 2004: 169). For hunting practices at Arslantepe, see Bökönyi 1993. On the two reliefs, see now Blanchard 2019a: 201–2, nos. 83-84 (V. Blanchard).

22 Mazzoni 1997: 319.

23 Istanbul, Ancient Oriental Museum 7716 (Orthmann 1971: Zincirli A/7; Gilibert 2011: Zincirli 8); 7718 (Orthmann 1971: Zincirli A/8; Gilibert 2011: Zincirli 9); 7710 (Orthmann 1971: Zincirli A/9; Gilibert 2011: Zincirli 10). See also Orthmann 1971: 60; Gilibert 2011: 58–61. On the state of preservation, see Orthmann 1971: 537.

24 For a religious interpretation of the hare, see Crepon 1981: 147.

Figure 35. Deer hunt on a relief from Arslantepe. Paris, Musée du Louvre AM255. Photo © RMN-Grand Palais (musée du Louvre) / Les frères Chuzeville.

Figure 36. Orthostats from the Southern City Gate of Zincirli. (a) Archer with hare. Istanbul, Ancient Oriental Museum 7716. D-DAI-IST-71/12 (Photo: W. Schiele 1971). (b) Deer and dog. Istanbul, Ancient Oriental Museum 7718. D-DAI-IST-71/16 (Photo: W. Schiele 1971).

not connected with the other hunt reliefs of the gate.[25] However, the first two reliefs are relevant, as the presence of a dead hare behind the archer suggests the first stage of the hunt has already been completed, and the stag is the hunter's next victim. Therefore, the archer is depicted in the act of hunting prey of different species. The multiple-quarry hunt iconography would be emphasised if the relief with lion and stag belonged to the sequence.[26]

At Tell Halaf (ancient Guzana) the West Palace is of interest. The importance of hunting in the ideology of power is demonstrated here by the widespread presence of hunting scenes in the decoration of the hilani which is linked to the name of Kapara and generally dated to the ninth century BC. Scholars have generally called this building a "temple-palace".[27] The north side of the hilani, with the main façade, was decorated with large orthostats carved at the same time as the building. Two bow hunts, one of a bull (Fig. 37) and the other of a deer, each carved on a separate relief, were arranged symmetrically around the axis of the portal.[28] On the outer southern wall and on the southern part of the west and east walls of the hilani were the so-called "small orthostats", carved in limestone and basalt, and they chiefly depict men and animals. The "small orthostats" are generally dated to the first half of the ninth century BC, so a little earlier than those of the main façade. They were possibly originally created for a temple of the Storm God.[29] These reliefs were adapted for the hilani and arranged in a typological rather than a narrative sequence (for example, the series of archers and animals).[30] The iconographies are diverse. Some orthostats feature hunting scenes of lions and bulls conducted from chariots (A 3,56–58) or on foot (A 3,52); other reliefs show combats between men and real or imaginary animals (A 3,51 and 53–55).[31] Lastly, there are orthostats of the same series showing only men armed with bows, spears and slings, or animals of different species, such as deer, lions, bears and birds, depicted in profile to the right or left. A. Özyar combined two blocks pertaining to a single hunting scene (A 3,57 and 101), and hypothesised that A 3,58 and A 3,8 were originally part of hunting narrative segments as well.[32]

The case of Tell Halaf thus reinforces the connection between hunts and the ideology of power. As for the compositional strategies adopted here, the hunts were either represented on one slab or developed on more than one block, as at Zincirli. Some of these reliefs can be traced back to multiple-quarry hunt scenes, although the original display of the slabs and the length of the original sequence of hunts are uncertain.

In Hittite and Syro-Hittite contexts, the combining of hunts of different species of prey appears to be widespread, but a dominant compositional device cannot be traced. Generally, as discussed, two strategies can be identified: different animal species for distinct hunt episodes and the coexistence of several prey in a single hunt episode. These episodes may occupy either distinct figurative fields or portions of the same figurative field. This flexibility in using the figurative fields is particularly remarkable in monumental art, where hunting images occupy more blocks in a sequence of prey chased by the hunter. In Syro-Hittite art, in particular, the hunting scene is organised in a way that reveals a temporal sequence in the pursuit of prey, as in the case of the Southern City Gate of Zincirli (first the hare, then the stag). These strategies will also be considered later for the context concerned here.

3.1.2. The Assyrians

The Assyrian context may appear distant from the Eastern Mediterranean in the Persian period, but it is worth recalling that the neo-Assyrian Empire included the Syro-Levantine area, which is of relevance to this study. Moreover, representations of city sieges in the neo-Assyrian art have been mentioned as a possible forerunner of the so-called city-wall reliefs, a specific feature of Lycian art.[33]

Hunting is – alongside war – the main activity associated with Assyrian kingship. The motif of hunting became part of the Assyrian ideological discourse in the Middle Assyrian period (fourteenth-eleventh centuries BC).[34] Alongside scenes connected with cosmic implications of the hunt, during this period glyptic allowed room for real figures (herbivorous animals, lions, humans) and narrative scenes, as shown on a twelfth-century BC clay tag with the impression of a chariot hunt.[35] Hunting was also present as a theme in Middle Assyrian textual production. At the time

[25] Pucci 2015: 50.

[26] On the Outer Citadel Gate there is a scheme of hunting multiple deer in a definite direction (Zincirli B/6–8; Orthmann 1971: 424; Gilibert 2011: 65–7). Even the reliefs of the Karkemish King's Gate (early tenth century BC) show the hunt of two deer on two blocks (Karkemish H/6–7; Orthmann 1971: 511); on the order of these two slabs, see Gilibert 2011: 43.

[27] On the West Palace, see lastly Blanchard 2019a: 337–9, no. 178 (N. Cholidis). For the chronology of Kapara, see Pucci's summary table (2008: 125 note 704), where a dating to the eighth century BC is proposed. See also Cholidis and Martin 2010: 354–62. "Temple-palace": von Oppenheim 1955: 26; Parrot 1961: 83–6. Palace: Mazzoni 1997: 329. Political-cultic centre: Niehr 2014: 139. In the context of the West Palace decoration one must also consider the hunting scene that decorated the space between the legs of the griffin Bb,3 (Cholidis and Martin 2010: 130, fig. V.112; Blanchard 2019a: 349, no. 186 [N. Cholidis]).

[28] Bull hunt: Ba,1; deer hunt: Ba,6. Von Oppenheim 1955: 99–100, 104–5; Mellink 1974: 209; Cholidis and Martin 2010: 256.

[29] Winter 2010b: 383–8; Mazzoni 1997: 327. For various reconstructions of the history of "small orthostats", see Özyar 1992: 209–18, and Cholidis and Martin 2010: 145–6. See now Blanchard 2019a: 356–8, no. 193 (L. Martin).

[30] See Özyar 2008: 409 for a distinction of the types of reuse. See also von Oppenheim [n.d.]: 142–4; 1955: 15–7; Orthmann 1971: 120–2; Pucci 2008: 108. For the number of orthostats, see Özyar 2008: 404 and note 30.

[31] See von Oppenheim 1955 for the numbering of the orthostats. For the motifs on the orthostats, see von Oppenheim 1955: 17–9. Chariot hunt scenes are also present on the Nimrud ivories from Fort Shalmaneser and the Burnt Palace, related to the north Syrian area (Herrmann and Laidlaw 2008: 92; Winter 2010a: 250; 2010b: 390).

[32] Özyar 1992: 186–8, 195–6 and 201–2.

[33] Childs 1978: esp. 107–8. On the knowledge of Assyrian sites and art in later periods, see Reade 2001; 2018: 77.

[34] On this period, Jakob 2017a; 2017b. On the king as hunter, Pongratz-Leisten 2015: 244–58.

[35] Matthews 1990: 91–8; Harper *et al.* 1995: 102–3, no. 65 (J. Aruz).

Figure 37. Orthostat Ba,1 from Tell Halaf with a bull hunt (photo taken in 1912-1913, before destruction). Max Freiherr von Oppenheim Foundation, Cologne.

of Tiglath-Pileser I (1115–1077 BC) royal inscriptions celebrated both royal hunting and military exploits. Against a yearly organisation of the military campaigns, hunts are at the centre of a discourse based on geographic criteria: the different species of prey are listed distinctively according to the new territories included by the Assyrian king into the empire, making it clear that the sequence of hunts pinpoints the progressive struggle of the king against chaos.[36] That the hunt was part of the ideological discourse of the time is demonstrated by the epic-style poem *The Hunter*, often associated with Tiglath-Pileser I, where a king's military campaign is metaphorically recounted as a hunt.[37]

The White Obelisk from Nineveh, dating to 1050 BC or shortly thereafter, is considered a starting point to analyse hunting representation in Assyrian monumental art. According to H. Pittman it could reflect the narrative programme of the throne room of a palace in Nineveh that later inspired Ashurnasirpal II's Throne Room B at Nimrud.[38] Onager, caprid and bull hunts carried by a king occupy three sides of the lowest register of this obelisk, while the fourth side at this level bears an eroded relief showing the royal figure in a chariot approaching a city, with a rampant lion behind him.[39] Each of the four sides of the monument shows a distinct scene, in which one species – onagers and caprids, but only one bull – occupies a single field delimited by a frame. The figurative programme of the White Obelisk therefore shows multiple-quarry hunts, the organisational logic of which assigns a distinct figurative field to each species.[40]

In the neo-Assyrian period (tenth-seventh centuries BC), hunting was the royal activity *par excellence*:

> The gods Urta (*NIN-UR*) and Nergal (*IGI-DU*), who love my priesthood, gave to me the [beasts] of the field, and commanded me to follow the chase. 360 lions I slew from my hunting (?) chariot, by my strong attack,

[36] Grayson 1991: 25–6 (A.0.87.1: vi 55–84). Pongratz-Leisten 2015: 250.

[37] The interpretation and the dating of this poem is not unanimous (Pongratz-Leisten 2015: 252; Foster 2005: 336–7).

[38] Pittman 1996. Scholars debate on the dating of the White Obelisk by attributing it to Ashurnasirpal I (1049–1031 BC) or Ashurnasirpal II (883–859 BC). See also Russell 2017: 471.

[39] London, British Museum 118807. Pittman 1996: 355.

[40] See Russell (2017: 471) on the arrangement of the registers.

and on my swift feet, with the javelin (?). 240 wild oxen I slew. Seven mighty wild bulls, charging (*lit.*, running), I caught alive. Six elephants I killed on the rush. Into pits I cast them. Four live elephants I captured. Five *ashkippu* I captured. Lions, wild oxen, elephants, deer, wild goats, wild asses, gazelles, MAL-SHIR-birds, herds of (them), I gathered into cages (?).[41]

In this celebratory text the king Adad-nirari II (911-891 BC) is praised for his hunting exploits. He has killed different species of prey, listed according to the decreasing challenge of the hunt or symbolic value of the animals, with the lion in first place. In addition, the description is characterised by a precise tally of the prey killed and captured by the king.[42]

The most important visual evidence from the neo-Assyrian period comes from palatial figurative cycles in which the values of kingship are expressed by different themes, in particular war and the hunt. In the neo-Assyrian palace hunts, characters of royal rank chase different species of quarry, a feature that is consistent with the catalogues of different prey in the encomiastic texts.

This principle is fully embraced by the lion and bull hunts belonging to two different palace contexts from the reign of Ashurnasirpal II (883–859 BC). The first example are the bronze bands decorating the palace gates of Ashurnasirpal II at Balawat, the ancient site of Imgur-Enlil. Two of these bands represent a royal lion hunt, and the other two, bull hunts.[43] It is likely that the bands were arranged symmetrically on the two doors, so that when they were closed they formed long uniform strips, each showing many hunters and prey, but only one species per strip.[44] The positioning of these bands at eye-level, amid a number of other themes such as tribute scenes, campaigns and processions, led scholars to consider hunting scenes of particular importance.[45]

The second example, perhaps directly connected to the possible model for the White Obelisk, is the decoration of Throne Room B of Ashurnasirpal II in the Northwest Palace at Nimrud (Fig. 38). Here, hunts were represented on the eastern section of the south wall, nearest the throne, a location that suggests the importance of these depictions.[46] The upper register represents the king in his chariot chasing bulls and lions from his chariot in two distinct scenes, each of which represented one species (Fig. 39).[47] In the lower register, two libation scenes show the corpses of the animals killed above.[48] These reliefs therefore offer a double reading: the upper register, horizontally, presents a sequence of two different animal hunts, paratactically side by side, with a repetition of the main character. However, read vertically, each hunt has a ritual companion, suggesting a temporal sequence.

The palace reliefs at Khorsabad, ancient Dur-Sharrukin founded by Sargon II (722–705 BC) as the new capital, reveal a change: the hunting themes were transferred from the public to the residential rooms. Interestingly, this feature is accompanied by other innovations. Firstly, the change of location within the palace complex implies that lion and bull hunts, gave way to the quieter stalking of game in the woods.[49] Two reliefs with multiple-quarry hunts of birds and quadrupeds come from the Pavilion of the Palace of Sargon II.[50] Here, different prey are represented in the same scene. On one of the hunting reliefs, three men appear in a landscape characterised by coniferous trees of different sizes. To the left, a hunter, identified as Sennacherib, the crown prince, aims his bow at birds;[51] in the centre, a bearded figure holds a bow and arrows; on the right, a third character carries a gazelle on his shoulders (perhaps still alive), grabbing its legs with his left hand and holding a small hare or rabbit with his right.[52] This representation implies an explicit chronological sequence with the various hunts led by the same characters. The hunting theme was also present on the reliefs of the lower register of Room VII (Fig. 40). Here, according to E. Guralnick, there were royal hunt events depicted in several moments, in which the king must have been at the centre of the room's three decorated walls. In this case, therefore, prey of different species coexisted in the scenes that filled an entire room.[53]

With Ashurbanipal (669–627 BC) and his North Palace at Nineveh, the last neo-Assyrian palace, the hunt as a royal activity assumed a central role in the visual celebration.[54] The king or the crown prince is surrounded by a large retinue of attendants, showing his ability at chasing prey.[55] While the reliefs of Room C depict the king preparing for

[41] Luckenbill 1989: 116, no. 375.

[42] For an overview of the literary testimonies on the hunting exploits of Assyrian kings, see *RAVA* V: 234–5. There were also similar lists in the Hittite tradition (Archi 1988: 32).

[43] The hunts can be traced back to specific historical and geographical coordinates thanks to the inscriptions on the door and naturalistic elements in the scenes. The hunt for wild bulls took place by the River Euphrates; for lions at the River Balikh, a small tributary of the Euphrates in northern Syria, see Bienkowski and Millard 2000: 46; Thomason 2001: 70.

[44] Bull hunts: London, British Museum 124697, 124700. Lion hunts: London, British Museum 124698, 124699. See Davies *et al.* 2008: 33–4 and 41–2. According to a recent reconstruction, the bands with scenes of bull and lion hunts occupied, respectively, the IV and V registers from the top, at a height of 1.5–2.2 m above the ground (Curtis and Tallis 2008: 26–9). On the Balawat findings, see Curtis 2013: 24–5.

[45] Curtis and Tallis 2008: 29.

[46] Reade 2018: 56.

[47] London, British Museum 124532 and 124534. This representation is the oldest neo-Assyrian palace relief of a lion hunt. Thomason, despite the absence of inscriptions and landscape elements and based on a comparison with the gates of Balawat, believes that these lion hunts were conducted in northern Syria (Thomason 2001: 75–6). For observations on the figurative programme of the Palace of Ashurnasirpal II, see Russell 1998.

[48] London, British Museum 124533 and 124535. Pittman 1996: 345–6; Ataç 2010: 15–9.

[49] Matthiae 1996: 198. On the palace, see Caubet 1995.

[50] On the discovery of these two reliefs, see Reade 1994: 124–6.

[51] Parrot 1961: 369, no. 66.

[52] London, British Museum 118829. See also Ataç 2010: 51–3.

[53] Guralnick 1976: 6. For the role of the landscape in these reliefs, see Mazzoni 1992: 159.

[54] Brereton 2018: 16.

[55] Matthiae 1996: 198. See also Ataç 2010: 74.

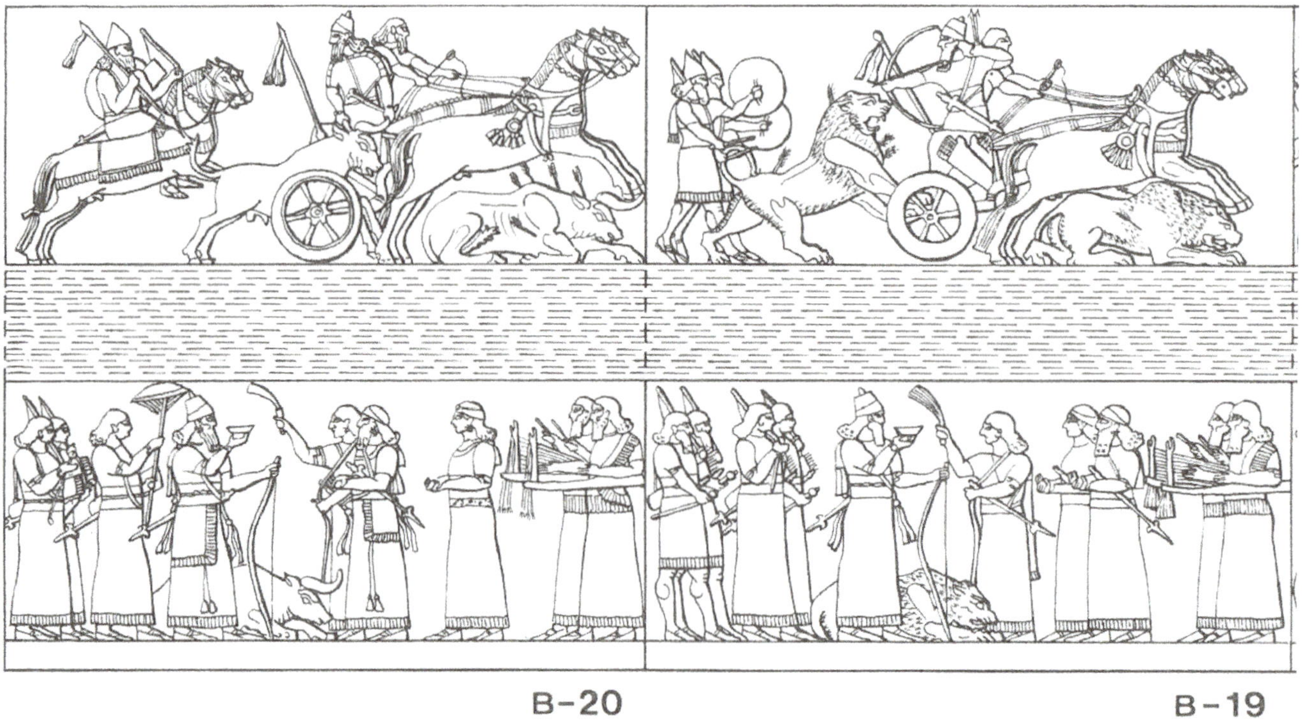

Figure 38. Ashurnasirpal II's hunts from the Northwest Palace of Nimrud. Reconstructive drawing by H. Lewakowa. After Meuszyński 1981: pl. 1,3, nos. B-20 and B-19.

Figure 39. Ashurnasirpal II's lion hunt. London, British Museum 124534. © Trustees of the British Museum.

the hunt and shooting lions and lionesses from his chariot in a dedicated space, Room S, "the apogee of ancient Near Eastern narrative art" according to R.D. Barnett, stands out in the neo-Assyrian hunting representations for the variety of episodes of a proper multiple-quarry hunt.[56] On the south-east wall of this room, with a rear entrance probably used for hunting, a character of royal rank – the king or the crown prince – chases different species.[57] The scenes were arranged in independent narrative segments,

[56] Barnett 1976: 19. See also Meissner and Opitz 1940; Nadali 2006: 136–43. On Room C, the decoration of which is entirely devoted to royal lion hunt, see Watanabe 2018: 222–9.

[57] On the identification of the main hunter as the king, see Barnett (1976: 19), Nadali (2006: 136) and Reade (2018: 71); Matthiae (1996: 201) and Schmidt-Colinet (2005: 31) hypothesise that the character may represent the crown prince.

Figure 40. Reliefs from Room VII of the palace of Khorsabad. Drawing by E. Flandin. After P.E. Botta and E. Flandin, *Monument de Ninive*, Vol. 2. *Architecture et sculpture*, Paris, 1849, pl. 111.

divided into superimposed registers, devoted to different species of fauna: the upper and median ones represented lion hunts, the lowest one depicted gazelles and onagers, grouped in distinct parts of the register (Fig. 41).[58] In other words, each species occupies distinct figurative fields or a well-defined segment of figurative field, and the variety of quarry implies different weapons and techniques.[59]

This brief survey on Assyrian hunt scenes highlights the importance of the multiple-quarry hunt theme in both literary and in visual evidence. Visual evidence shows a variety of devices, which reflects the flexibility of Assyrian narrative art: for example the practice of isolating each species of prey in distinct figurative fields (Balawat bronze strips; Ashurbanipal's palace reliefs); the coexistence of different prey with an explicit temporal sequence (Sargon II's palace reliefs) and different hunt scenes with the main hunter repeated not only in different figurative fields but also in one single register (Ashurbanipal's palace reliefs). Some of these strategies will be taken into account for the representations of multiple-quarry hunt in the context concerned here.

3.1.3. The Levant and Cyprus

The multiple-quarry hunt in a continuous figured field often occurs in Cypro-Levantine art. The use of a long figured field to arrange a series of different species of quarry can be seen already in the second millennium BC, when different prey hunted by one figure were depicted in the circular figured field on the gold patera of Ras Shamra (fifteenth to fourteenth century BC) (Fig. 42) and on the Sîn-rabû seal (thirteenth century BC).[60] At Enkomi, the

[58] On the southern corner of the room, instead, a lion hunt from boats is represented.

[59] See Nadali 2006: 276; Czichon 1992: 62.

[60] Ras Shamra patera (Paris, Musée du Louvre AO17208): Schaeffer 1949: 3–23; Frankfort 1996: 260–1. Sîn-rabû seal: Mazzoni 2005: 237–8.

Figure 41. Ashurbanipal's hunts from the North Palace of Nineveh, Room S. London, British Museum 124881. © Trustees of the British Museum.

Figure 42. Hunt on the patera from Ras Shamra. Paris, Musée du Louvre AO17208. Photo © RMN-Grand Palais (musée du Louvre) / Franck Raux.

long sides of an ivory game-box show a hunting scene, maybe of royal rank, which also depicts several quarry in the same figurative field (Fig. 43).[61]

This tendency is further confirmed by later evidence. The Phoenician metal bowls, a corpus dated to the ninth to seventh centuries BC, show well-defined compositional characteristics.[62] Concentric bands decorating the interior surface facilitated a flexible use of the space for narrative depiction, and hunting appears in several examples.[63] A "continuous" style is present both on the Praeneste gold-plated silver shallow bowl (late eighth to early seventh century BC) (Fig. 44) and on the silver shallow bowl from Kourion in Cyprus. The outermost register of both is decorated with a royal hunt sequence of mythological nature, called "the Ape Hunt" or "Hunter's Day" sequence, with nine episodes, in which the leading figure is repeated several times.[64]

Phoenician bowls showing hunting scenes with various types of quarry in the same figurative band were perhaps known up to the Persian Achaemenid period. This may be the case of the bronze bowl from a tomb in Armou, in Cyprus, decorated inside with an embossed and engraved hunting scene, in which a kneeling archer has already killed a gazelle and a stag, and is actively shooting at gazelles and ibexes (Fig. 45). The object can be dated to the seventh century BC, but the context of discovery and an incised inscription below the rim seem to attest to it being reused later, up to the sixth century BC.[65]

These models therefore might be available later than the period of their production, a direct use of earlier patterns thus may be taken into account for the Achaemenid Eastern Mediterranean. It is not a coincidence that an object from Cyprus – the so-called Golgoi Sarcophagus – seems to be one of the first cases of this type of hunt in the

[61] London, British Museum 1894.4–1.996. Tatton-Brown 1997: 41, fig. 38; Karageorghis 2002: 100, fig. 205; Frankfort 1996: 261.

[62] Markoe 2000: 148; Matthäus 2009, with a history of studies.

[63] For general observations, see Markoe 1985: 60–5.

[64] Rome, Museo Nazionale Etrusco di Villa Giulia 61565 (bowl from Praeneste); New York, Metropolitan Museum of Art, Cesnola Coll. 74.51.4556 (bowl from Kourion). Güterbock 1957: 69–70; Markoe 1985: 177, cat. Cy7; 191, cat. E2; Hermary 1992; Karageorghis 2000: 186–7, no. 305; 2002: 174–5.

[65] Nicosia, Cyprus Museum 1980-XII-18-2. Karageorghis 1981; Markoe 1985: 187–8, cat. Cy22; Matthäus 1985: 168–9, no. 442. On the difficulty in considering the archaeological context, see Feldman 2014: 121.

Figure 43. Hunting representation on the ivory game-box from Enkomi. London, British Museum 1897,0401.996. © Trustees of the British Museum.

Figure 44. Bowl from the Bernardini Tomb in Praeneste. Drawing by O. Sörling. After O. Montelius, *La civilisation primitive en Italie depuis l'introduction des métaux*, Vol. 2.2. *Italie centrale. Planches*, Stockholm, 1904, pl. 368 fig. 5.

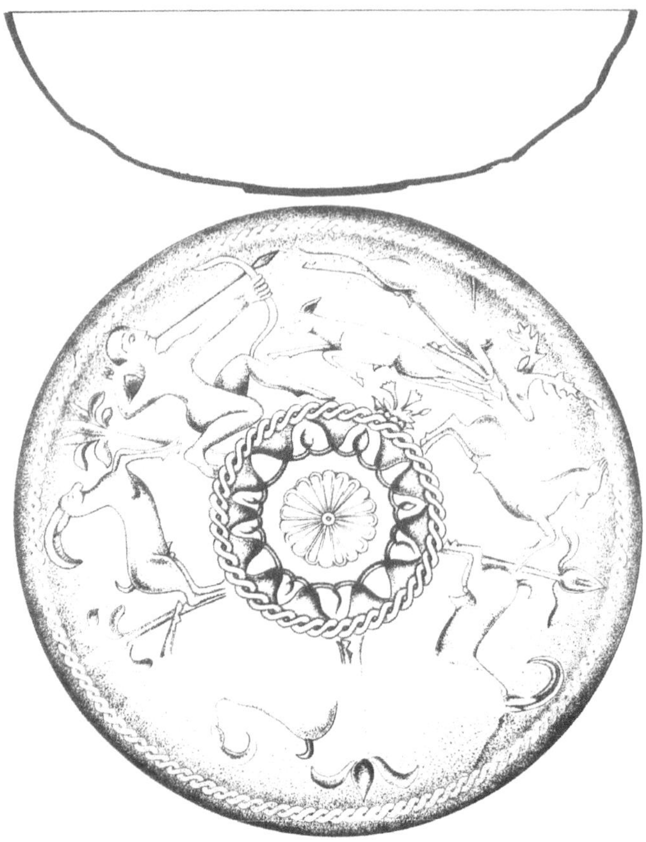

Figure 45. Bronze bowl from Armou with hunting representation. Lefkosia, Cyprus Museum 1980-XII-18-2. Drawings by A. Papadopoulos. After Karageorghis 1981: pl. XXII. Courtesy of Vassos Karageorghis.

Eastern Mediterranean from the Achaemenid period. The sarcophagus, probably from Golgoi, is dated to the first half of the fifth century BC (Fig. 46).[66] Its long sides combine a hunt and a banquet scene, as on the Satrap Sarcophagus of Sidon and other Lycian dynastic monuments. Two hunting scenes develop around two prey, a bull and a boar, the first of which has collapsed; two hunters armed like hoplites move around each animal, and an archer is also involved in the bull hunt. The composition is enlivened by three trees, represented in the background behind a horse, the bull and the boar, the horse and a gazelle graze placidly, and a cock is seen between the two hunts. The role of vegetation in the hunting scene on the Golgoi Sarcophagus is remarkable, since it appears as an antecedent of the solution adopted on the socle of the Mourning Women Sarcophagus from Sidon. As for the banquet scene, the Cypriot sarcophagus shows four banqueters on *klinai*, as well as hetaerae, a musician and a young servant.[67] The Cypriot model may have been important for the adoption of the sarcophagus decorated by bas-reliefs as a typology of royal burials in Sidon. Another fifth-century BC sarcophagus from Cyprus, indeed, the Amathus Sarcophagus, was for a figure of royal rank.[68]

Therefore, in the Cypro-Levantine context it is possible to detect the use of long friezes mainly on portable objects with one hunting scene and prey of different species or multiple hunting scenes. In the Persian period there is however a transfer to larger scale artefacts.

3.2. The multiple-quarry hunt in Persia

Before taking into account the role of hunting in Persian Achaemenid ideology, it is useful to mention two metal bowls from Iran dating to the first half of the first millennium BC: they offer the opportunity to consider the wide geographical impact of the Phoenician metal bowls and consequently of the sequence of hunting scenes within one figurative field. A bowl found in Luristan, dated to the first half of the seventh century BC, shows two archers, a bird and fleeing animals (a mountain goat, ibexes, a hare), two of which are explicitly the targets of the two hunters (Fig. 47).[69] Here, the interest in the rendering of the landscape through a representation of high ground and vegetation is discernible. The tradition of the Phoenician bowls – alongside the echoes of other cultural elements – is reflected also in the Arjan bowl, found in Iran in a late neo-Elamite burial of the first half of the sixth century BC. The rich iconographic apparatus of this bowl, including several activities involving a royal figure, such as the return from the hunt, proves that this type of artefact was known at least until the onset of the Achaemenid Empire.[70]

With the establishment of the Persian Achaemenid Empire in the mid-sixth century BC, hunting was part of the ideology of power, an element of continuity with the neo-Elamite world. In the Persepolis Fortification Archive the impressions of PFS 51 reveal that this seal was used by Irdabama, a woman of the royal family (Fig. 48).[71] Here, a horseman wears a crown-shaped headdress and pursues two animals in flight; these two prey – a deer and an onager – have already been hit.[72] This seal belonged to the late neo-Elamite or, as defined by Garrison, the early Persian period, since it may be associated stylistically with seal PFS 93*, which is dated by the presence in Elamite of the name of Cyrus I (Cyrus of Anshan, son of Teispes), grandfather of Cyrus the Elder.[73] The seal thus has a double value: first, the hunter's headdress proves that even before the Achaemenid period multiple-quarry hunts were associated with royalty. Secondly, its use was transmitted within a royal context: a woman used this seal not so

[66] New York, Metropolitan Museum of Art, Cesnola Coll. 74.51.2451. Schollmeyer 2007.

[67] Karageorghis 2000: 204–6, no. 331; Hermary and Mertens 2014: 363–70, no. 491.

[68] Stylianou 2007; Hermary and Mertens 2014: 353–63, no. 490.

[69] Tehran, National Museum 75/3. Markoe 1985: 212–13, cat. Ir9; Haerinck and Overlaet 1998: 25; Gunter 2009: 81.

[70] For dating prior to the sixth century BC: Majidzadeh 1992; Karageorghis 2005: 110; Matthäus 2009: 443–4. For dating around 600 BC and to the sixth century BC: Garrison 2002: 92 note 67; Stronach 2003; 2004: 712; Álvarez-Mon 2010: 273. See also Henkelman 2008: 31.

[71] Garrison 1991: 3–4; Root 1991: 21. She has been identified as the Gaubarva's daughter, who married Darius before he took the throne (Koch 1992: 238–9).

[72] Koch (1992: 239) considers both prey to be wild asses.

[73] Kuhrt 2007: 54–5, no. 3; Garrison 2011: 383. See also Root 1979: 27 and 120, no. 1.

Figure 46. The "Golgoi Sarcophagus", side with hunts. New York, Metropolitan Museum of Art, Cesnola Coll. 74.51.2451. Public Domain from https://www.metmuseum.org/art/collection/search/242004.

much for its iconography as for the dynastic value it assumed.[74]

Glyptic seems to be the privileged medium for hunting depictions in connection with power. The cylinder seal of Darius I, supposedly from Egypt, embodies a marked connection between the hunt and kingship (Fig. 49).[75] Here the Great King Darius I is clearly identified by the inscriptions in Old Persian, Elamite and Babylonian, the presence of the divine symbol of Ahuramazda, the winged solar disc that ensures the protection of the monarch, and Darius' headpiece. He is depicted in his chariot shooting arrows at a lion, after having mortally wounded another one: this reaffirms the royal value of the hunt, in particular the lion hunt.[76] However, there is no certain depiction of royal multiple-quarry hunts, but a blue chalcedony scaraboid seal shows a lion and a fox, fleeing in the same direction, and dominated by the symbol of Ahuramazda (Fig. 50). The presence of the lion and the sun disc, two elements included on Darius' seal, points to the hunter's royal rank, the figure of which however has been omitted here as on other "Graeco-Persian" contemporary seals.[77] In glyptic, however, the hunt was also associated with Persian officers, such as the grain/flour supply seal and the seal of Irdumartiya, a high ranking officer in Persepolis during the period of Darius.[78]

Hunting scenes associated with kingship appear more frequently on portable artefacts such as seals than in monumental art.[79] In Persian monumental art, with the exception of apotropaic-type duels in buildings at Persepolis, narrative hunt scenes are absent. It has been argued that this is because these themes were represented on perishable artworks such as tapestries, but analysis of the Great Kings' funerary monuments shows that hunting representations were not a priority in such contexts: this is a marked difference from the contemporary Eastern Mediterranean funerary monuments.[80]

Unfortunately, archival records from Persepolis, which are valuable in reconstructing many aspects of the central administration, did not produce much evidence of hunting practices.[81] The nexus between the hunt and Persian kingship, however, was well present in Greek sources. The ancient geographer Strabo, who lived between the first century BC and the first century AD, mentions the epitaph of a figure of royal rank named Darius according to the formulation provided by Onesicritus, Alexander's fourth-century BC historian:[82]

[74] Some scholars interpret the seal as evidence of female participation in the hunt (Rashad 1996: 242–3), but it is more likely that it was an indication of the role of women of royal rank in the imperial administration (Fornasier 2001: 208).

[75] London, British Museum 89132. For a recent discussion on this seal, see Garrison 2014: 82–4.

[76] For the link between lion and kingship in earlier times, see Cassin 1981.

[77] Furtwängler 1900: II, 58, no. 2 (the scholar interprets the second animal as a dog instead of a fox); Delaporte 1923: 216, cat. A. 1229; Boardman 1970b: 354, pl. 908.

[78] Garrison 2017: 531–2, 533, figs. 1 and 2, and 535–6, figs. 3 and 4.

[79] Briant 1996: 244; on portable objects, see Thomason 2014.

[80] Poggio 2012: 229.

[81] Henkelman 2008: 84. However, Hallock (1969: 8) interprets two texts as providing rations to people, including servants, and dogs involved in hunting.

[82] Str. 15.3.8 = *FGrH* 134 F 35.

Figure 47. Hunting representation on the bowl from Chamahzi Mumah, Luristan, with drawings. Tehran, National Museum 75/3. After Haerinck and Overlaet 1998: pl. 58 and p. 29 ill. 12. Courtesy of the authors.

> "I was friend to my friends; as horseman and bowman I proved myself superior to all others; as hunter I prevailed; I could do everything".[83]

Scholars have considered Onesicritus' epitaph as spurious and inspired by Herodotus (Hdt. 1.136), in turn influenced by the Naqsh-i Rustam inscription.[84] Although it is not possible to establish the identity of the Darius discussed by Onesicritus, the mention of the hunt, however, does not appear to be isolated, but finds an exact correspondence, along with other similarities, in the portrait of Cyrus the Younger found in Xenophon's *Anabasis* 1.9.[85] This excursus sets out the qualities of the deceased of royal rank.[86] For instance, the skills of riding (φιλιππότατος καὶ τοῖς ἵπποις ἄριστα χρῆσθαι), archery (τοξική) and hunting (φιλοθηρότατος ἦν καὶ πρὸς τὰ θηρία μέντοι φιλοκινδυνότατος) appear in the same order as in Onesicritus' epitaph, with a similar use of superlatives to describe superiority. This portrait by Xenophon interrupts the narrative after the mention of the death of Cyrus the Younger, and the function of this passage thus does not seem to be very different from that of an epitaph.[87] There is also an unusual first-person intervention by the author, to emphasise the direct source of his information (Xen. *An.* 1.9.28): indeed, Momigliano, while underlining the

[83] φίλος ἦν τοῖς φίλοις· ἱππεὺς καὶ τοξότης ἄριστος ἐγενόμην· κυνηγῶν ἐκράτουν· πάντα ποιεῖν ἠδυνάμην. Text and translation from Jones 1961.

[84] Briant 2003: 283 note 144; Biffi 2005: 285. See also Leroy 2016: 270 note 854.

[85] Most scholars identify this Darius as Darius I, while Allsen speaks of Darius III (for interpretations: Allsen 2006: 126; Asheri 1983: 102; Briant 2003: 283 note 144). One must bear in mind that this name was widespread in the Persian royal family, given that at least two other princes were given it, although they never sat on the throne (Schmitt 2011).

[86] See Lendle 1995: 76.

[87] Some scholars have speculated that it was added later. For some considerations and the debate on this passage, see Bevilacqua 2002: 160.

Figure 48. Collated line drawing of PFS 51 from the Persepolis Fortification Archive. Drawing by Mark B. Garrison. Courtesy of the Persepolis Seal Project and the Persepolis Fortification Archive Project.

Figure 49. Cylinder seal with Darius I as hunter. London, British Museum 89132. © Trustees of the British Museum.

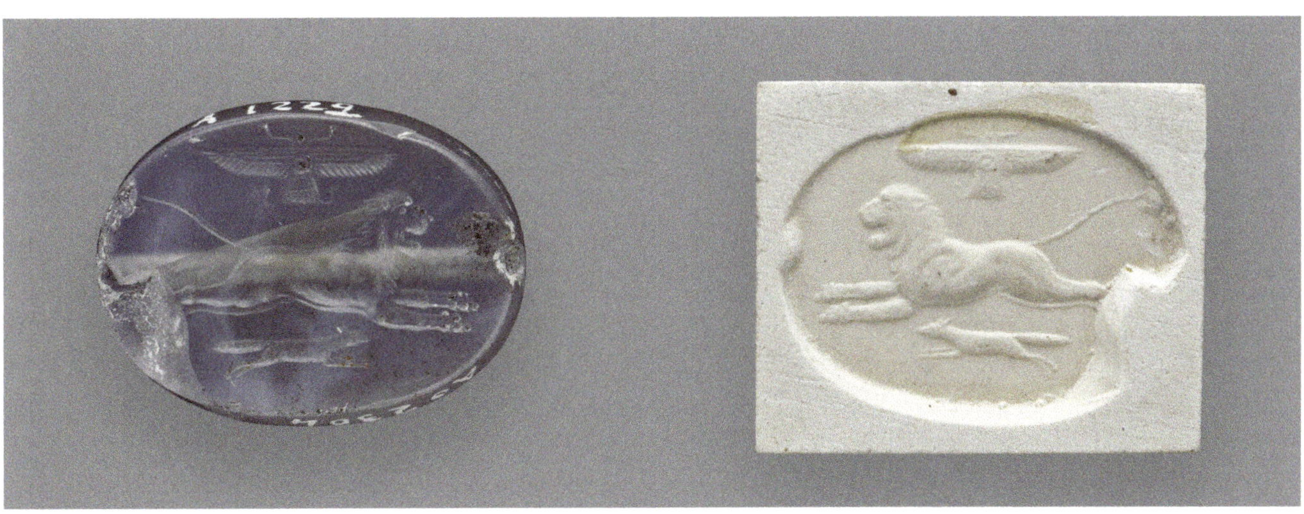

Figure 50. Fleeing animals on a scaraboid. Paris, Musée du Louvre AO2304. Photo © RMN-Grand Palais (musée du Louvre) / Mathieu Rabeau.

tendency towards idealisation, states that the portrait of Cyrus the Younger is based on authentic details about court life in Persia.[88] The similarities between the texts of Onesicritus and Xenophon, both dating back to the fourth century BC, may refer to a tradition of Persian eulogy commemorating figures of royal rank, in which hunting appeared according to a stereotyped pattern.[89]

As for multiple-quarry hunts, Greek sources have highlighted their role within Persian Achaemenid ideology. Herodotus, recounting a hunt led by Darius, speaks of beasts (θῆρες), in the plural (Hdt. 3.129). We know from literary sources and archaeological evidence about the existence of gardens – the famous *paradeisoi* – that were part of Persian sites such as Pasargadae, Persepolis and Susa. Here, the variety and the richness of the Great King's domains were expressed through diverse species of flora and fauna, providing the setting for royal hunts. This model was also exported to the periphery of the empire, as will be made clear in Chapter Four.[90]

Additionally in Xenophon's fictional biography of Cyrus the Elder, *Cyropaedia*, multiple-quarry hunting plays an important role, as the episode of the young Cyrus the Elder's first hunt shows (Xen. *Cyr*. 1.4.8–9):[91]

> (8) All these lessons Cyrus eagerly learned. But when he saw a deer spring out from under cover, he forgot everything that he had heard and gave chase, seeing nothing but the direction in which it was making. And somehow his horse in taking a leap fell upon its knees and almost threw him over its head. However, Cyrus managed, with some difficulty, to keep his seat, and his horse got up. And when he came to level ground, he threw his spear and brought down the deer – a fine, large quarry. And he, of course, was greatly delighted; but the guards rode up and scolded him and told him into what danger he had gone and declared that they would tell of him. Now Cyrus stood there, for he had dismounted, and was vexed at being spoken to in this way. But when he heard a halloo, he sprang upon his horse like one possessed and when he saw a boar rushing straight toward him, he rode to meet him and aiming well he struck the boar between the eyes and brought him down. (9) This time, however, his uncle also reproved him, for he had witnessed his foolhardiness. But for all his scolding, Cyrus nevertheless asked his permission to carry home and present to his grandfather all the game that he had taken himself. And his uncle, they say, replied: "But if he finds out that you have been giving chase, he will chide not only you but me also for allowing you to do so." "And if he choose," said Cyrus, "let him flog me, provided only I may give him the game. And you, uncle," said he, "may punish me in any way you please – only grant me this favour." And finally Cyaxares said, though with reluctance: "Do as you wish; for now it looks as if it were you who are our king."[92]

Although set in the context of narrative invention driven by moralistic intentions, the multiple-quarry hunt is here a source of the legitimation of power: the narration highlights the natural inclination of the royal hunter facing different prey, one after another, tirelessly, in a crescendo of difficulties and dangers, as Chapter Four will make clear.[93]

A multiple-quarry hunt with more scenes within one figurative field is represented on a partly gilded silver disc – perhaps a shield-boss – of the fourth century BC, which is part of the Oxus Treasure (Fig. 33).[94] The circular figurative field is organised as a band encircling the boss, in which there are three hunters in Persian garb. Two ride anticlockwise, in pursuit of two deer and two ibexes, while the third hunts a hare, in a clockwise direction.[95] This is the only depiction in a Persian Achaemenid context to adopt the compositional motif of the juxtaposition of hunting scenes in one figurative field, which possibly is due to the enduring impact of the Phoenician bowls, as discussed above.

This means that the corpus of visual evidence from Persia is poor regarding depictions formed of a sequence of juxtaposed hunting scenes, which is the most common compositional motif on the dynastic tombs of the Eastern Mediterranean. More frequent, instead, is the motif of one hunter chasing two prey of different species, which fitted with the limited figurative field provided by glyptic.

3.3. The multiple-quarry hunt in the Greek world

In the second half of the twentieth century hunting in the Greek world has been at the centre of a kaleidoscopic approach, from the reflection on the *realia* and ancient hunting practices to the analysis of hunting images in

[88] Momigliano 1993b: 133. See also the paideutic model in the Greek poem found in the Letoon near Xanthos, contemporary to Xenophon's and Onesicritus' texts (on the Letoon inscription, see § 1.2.). For some thoughts on the Persian paideutic *trivium*, see Asheri 1983: 102–3 and 169–70, no. 3.

[89] For the role of the encomium of Cyrus the Younger in the Greek context, see Alexiou 2010: 29. The dependence of Greek sources on the vocabulary of dynastic glorification has been acknowledged in other cases as well (Asheri, Lloyd and Corcella 2007: 170).

[90] For *paradeisoi* of the Persian period, with analysis of ancient sources and archaeological evidence, see Fauth 1979; Stronach 1989; 1990; Tuplin 1996: 80–131; Carroll 2003: 45–50; Lincoln 2003; Kuhrt 2007: 87–90, no. 29; 510–4, no. 21; 615–6, no. 46; 753, no. 19; 803, no. 41(i); 806–8, nos. 43–47; for a new assessment of the functions, see Henkelman 2008: 427–41. See now Tuplin 2018.

[91] Ferrari 1997: 18.

[92] Translation from Miller 1968.

[93] On the comparison with Herodotus and Ctesias' accounts, see Ferrari 1997: 5–23. In Herodotus, though in a different form, Cyrus' taking of power is also connected to hunting: Harpagus sends a message to Cyrus in the belly of a dead hare, a prelude to his rise to power; the lifeless animal is brought to Cyrus by a servant disguised as a hunter, carrying nets so as to go unnoticed (Hdt. 1.123).

[94] On the Oxus Treasure, see Curtis 2012.

[95] Dalton 1964: 13, no. 24.

different media and specific genres.[96] A progressive renovation of the field began due to the analysis of the social meaning of hunt. In 1968, P. Vidal-Naquet, representative of the French school that promoted the study of the ancient Greek culture from an anthropological perspective, published his article *Le chasseur noir*, in which he proposed an interpretation of the role of hunt in the formation of the Greek citizen.[97] Afterwards, a marked interest in painted pottery developed, which constitutes a meaningful corpus of hunting images from the Greek world.[98]

It is not however, easy to find examples of the association of different types of hunts in the monumental art of the Greek world. In the sixth century BC the figurative programme of the throne of Apollo at Amyclae, near Sparta, combined numerous encounters between heroes and real or fantastic creatures, including the Calydonian Boar Hunt (Paus. 3.18.9–16).[99] It is important to note that the throne's artist, Bathycles of Magnesia, came from Anatolia.

There are more occurrences on pottery that are dated prior to the development of multiple-quarry hunt iconography in the Eastern Mediterranean. Examples are quite varied and there is no true iconographic tradition. On two Attic Siana cups, dated to the second quarter of the sixth century BC and considered the oldest Greek examples of horseback hunting, one can see the hierarchical differentiation between the boar hunt, occupying the main figurative field, and the hare hunt, which decorates the rim (Fig. 51).[100] While the dangerous boar hunt involves five hunters on horseback, the easier hare hunt is undertaken by just a dog, which is absent from the boar hunting scenes below, as A. Schnapp noted.[101]

From a thematic point of view, deer and boar were associated as prey and a particular solution is that connected with circular figurative fields. On the cover of a Vulci amphora dated to the mid-sixth century BC, two episodes are painted in the circular band around the knob: a deer hunt occupies two-thirds of the figuration, while a boar hunt fills the rest (Fig. 52).[102] However, boar and deer hunts may be given the same importance within a more balanced structure, such as on the fourth-century BC Cista Ficoroni, where deer and boar hunts are engraved on the external circular band of the cover.[103]

The black-figure amphora of Basel, on the other hand, dated to around 540 BC, presents a multiple-quarry hunt in a single scene, unique in Attic iconography (Fig. 53).[104] On the rim of the B side is a scene where four hunters on horseback, armed with spears, surround a boar, a doe and a stag, fleeing to the right. A bird is shown in the remaining space above the boar, but seems to be a detail of the setting rather than a potential prey.[105]

Thus, in the Archaic age, there was a wide variety of compositional solutions for representing hunts with different species of prey. The Classical age offers further examples, such as a red-figure kylix dating back to 470 BC.[106] Both sides of the vase are painted with two encirclement hunts on foot, one for a deer and the other for a boar (Fig. 54).[107] The identical setting consists of a rocky landscape and a tree in the background, set back from the two animals. Compared with the Greek vases analysed so far, these two hunt scenes are indistinguishable, both in iconographical and compositional terms which is a novel feature. This confirms the equal significance given to the hunting of boar and of deer.

In conclusion, as for the examples analysed so far, the two hunting scenes on the cover of the Vulci amphora occupy different portions of the circular field since the number of participants differs, but the Basel black-figure amphora shows a fusion of the two different types of hunting in the same scene. Finally, the two main scenes shown on the two sides of the early Classical kylix are clearly separated, composed from the same pattern.[108]

Greek evidence for the incidence of multiple-quarry hunts seems minimal, which suggests that the dynastic hunting representations in the Eastern Mediterranean were determined more by local contexts. The wide variety of examples in the small sample discussed, however, is noteworthy, as it is a sign of the great ductility of the Greek artistic language.

3.4. Conclusion

Hunt images on dynastic tombs in the Eastern Mediterranean corresponded to an ideology of power widespread in the Near East and the Levant. The practice of combining different prey in one figurative programme

[96] Hull 1964; Daltrop 1966; 1969; Schauenburg 1969; Zazoff 1970; Anderson 1985.

[97] Vidal-Naquet 1968.

[98] Schnapp 1979a; 1979b; Schmitt Pantel and Schnapp 1982; Schnapp 1997; Barringer 2001; Fornasier 2001; Sachs 2012.

[99] For an analysis of Pausanias' passage, see Musti and Torelli 1991: 236–45. For the throne of Amyclae, see Faustoferri 1996; Delivorrias 2009.

[100] Hamburg, Museum für Kunst und Gewerbe 1908.255; Copenhagen, National Museum Chr. VIII 959. See Schnapp 1997: 224; Barringer 2001: 33 and 96.

[101] Schnapp 1997: 225. See also Daltrop 1966: 18; Schnapp 1979a: 204–6.

[102] London, British Museum 1839.11-9.1 (B 147). *ABV* 135, no. 44; *Para* 55; *BAdd*² 36; *CVA* British Museum 3 [Great Britain 4]: 3; *LIMC* II.1: 987, no. 349; Schnapp 1997: 234. For later dating, at 520 BC, see Anderson 1985: 25, fig. 11.

[103] Bordenache Battaglia and Emiliozzi 1990: 218.

[104] Basel, Antikenmuseum BS 495. *Para* 187, no. 3; *BAdd*² 111 (433.3); Schnapp 1997: 488, no. 107; Fornasier 2001: 292, cat. EA 11. I agree with Fornasier's dating.

[105] See also Schnapp 1979a: 211; Durand and Schnapp 1984: 61. See also the black-figure lekythos dated to the late sixth century BC (Munich, Staatliche Antikensammlungen 1966; Barringer 2001: 211 note 28).

[106] Copenhagen, National Museum 6327. *ARV* 271, no. 14; *ARV*² 413, no. 16.

[107] *CVA* Copenhague, Musée National 3 [Danemark 3]: 111, pl. 143. The main difference is the direction in which the two animals are shown: the deer turned to the left and the boar to the right.

[108] See also the identical representations on the Louvre cup, § 5.5.

Figure 51. Hunts on a black-figure Siana cup. Hamburg, Museum für Kunst und Gewerbe 1908.255. Museum für Kunst und Gewerbe Hamburg.

Figure 52. Hunt scenes on the cover of a black-figure amphora from Vulci. London, British Museum 1839,1109.1. © Trustees of the British Museum.

Figure 53. Hunt scene on the rim of a black-figure amphora, side B. Basel, Antikenmuseum BS 495. Antikenmuseum Basel und Sammlung Ludwig / Andreas F. Voegelin.

was not new in the Eastern Mediterranean. In particular, in the Hittite and Syro-Hittite contexts there was a practice of depicting the hunt on a monumental scale as part of public display, whereas in the neo-Assyrian world palaces were the privileged setting of royal hunts. In Persian monumental art there is no narrative hunting images.

Less usual was the juxtaposition of autonomous hunting scenes in the same figurative field: this solution was adopted in Ashurnasirpal II's palace reliefs and on Phoenician metallic bowls, whereas the contribution of Persian Achaemenid imagery appears minimal in this aspect.

Phoenician metallic bowls were probably known in the Archaic period at least, and in the fifth century BC the Golgoi Sarcophagus possibly shows the transfer of a sequence of hunting scenes to stone. Since Cypriot art impacted on the royal sarcophagi from Sidon, one of which, the Satrap Sarcophagus, seems to be on stylistic basis the oldest dynastic tomb with a multiple-quarry hunt in the corpus here, the Cypro-Levantine region might have guaranteed the transmission and the original elaboration of the multiple-quarry hunt motif in the Persian Achaemenid period in the Eastern Mediterranean.

The importance of fifth-century BC Cyprus for the artistic language of the Persian Achaemenid Eastern Mediterranean may also be demonstrated by the discovery in 2006 of the sarcophagus of Palaipafos, dated to approximately 480 BC.[109] Here, the representation of a city wall may provide a model for the so-called city-wall reliefs of Lycia, which generated an important debate about the origin of the distinctive art of this Mediterranean region.[110] This sarcophagus reveals the importance of Cyprus and the Levantine area for the dynastic language of the Persian-period Eastern Mediterranean, and hunting representations may be part of this heritage.

If the tradition of the multiple-quarry hunt and its visual expression seem well-rooted in the Eastern Mediterranean, the Hellenic contribution cannot be underestimated. In fact, on one hand, as already highlighted in Chapter Two, the stylistic features of the dynastic tombs under Persian rule reveal the activity of Greek or Greek-trained artists. On the other hand, multiple-quarry hunting imagery arose between the fifth and the fourth centuries BC, when the impact of the Hellenic artistic language in the Eastern Mediterranean increased, also illustrated in Chapter Two. Some scholars have noted that after hunting imagery declined in Greece at the end of the fifth century BC, it made its appearance in the Eastern Mediterranean, on local monumental funerary cycles.[111] Certainly, the

[109] Flourentzos 2007.
[110] Childs 1978.
[111] Barringer 2001: 174–5.

a

b

Figure 54. Kylix from Capua, sides A and B. Copenhagen, National Museum of Denmark 6327. Courtesy of the National Museum of Denmark.

multiple-quarry hunt was not a common theme in the Greek world, but compositional similarities to the Eastern Mediterranean multiple-quarry hunts are traceable on those parts of Greek vases that can accommodate lengthy scenes and allow a concurrent reading of the whole story, such as the rim and the cover. The results are similar to the sculptural reliefs on architraves, crest beams and socles of the dynastic monuments of the Eastern Mediterranean. In addition, if one considers the Marathonomachy painting in the Stoa Poikile (Paus. 1.15.3) and the Parthenon frieze, it will be noted that the arrangement of a continuous figured field in scenes set in a time sequence was a formal solution adopted in Greek monumental art close in time to the Eastern Mediterranean dynastic tombs.[112] Therefore, the juxtaposition of different autonomous hunting scenes in a sequence within a figurated field – which will be analysed in depth in the next chapter – may be due to the contribution of artists of Hellenic training.

Such contribution thus appears crucial in shaping a new artistic language on a monumental scale that combined a mature store of artistic knowledge of Hellenic style with local values and visual traditions. The result is highly original and peculiar to the Eastern Mediterranean in the Persian Achaemenid period.

[112] For considerations on the organisation of the Stoa Poikile painting, see de Angelis 1996: 122–3; on the Parthenon frieze, see Hanfmann 1957: 76.

Figure 55. (following page) Detail of the socle of the Mourning Women Sarcophagus from Sidon. Istanbul, Archaeological Museum 368. D-DAI-IST-R1771 (Photo: W. Schiele 1978).

A1 A2 A3 A4 A5 A6

4

Images of Multiple-Quarry Hunts in the Eastern Mediterranean

This chapter will analyse the fifth- and fourth-century BC dynastic hunting representations in detail, focusing on the iconographic aspects of these representations and their meaning. From the observations in Chapter Two the multiple-quarry hunt emerged as the favourite iconography adopted for the dynastic self-representation, when hunting images were included in the funerary figurative programmes. As will be made clear, the present analysis will take into account the representation of more than one prey not only in the same figurative field, but also in the same figurative programme. Therefore, at first the dynastic meaning of hunt in the area will be stressed. Then a visual analysis will be conducted not only through the corpus of dynastic tombs outlined in Chapter Two, but also through other types of elite tombs from this area and from other regions of Anatolia. Moreover, the transmediality of the multiple-quarry hunt will be investigated due to other types of objects, notably Graeco-Persian tabloid glyptic.

4.1. The hunt and dynastic ideology in the Eastern Mediterranean

As emphasised, the figurative programmes of seven out of eight dynastic funerary monuments in the Eastern Mediterranean dating from the late fifth and fourth centuries BC are characterised by the presence of hunt scenes: the Mausoleum of Halicarnassus, the Nereid Monument of Xanthos, the Heroon of Trysa, and the four marble sarcophagi of Sidon; the Heroon of Limyra does not have any explicit reference to the hunt.[1]

Consistently with other ancient contexts, the hunt played an important role in the dynastic ideology of this wide area. A few km from Xanthos the Letoon sanctuary was dedicated to the triad of Leto, Apollo and Artemis.[2] Here, presumably near the temple of Artemis, the Lycian dynast Arbinas – thought to be the patron of the Nereid Monument – offered a statue of the goddess with a socle carrying a bilingual dedication to Artemis (*Ertẽmi* in the Lycian text). The goddess is defined as Θηροφόνα ("killing wild beasts") in the Greek text.[3] This dedication may provide important evidence of the dynastic interest in hunting in Lycia. Lycia had a privileged connection with hunting.[4] The god Apollo, defined in Classical sources as a hunter (Aesch. *TGF* Fr. 200; Soph. *OC* 1091) or the inventor of game and hounds alongside Artemis (Xen. *Cyn.* 1.1), was connected to Lycia with certainty from the sixth century BC.[5] Apart from Homer's problematic epithet Λυκηγενής referring to Apollo, in the *Homeric Hymn to Apollo* the god is lord of Lycia, Maeonia (Lydia) and Miletus (*Hom. Hymn Ap.* 179–180).[6] This early connection between Apollo and Lycia cannot be accidental since Herodotus, without mentioning the god, cites the oracle of Patara (Hdt. 1.182), of which there is certain attribution to Apollo in written sources from the second and first centuries BC.[7] Later on, Statius set Apollo's hunting in Lycia (Stat. *Achil.* 1.165–166).[8]

Such a dynastic connection with the hunt is less evident in other coastal regions of southern Anatolia. There was a sanctuary of Artemis also at Cindya, the Carian settlement mentioned in Chapter One as the city of the probable Hecatomnid ancestors. Cindya is considered to be the fifth-century BC dynastic seat of Caria, before its replacement by Mylasa and Halicarnassus. It is tempting to connect the cult of this goddess to the importance of the hunt for the local dynastic ideology, which is confirmed by the presence of this theme on the Hecatomnus Sarcophagus and the Mausoleum of Halicarnassus. Moreover, it has been hypothesised that the marble slab depicting a boar hunt from Bodrum Castle, which matches the horsemen relief now in Vienna, might be part of the original decoration of the Palace of Mausolus.[9] Similarly, J. Borchhardt has proposed that two blocks from Silifke, in Cilicia, formed a hunting frieze decorating the palace of a local dynast or

[1] As already mentioned, the Hecatomnus Sarcophagus in Mylasa should be included among the dynastic tombs of this area displaying a hunting scene of a single-prey lion hunt.

[2] Des Courtils 2003: 130–66.

[3] Asheri 1983: 97–8 and 168–9, no. 2; see also Kolb 2018: 628. For Artemis, see Bryce and Zahle 1986: 181–2; Schürr 2013: 219–20. Moreover, a cult of Artemis Kynegetis (Huntress) is attested on the so-called Twelve Gods reliefs, a Lycian production dating back to the Roman period. The interpretation of the Lycian Twelve Gods is not unanimous, although the most common hypothesis is that they should be interpreted as hunter gods (Renberg 2014). The Twelve Gods are mentioned already in the fifth-century BC Greek epigram of the Inscribed Pillar with reference to the "agorà" of Xanthos: if these Xanthian Dodekatheoi were generally inserted into a long-standing tradition from the Hittite to the Roman times, in recent years they have been considered in connection with Athens due to their agoraic feature (Schürr 2013: 218–9). However, in light of the dynastic devotion to Artemis Θηροφόνα in the Letoon, it would be interesting to explore a connection between a place for dynastic burials (the Xanthian "agorà", which – due to its marked funerary character – should not be considered necessarily as a public space in Greek terms) and a possible interpretation of the fifth-century BC Twelve Gods as hunter gods.

[4] On hunting scenes in Lycia, see Pekridou-Gorecki 2012: 73–9. See also Hoff 2017: 233.

[5] See Hor. *Carm.* 3.4.62–64; Nisbet and Rudd 2004: 75, vv. 62–64. For other observations on Apollo the hunter, see Guidorizzi, Avezzù and Cerri 2008: 334, vv. 1088–1093.

[6] Keen 1998: 198; for dating the *Hymn*, see Càssola 1991: 101.

[7] Herodotus mentions "the prophetess of the god at Patara in Lycia" (translation from Godley 1966). See also Pind. *Pyth.* 1.39; Gentili *et al.* 1995: 341, v. 39. On Apollo and Lycia, Càssola 1991: 85; Keen 1998: 197–200.

[8] See also Nuzzo 2012: 62–3, vv. 163–166; Uccellini 2012: 144–5, vv. 165–166.

[9] See Pedersen 2009: 329–30. See also Borchhardt 1968: 190.

Persian governor.[10] These hypotheses are very attractive, although little is known about palace decoration in this context, other than the relief of Meydancıkkale in Rough Cilicia.[11]

It is known that many residences of royal and satrapal rank in the Eastern Mediterranean had *paradeisoi*, parks that were rich both in flora and in fauna: in Anatolia, Sardis (Xen. *Oec.* 4.20–21), Celaenae (Xen. *An.* 1.2.7), Dascylium (Xen. *Hell.* 4.1.15–16); in Phoenicia, Sidon (Diod. Sic. 16.41.5).[12] For this reason, it has been hypothesised that an Aramaic rock inscription in Rough Cilicia, recalling the resting place of a person of high rank – perhaps a local dynast – during hunting trips, may refer to a *paradeisos*, although there is no evidence to support this interpretation.[13]

Finally, a hunting theme may be present on several drachmas from Aspendos, in Pamphylia, which was the region east of Lycia. Here, a wild boar on the obverse is paired with a horseman on the reverse. L. Robert considered that the two images were related iconographically: the horseman would be Mopsus, the hero and founder of the city, depicted hunting the wild boar on the obverse.[14] In this case, the hunting representation would have a specific local meaning.

This range of evidence suggests that this area fully belongs to that wider area in which a tradition of "political hunting" developed.[15]

4.2. The iconography of the multiple-quarry hunt

4.2.1. Dynastic funerary monuments

Five out of the seven dynastic tombs with hunts display a coexistence of prey of different species in one figurative field: the Nereid Monument, the Heroon of Trysa, the Satrap Sarcophagus, the Mourning Women Sarcophagus, and the Alexander Sarcophagus. On the Mausoleum of Halicarnassus it is possible that different species were represented on each side of the podium's step dedicated to the hunt theme. On the Lycian Sarcophagus, instead, two hunting scenes are each on opposite sides of the coffin.

The earliest representation of hunting in this corpus is on the Satrap Sarcophagus from the Royal Necropolis of Sidon, a complex composition in a frame-type arrangement. A deer occupies the first position from the left, its legs bowed under, and all the attention and tension of the scene focuses on a panther, whom the main hunter is intent on killing (Fig. 56).[16] Two horsemen, one of whom is the dynast, are arranged symmetrically in the central scene of the panther hunt, and this is flanked by two challenging moments for the other members of the hunt. On the left, a rider tries to control his horse before the dying deer; on the far right, a horse runs from the centre of the scene, startled by the dangerous beast facing the dynast. Since the horseman on the left seems intent on reining in his horse rather than making a hunting gesture, the whole depiction could be read as a sequence of hunts immortalised in one moment: the dynast has struck a deer and is moving on to the more dangerous panther, like the young Cyrus in his first hunt with deer and boar (Xen. *Cyr.* 1.4.8).[17]

The Lycian Sarcophagus shows two distinct hunting scenes on each of the long sides (Figs. 19 and 57). As already discussed in Chapter Two, on one long side four clean-shaven horsemen and one bearded surround a boar, whereas opposite are hunters in chariots, who have been identified as princes or Amazons, pursue a lion.[18] If we observe two hunting scenes with different prey on distinct sides of the coffin here, it is useful to highlight that the representation of Centaurs struggling over a dead deer on one of the short sides of the sarcophagus may amplify the hunting imagery of the two long sides, adding a third prey to the overall programme of the coffin (Fig. 20).[19]

The hunt on the Nereid Monument of Xanthos – represented on three slabs of the eastern architrave – has a tripartite composition similar to the Satrap Sarcophagus (Fig. 58a).[20] The first two slabs (Sculptures 889 and 887), in a centripetal scheme, revolve around the hunting of two dangerous prey, respectively a bear and a boar (Figs. 58b-c). The third slab (Sculpture 888) differs from the other two, since the figures are organised in a wave that flows from right to left, except for a runaway horse, which moves to the right (Fig. 58d).[21] This means that the pace of the continuous figurative field is similar in Sidon (Satrap Sarcophagus) and Xanthos: two narrative units are centred on one prey each; the third one has an incident as its focus.[22] Another similarity between the Nereid Monument and the Satrap Sarcophagus is the presence of a time sequence: in Xanthos on slab 889 the lifeless body of a deer is carried by one of the attendants accompanying the hunters on horseback, suggesting that the same characters are participating in a sequence of hunts.

[10] Borchhardt 1968: 190. Fleischer (1984: 92–8) and Kubala (2000), instead, attribute these reliefs and another one to one Cilician funerary monument in the Graeco-Persian style.

[11] Laroche and Davesne 1981; Davesne and Laroche-Traunecker 1998; Gates 2005: 62–3. On palace structures, see Marksteiner 2002: 81–97, and, for Halicarnassus, Pedersen 2009.

[12] See § 3.2.

[13] Scholars date this inscription to the sixth to fourth century BC. See Friedrich 1957–8; Jensen 1958: 284; Donner and Röllig 1973: 309, no. 261; Gibson 1975: 155, no. 35; Lemaire and Lozachmeur 1996: 102; Lemaire 2000a; Casabonne 1996: 111–5; 2000: 93–6; 2004: 148–9 and 241, cat. IAC 1; Lemaire 2014: 322.

[14] Robert 1960: 177–8; *SNG v. Aulock* XI: nos. 4487–4499; *LIMC* VI.1: 653, no. 4.

[15] Allsen 2006: 8 and 14.

[16] For the panther hunt in the Persian context, see Borchhardt 1968: 166–71.

[17] See § 3.2.

[18] Langer-Karrenbrock 2000: 88–95.

[19] Schmidt-Dounas 1985: 71.

[20] London, British Museum 1848,1020.113 (Sculpture 889); 1848,1020.115 (Sculpture 887); 1848,1020.116 (Sculpture 888).

[21] Poggio 2011: 480–1.

[22] For the interpretation of Sculpture 888 of the Nereid Monument, see § 5.5 and Poggio 2011: 485.

Figure 56. Hunt relief on the Satrap Sarcophagus from Sidon. Istanbul, Archaeological Museum 367. D-DAI-IST-70/42 (Photo: W. Schiele 1970).

In other examples, longer sequences of hunting scenes are depicted in the same figurative field. The Heroon of Trysa presented the longest series of hunt scenes in this context. In the upper register of the northern wall were nine hunt scenes showing different kinds of prey, interspersed with trees used as a formal device to conceal the joints between the slabs (Fig. 59).[23] The sequence of hunts is polycentric, with centripetal scenes placed side by side paratactically, an arrangement that resulted in one continuous frieze. The various scenes differ in the prey, the technique and the number of figures. Although no temporal sequence can be detected, unlike the Satrap Sarcophagus and the Nereid Monument, where the deer hunt clearly enjoyed priority, at Trysa the representation of fleeing ibexes chased by hunters armed with javelin and bow occupies the first position from left and a third fleeing ibex climbs up (B9).[24] By contrast, panthers and boars are represented as surrounded by hunters on horseback and on foot. Dogs are shown in two feline hunts, perhaps panthers (A14 and A18), and in that for a wild boar (A19 and A20), and a bear hunt (A15) is also represented.[25] As will be seen, even in these images a hunting accident is presented when one of the hunters is attacked by a feline, perhaps a lion (A17).[26]

The representation of hunting on the Mourning Women Sarcophagus from Sidon is similar (Fig. 55). It appears as a very low bas-relief frieze on the lower socle of this miniature temple and shows precise compositional strategies. The arrangement of the figures in diagonals contributes to the impression of excitement, movement and running. Like the use of repetition in rhetoric, the effect is reinforced by the use of recurrent *schemata*. The interruption of this pace serves to separate the individual episodes. For example, while B1, B2 and B3 advance "diagonally" to the right, B4, B5 and B6 turn to the left, creating a triangular composition at the centre, defined by B3, B4 and the prey, shown twisting: the panther, which hurls itself to the right, turning its head in the opposite direction, invites the observer to consider both portions of the scene (Fig. 32). In another example, the focal point is signalled by two devices: the first is the vertical axis of the tree between B9 and B10; the second is the interruption of the pace created by the boar and two dogs between B9 and B10. Similar patterns are found in other episodes.

Unfortunately, little can be said about the Mausoleum of Halicarnassus. Surviving fragments of statuary representing boar, panthers and dogs may suggest there were hunting scenes on the western and southern sides of the podium's lower step. Scholars have also identified the fragmentary horseman in Persian attire as the main hunter (Fig. 60), but this is not certain.[27] It is worth noting that

[23] Gschwantler 1993.
[24] Although this third ibex is represented on the lower register, it is highly probable that it should be connected with the hunting scene of the upper register. See also the position of the second deer on the hunt relief of the 'Eshmun Sanctuary near Sidon (Stucky 2005: 171, fig. 101, figure no. 5).
[25] Benndorf and Niemann 1889: 169; Eichler 1950: 68–9.
[26] A lioness, according to Landskron (2015: 175). For hunt accidents, see § 5.5.

[27] London, British Museum 1857,1220.234 (sculpture 1045). On the Mausoleum sculpted hunting group, see Jeppesen 1958: 51–2; Waywell 1978: 45–6; 110–2, no. 34; Lucchese 2009: 33.

Figure 57. Mounted boar hunt on the Lycian Sarcophagus from Sidon. Istanbul, Archaeological Museum 369. D-DAI-IST-71-59 (Photo: W. Schiele 1971).

here the hunt was not rendered as a relief, but through free-standing sculptures.

On the Alexander Sarcophagus the hunting depiction occupies two different sides of the coffin. On one of the long sides is the well-known lion hunt, which occupies the centre of the frieze (Fig. 61). On the right of the same frieze, two hunters on foot surround a deer, one of them seizing it by its antlers. Moving around the sarcophagus in an anticlockwise direction, on the short side is a panther hunt (Fig. 62). In the centre the main hunter, dressed in Persian clothes, raises his arm to hit the wild beast, which threatens him with its paw. Three more hunters in Persian dress surround the quarry, and they too are ready to attack with their weapons. On the left, behind the main hunter, a member of the entourage struggles to restrain a horse.

Figure 58. Hunt expedition on the architrave frieze of the Nereid Monument. (a) Drawing. After Childs and Demargne 1989: pl. 88 (detail). Courtesy of William A.P. Childs. (b) The bear hunt, Sculpture 889. London, British Museum 1848,1020.113. © Trustees of the British Museum. (c) The boar hunt, Sculpture 887. London, British Museum 1848,1020.115. © Trustees of the British Museum. (d) The startled horse, Sculpture 888. London, British Museum 1848,1020.116. © Trustees of the British Museum.

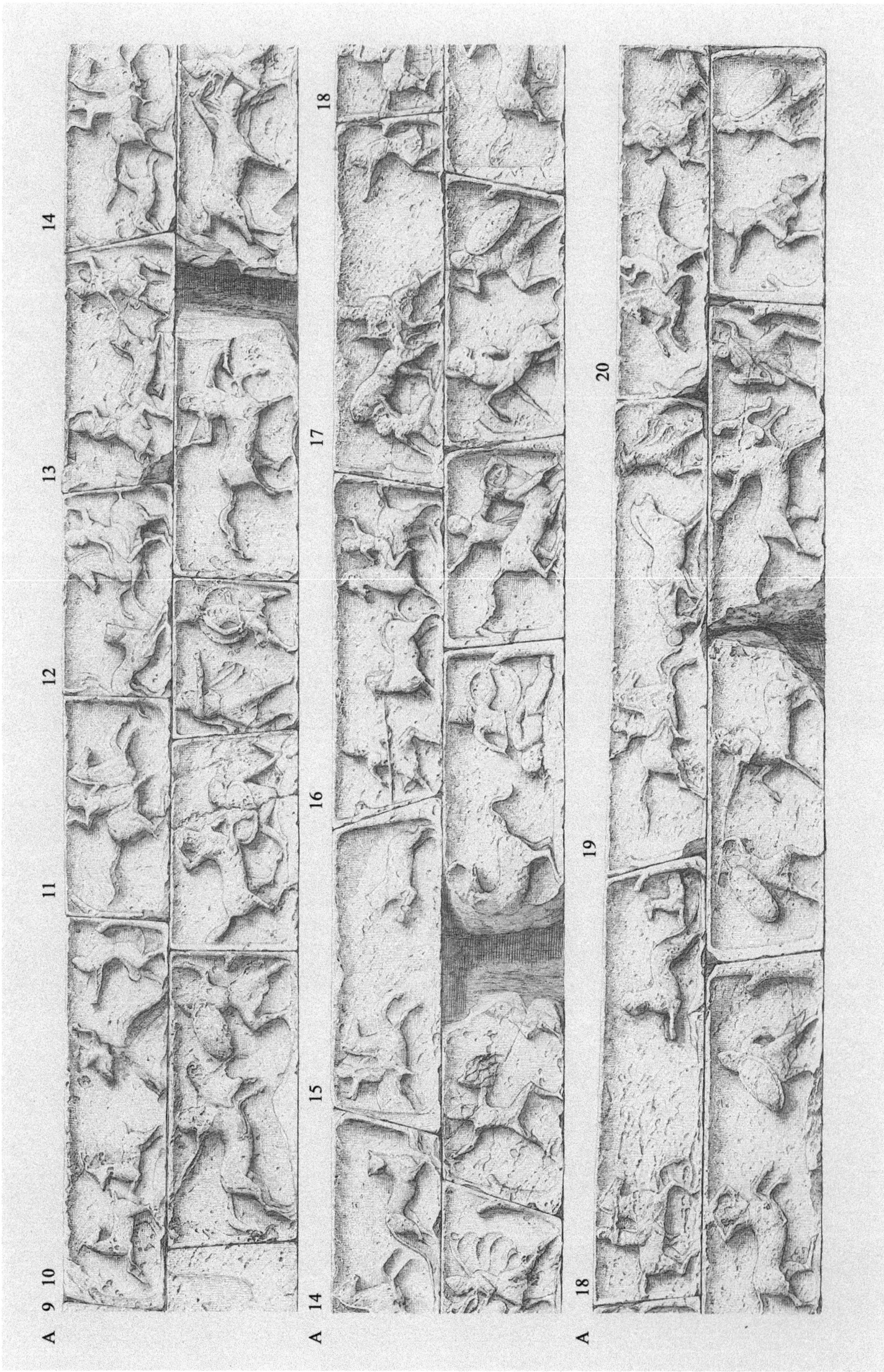

Figure 59. The multiple-quarry hunt of the Heroon of Trysa (register A). Modified after Benndorf and Niemann 1889: pl. 17.

Figure 60. Statue of a rider interpreted as hunter from the Mausoleum of Halicarnassus, Sculpture 1045. British Museum 1857,1220.234. © Trustees of the British Museum.

Figure 61. The hunt representation on the long side of the Alexander Sarcophagus from Sidon. Istanbul, Archaeological Museum 370. D-DAI-IST-8120 (Photo: Sébah & Joaillier about 1900).

Figure 62. The hunt representation on the short side of the Alexander Sarcophagus from Sidon. Istanbul, Archaeological Museum 370. D-DAI-IST-8126 (Photo: Sébah & Joaillier about 1900).

On the long side at least the principle of the multiple-quarry hunt in the same figurative field was followed. Thus, this sarcophagus – the latest of the royal sarcophagi from Sidon – maintains the hunting iconography that was current in Sidon, somehow recovering the example of the Satrap Sarcophagus, which represented two types of prey in the same figurative field.

4.2.2. Further sculptural evidence from western Anatolia

The present research is focused on multiple-quarry hunt as it is the most common hunting iconography on the dynastic tombs of the area under analysis. However, this iconography was also used on tombs that cannot be related to dynastic rank: in Lycia this iconography is observed in particular on tombs attributed to aristocracy mostly in the main dynastic seats of Xanthos and Limyra. This demonstrates the spread of this iconography through different components of society. Other pieces of evidence from north-western Anatolia will be considered, although this is outside of the scope of this work.

4.2.2.1. Lycian tombs

The hunting theme is significant in the funerary imagery of Lycia, possibly because of the special connection of this region with hunting gods such as Apollo and Artemis, as was noted at the beginning of this chapter. In addition to multiple-quarry hunts, there are representations of hunts with one quarry such as the boar hunt on the lid fragment of a sarcophagus from Xanthos and the bear hunt on the tomb of Muskar.[28] There are also representations of many quarry of the same species, as on the so-called sarcophagus of dancers at Xanthos, where two hunters face a wild boar each, all in the same figurative field.[29] Since the focus here is on the multiple-quarry hunt theme, only those hunting representations that combine quarry of diverse species will be considered.

One of the most representative examples is the Payava Tomb (370–350 BC), from the funerary area to the north-east of Xanthos, now in the British Museum, London. This limestone monument bears inscriptions that allow the figures depicted to be identified.[30] The name of the owner, Payava, certified the iterative presence of this figure in the complex programme of the sarcophagus, a device that is consistent with the repetition of the dynast in the figurative programme of the Nereid Monument.

Payava was the local representative of the satrap Autophradates, who is represented on the podium. The deceased belonged thus to the local elite, but, due to his position, adopted the figurative imagery and the conventions used in dynastic tombs. The dynastic tone of the tomb is also inferred from its scenic location, a feature that connects it with the Nereid Monument, though this sarcophagus was less isolated.[31]

The figurative programme on the podium includes a man presenting a young athlete with a wreath, an audience scene probably with the satrap Autophradates seated, two armed figures and a battle involving cavalry and foot soldiers. On the lid, the curved sides are decorated with *apobatai* chariots and the gable ends with pairs of sphinxes; on one of the gable ends is a seated couple while on the other only a seated woman is preserved. The two sides of the crest beam represent a battle between cavalry and foot soldiers, and a tripartite multiple-quarry hunt organised around three prey: a deer, a boar and a bear (Fig. 27). The species of these animals and the position of this iconography on the uppermost level of the monument recall the hunts on the architrave of the Nereid Monument. The crest beam of the Caeneus Sarcophagus of Limyra is also decorated with two sculpted continuous friezes: on one side is a Centauromachy, on the other a tripartite multiple-quarry hunt with three prey, two real and one mythological: a panther, a boar and a winged griffin (Fig. 63).

Returning to Xanthos, the Merehi Tomb (370–350 BC) presents a further example of hunt (Fig. 64a-b).[32] Here, the decoration is concentrated on the lid, which shows the standard themes of the Lycian funerary programmes. On one side of the crest beam a long series of foot soldiers is depicted, with a siege scene on the right. On the other side, instead, a sequence of peacetime scenes is presented: a banquet, the wreathing of an athlete, standing men and an audience scene. Hunts are represented on the curved sides of the lid: the *apobatai* model is used for hunting scenes where the prey are a panther and a Chimaera. On the Merehi Tomb as on the Lycian Sarcophagus of Sidon, then, different types of hunts occupy distinct figurative fields.[33]

The representation of hunts in distinct figurative fields is also found on the fragmentary socle block of the Islamlar Sarcophagus. Scholars have described it as decorated on the short right side with a bear hunt led by a horseman assisted by a dog, on the left side with a boar hunt on foot, and on the long side with a battle scene.[34] In the Lycian context the presence of this hunt-themed decoration on the socle of a sarcophagus is unique, since in the above examples hunting representations appear on the upper parts.

[28] For the sarcophagus from Xanthos, now in the Istanbul Archaeological Museum, see Demargne 1962: 37; Demargne and Laroche 1974: 46–60, esp. 57–9. For the Muskar Tomb, see Zahle 1979: 306–9; Benda-Weber 2005: 109, no. 7.

[29] Demargne and Laroche 1974: 97–103; Bruns-Özgan 1987: 285–6, cat. S 26.

[30] London, British Museum 1848,1020.142 (Sculpture 950). *TAM* I: 34–6, no. 40; Demargne and Laroche 1974: 137–9.

[31] On the Payava Sarcophagus, see Demargne and Laroche 1974: 61–87; Demargne 1974; Shahbazi 1975: 135–47; Jenkins 2006: 179–84; lastly, Prost 2012b. On Pajava, see also Pirson 2014: 134.

[32] London, British Museum 1848,1020.143 (Sculpture 951).

[33] On the Merehi Tomb, see Demargne and Laroche 1974: 88–96; Jenkins 2006: 176–9.

[34] Zahle 1979: 344–5, no. 69; Borchhardt 1996–7: 5–6; Borchhardt and Bleibtreu 2008: 64.

Figure 63. Part of the crest beam of the so-called Caeneus Sarcophagus from Limyra. Antalya, Archaeological Museum A.3773. D-DAI-IST-R708 (Photo: W. Schiele 1967).

It should also be noted that some fragments of a hunting scene from Limyra (Lycia), attributable to the second quarter of the fourth century BC, have been interpreted as a multiple-quarry hunt.[35]

4.2.2.2. Further evidence from north-western Anatolia

Another cluster of evidence with multiple-quarry hunt representations may be pinpointed to north-western Anatolia.[36] A multiple-quarry hunt and a battle scene are represented on the Çan Sarcophagus, found in 1998, midway between Dascylium and Ilion, dated to the early fourth century BC (Fig. 65).[37] This marble sarcophagus, attributed to a local dynast, displays two hunting scenes on one long side and a battle scene on one short side. The long side is divided into two figurative fields of the same size, separated by a tree. The left scene – damaged by grave robbers – depict two deer, chased by two horsemen: the deer are depicted fleeing to the right with a second collapsing, as shown by the folding legs, similar to the deer on the Satrap Sarcophagus.[38] The scene on the right, instead, shows a boar being attacked by a horseman and by two dogs. Here, the juxtaposition of two hunting scenes recalls the pattern of the dynastic monuments analysed above.

Multiple-quarry hunts appear on other Anatolian monuments of this period. A stele now in the Bergama Museum, which comes from Manisa, and probably dates from the late fifth to the early fourth century BC, is composed of two superimposed figured registers (Fig. 66).[39] The hunt register at the top seems to be a representation of Xenophon's passage about the first hunt of the young Cyrus the Elder in the open field. We see a hunter in the act of delivering a spear blow to a boar, while the first victim – possibly a deer – lies lifeless on the ground. There is much emphasis on the hunter's gesture with attention focused completely on his action rather than on the prey. In the lower register the same horseman is carved with an attendant on foot and a dog, perhaps a scene preceding or following the hunt.[40] From a stylistic analysis of the floral anthemion, W. Radt, taken up by J. Borchhardt and E. Bleibtreu, dated the stele to 500 BC. C.H. Roosevelt's later dating however is preferable, given that multiple-quarry hunt iconography on this sort of stele has no parallels in the Archaic period, as the stelae from Dascylium demonstrates.[41]

The second example is the stele from Çavuşköy, near Dascylium in Mysia, dating from the late fifth century BC (Fig. 67).[42] The scene is nicely arranged in two parts: on the left the horseman and his squire, on the right the tree with the prey. The interaction between the two sections comes from semi-circular compositional devices like that created by the curvilinear motion of the horse and the quarry leaping forward. Diagonal lines increase the dynamism of the scene, as in the hunter's long spear echoed by the two branches on the right. Lastly, the horseman and the tree, which have almost equal importance in the figurative balance, create the vertical emphasis of the composition. Here we see the pairing of a deer and boar once more, but unlike the previous example, the boar is the first prey to be attacked, while the deer, aware of the danger, prepares to flee.

[35] Seyer 1996; Pekridou-Gorecki 2012: 77.

[36] I have not included the fragmentary stele from Uşak with boar hunting since the presence of a second prey is plausible, but not certain (Polat 1994).

[37] Tevfikiye, Troy Museum 9025. Sevinç *et al.* 2001; Tombul 2004; Rose 2007: 254–6; Ma 2008; Wu 2014: 234–5; Rose 2014: 129–42.

[38] Conversely, the monument's editors speak of the motif of "versammelter Gallop" (Sevinç *et al.* 2001: 391).

[39] Bergama Museum 4394.

[40] Borchhardt and Bleibtreu 2008: 81. For Xenophon's passage on Cyrus' first hunt outside the reserve, see § 3.2.

[41] Radt 1983: 67; Borchhardt and Bleibtreu 2008: Taf. 11.5; Roosevelt (2009: 162, 255, no. 21.1) interprets both the prey as boar. For the Dascylium stelae, see Nollé 1992.

[42] Istanbul, Archaeological Museum 1502. Pfuhl and Möbius 1977: 30–1, no. 73; Dentzer 1982: 576, cat. R 68; Nollé 1992: 27–30, cat. S 7; Fabricius 1999: 33 and note 79; Karagöz 2013: 66, cat. 5. Miller (2003: 29) attributes this stele to a local dynast.

Figure 64. The two sides of the lid of the Merehi Tomb of Xanthos. Drawings by Sir G. Scharf. (a) London, British Museum 2012,5034.91. © Trustees of the British Museum. (b) London, British Museum 2012,5034.92. © Trustees of the British Museum.

Figure 65. Hunting scenes on the long side of the Çan Sarcophagus (Çanakkale Museum display). Tevfikiye, Troy Museum 9025. Courtesy of the Troy Excavation Project.

Figure 66. Stele from Manisa. Bergama Museum 4394. D-DAI-IST-PE.82/4-5 (Photo: E. Steiner 1982). Courtesy of the Pergamonarchiv, Deutsches Archäologisches Institut – Abteilung Istanbul.

In conclusion, six out of eight tombs among those just analysed have prey of different species in one figurative scene: the Payava Sarcophagus, the Caeneus Sarcophagus, the fragmentary relief from Limyra (from Lycia); the Çan Sarcophagus, the Manisa Stele and the Çavuşköy Stele (from north-western Anatolia). Two Lycian tombs have prey of different species on distinct figurative fields, the Merehi Sarcophagus and the Islamlar Tomb.

Figure 67. Stele from Çavuşköy. Istanbul, Archaeological Museum 1502. D-DAI-IST-68/87 (Photo: W. Schiele 1968).

4.2.3. A typological appraisal

There are seven dynastic tombs with multiple hunting scenes from south-western Anatolia and Phoenicia dating back to the fifth to fourth centuries BC. Moreover, among contemporary tombs of smaller scale, there are five cases from Lycia and three from north-western Anatolia.

In Lycia, other than the multiple-quarry hunt on the Heroon of Trysa, hunting scenes often decorate extensive figured fields in elevated positions, as on the architrave of the Nereid Monument and the lids of sarcophagi (curved surfaces or crest beams).[43] In this respect there was continuity with the Archaic age, since already on the Kızılbel Tomb the lion hunt decorated the inner lintel of the access door.[44] Hunts are present on the sides of sarcophagi coffins, not only in Sidon, but also in Anatolia, as evidenced on the Çan Sarcophagus and the Hecatomnus Sarcophagus. Hunting representations also appear on the lower elements of tombs, such as the socle of the Mourning Women Sarcophagus and, based on current reconstructions, the lower podium step of the Mausoleum at Halicarnassus.[45]

[43] On the Heroon of Trysa, however, the multiple-quarry hunt frieze occupied the upper register of the inner northern wall.
[44] Mellink 1998: 37–8, 61. The Kızılbel Tomb shows a multiple-quarry hunt on the east wall (Mellink 1998: 32–4, 60–1).
[45] Waywell 1978; Lucchese 2009: 61–2.

When prey of different species coexist in the same figurative field, two distinct typologies can be outlined from the corpus of dynastic and non-dynastic tombs. On the one hand, the coexistence of more than one prey in a single figurated field may imply an explicit timeframe if the prey are pursued in succession. A similar solution, which reveals a more complex construction of the image from a narrative point of view, has been observed in different cases in Chapter Three. I shall call these cases "hypotactic multiple-quarry hunts", since from a narrative point of view hunted prey are ranked in a precise chronological order. Among dynastic monuments this typology is in the minority, since only the Satrap Sarcophagus and the representation of deer on the Nereid Monument follow this principle, using different visual devices: in Sidon the prey are represented in succession, indicating a short timespan between the two hunting events. The representation of a series of prey with one hunter is not new in the Eastern Mediterranean, as seen in Chapter Three, but the fact that one of the prey has been struck and left behind by the main hunter is unusual and makes the temporal and spatial dimensions tangible in the image. In Xanthos, instead, the lifeless body of the deer indicates a more marked time break.[46] The strategy of prey pursued in succession seems more widespread on the north-western Anatolian stelae, since both of the two items described above – those from Manisa and from Çavuşköy, follow this principle.

On the other hand, the coexistence of diverse prey in the same field is a simple juxtaposition of hunting scenes. Since the rhetorical principle of coordinating accumulation seems to prevail, these cases will be termed "paratactic multiple-quarry hunts".[47] The following dynastic funerary monuments fall into this category: the Nereid Monument (for the sequence of bear and boar hunts), the Heroon of Trysa, the Mourning Women Sarcophagus and the Alexander Sarcophagus. Probably the Mausoleum of Halicarnassus could also be included in this group. Moreover, other Lycian examples should be included: the Payava Sarcophagus, the Caeneus Sarcophagus and the fragments from Limyra. In north-western Anatolia the Çan Sarcophagus must also be taken into account. Of the fifteen multiple-quarry hunts identified on Eastern Mediterranean monuments dated to the fifth and fourth centuries BC, nine thus accord with this principle. Obviously, the prevalence of the paratactic multiple-quarry hunt on large monuments and sarcophagi must be underlined and seems justified by the greater expanse of surfaces available for decoration.

The Merehi Sarcophagus of Xanthos, the Islamlar Tomb, the Lycian Sarcophagus of Sidon and the Alexander Sarcophagus (panther hunt), which display different prey on distinct sides of the monuments, may be considered as a specific type of multiple-quarry hunt, although they would not be included in B. Tripodi and M. Miller's definitions, which consider the representation of different kinds of quarry in one figurative field.[48] When different kinds of quarry are represented on distinct sides, the message of accumulation of prey within the overall figurative programme is however the same, thus these cases may be included in the analysis of multiple-quarry hunts ("multi-sided multiple-quarry hunts").

At the end of this section, one can thus say that in the multiple-quarry hunt more prey of different species are represented in the same figurative field or at least in distinct parts of the same figurative programme; the result is an accumulation effect. These representations mostly concern historical or generic hunts attributed to the dynast and his entourage, but they can include mythological hunts as heroic pendant.[49]

4.2.4. The contribution of glyptic: the Graeco-Persian tabloid seals

Within a transmedial perspective, the above analysis must be integrated with an examination of Graeco-Persian glyptic. In the Persian Achaemenid tradition, seals were used for administrative purposes, thus they were connected with specific functions.[50] It is difficult to state whether Graeco-Persian seals were actually used, however it is certain that they convey images and values connected with the owners' status.

The hunt is one of the main themes in Graeco-Persian glyptic, which seems to follow similar compositional schemes of the monumental art. There are hypotactic multiple-quarry hunts, such as the representation of the chalcedony scaraboid seal showing a Persian horseman brandishing a spear in his right hand and chasing a deer in flight, while the lower part of the field includes a fleeing fox (Fig. 68). Here are two different types of prey in the same scene, and the deer is destined to succumb first.[51] An example of paratactic multiple-quarry hunt is provided by a scaraboid showing two scenes arranged on two registers. In the upper register the rider is facing a lion and aiming a bow, while the lower register shows a man with a spear confronting a boar.[52]

As for the multi-sided multiple-quarry hunt, a small corpus of Graeco-Persian seals offers a case that deserves more attention here: a group of decahedral seals, which date from the same period as our monuments. In this series of

[46] See the relief from the Southern City Gate of Zincirli with a hunter and a dead hare behind (§ 3.1.1.2.).

[47] Lausberg 1998: 298–9, §666. For a different use of the term "paratactic" in ancient art, see Zupnick 1962–3.

[48] Tripodi 1991; Miller 2003.

[49] See *ultra*, § 4.3.4.

[50] The study of administrative archives both in Persia and in the provinces of the empire is being enhanced. As for personal seals, see for instance Root 1991: 19–21.

[51] London, British Museum 120332. Boardman 1970b: 353, pl. 888. For another representation of the fox as prey, which never appears on monuments, see § 3.2.

[52] Cambridge, Fitzwilliam Museum E.2.1864. It is dated unanimously as fifth-fourth century BC except by Middleton, who suggests the fourth century AD, in the Sassanid period (Middleton 1891: app. ix, no. 24; Furtwängler 1900: II, 55, no. 1; Boardman 1970b: 354, pl. 924; Munn-Rankin 1959: 35, no. 71; Henig 1994: 38–9, no. 62).

Figure 68. Hunting scene on a stamp seal. London, British Museum 120332. © Trustees of the British Museum.

seals, six faces are decorated, and the other four are left smooth. Two of these smooth sides host the string hole; the lower face, the widest, almost always bears figurative decoration.[53] The first attempt to classify this corpus was made by H. Seyrig in 1952.[54]

Many of these seals show an image that certainly refers to hunting on their lower side, probably the main one (Fig. 69).[55] These are scenes of hunting on horseback, typical of the Persian context, with the hunters in Persian attire. Most of the other faces show animals poised for flight or attack, as if facing the hunter depicted on the main side who, for brevity or reasons of space, is depicted only once. Moreover, as emphasised by P. Zazoff, wild beasts on seals, often in the act of fleeing or attacking, can be considered prey even though no hunter is represented, as seen in Chapter Three.[56]

Even among the seals that do not have hunting scenes on the main face, some of the animals on the smaller faces may be interpreted as quarry for human hunters or dogs used in hunts. It can be assumed that the horseback hunts on the larger faces carry the meaning of the entire object, these seals may thus be interpreted as representations of multiple-quarry hunts.[57]

These seals are a link between paratactic, hypotactic and multi-sided hunts: as in the paratactic and multi-sided patterns, each prey plays a crucial role in each scene, but, as in the hypotactic hunt representations, the hunter is represented just once, for brevity or for reasons of space.

Although most of these objects are unprovenanced, it is possible to say that they were produced in the same cultural milieu as the dynastic monuments already mentioned. Scholars agree that these seals can be traced to the fifth and fourth centuries BC, when the Graeco-Persian artistic language was at its height.[58] A. Procopé-Walter noted that the shape of these seals could be traced back to Hittite glyptic art and suggested Anatolia as the place of origin.[59] On a stylistic basis, provenance from Anatolia was also proposed by Richter and Seyrig.[60] N.M. Nikulina suggested a connection with the Syro-Hittite context, identifying a stylistic relationship with the art of Lycian and Phoenician funerary monuments, and concluding that the production of the seals should be linked to southern Anatolia, in particular to Lycia and Caria.[61]

H.-P. Francfort extends the possible area of production to northern Syria as well.[62] On the basis of the data available, indeed, there is a concentration of these artefacts in the Syro-Levantine area. Moreover, considerations about the role that the Levantine area may have played in the elaboration of the multiple-quarry hunts of the Persian Achaemenid period and the thematic affinities with the representations of multiple-quarry hunts on the funerary monuments analysed here may also support the provenance of the decahedral seals from the Syro-Levantine area. This may reinforce the iconographical association between

[53] Furtwängler 1900: III, 118; Procopé-Walter 1937: 23; Seyrig 1952: 195–8. For the comparison proposed by Seyrig, see Wroth 1889: pl. 29 fig. 10.
[54] Seyrig 1952. See also Poggio 2016a. My ongoing research is recording an increasing number of items in world collections.
[55] See also Fornasier 2001: 245.
[56] Zazoff 1970: 17–22. See § 3.2.
[57] For recognising the main face of these seals, Seyrig 1952: 195.
[58] Richter 1949: 293.
[59] Procopé-Walter 1937: 26.
[60] Richter 1949: 296; Seyrig 1952: 199.
[61] Nikoulina 1971: 100–1.
[62] See also the important observations in Francfort 1975.

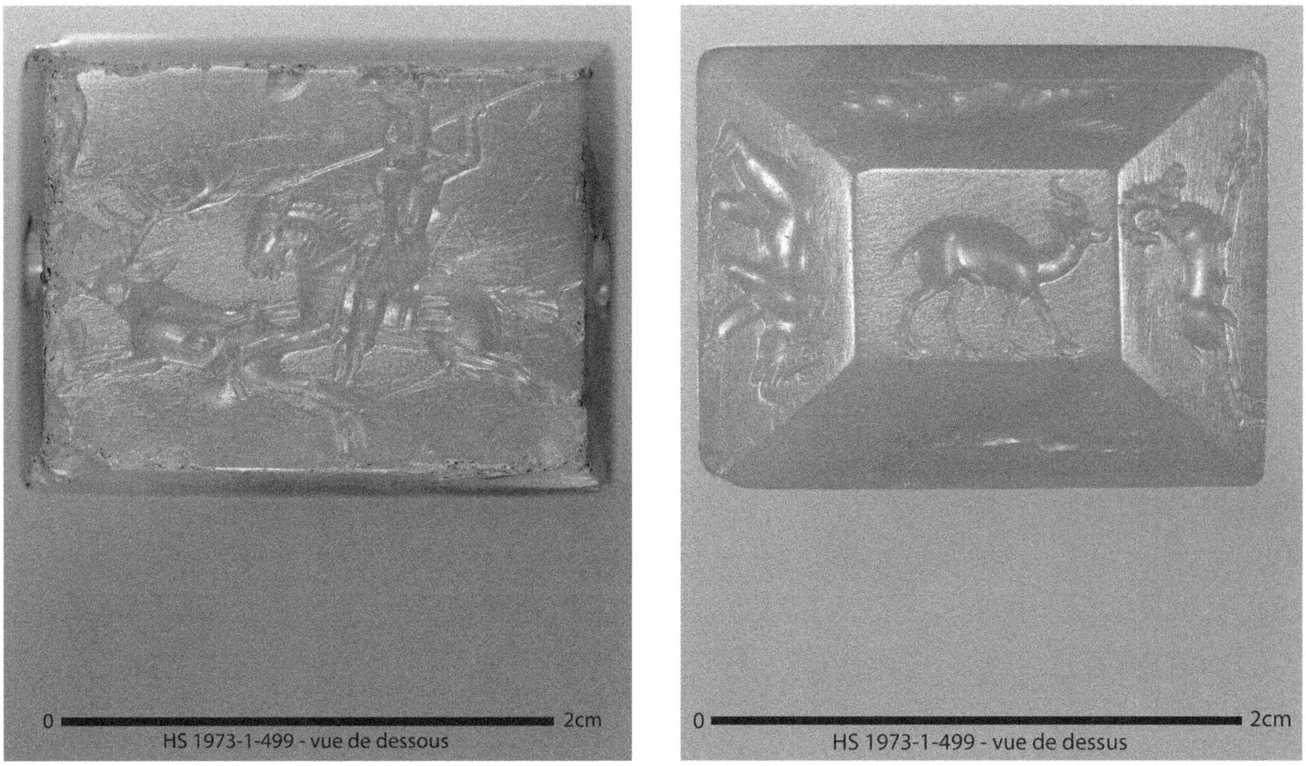

Figure 69. a-b Tabloid seal, lower and upper faces. Paris, Bibliothèque nationale de France HS 1973-1-499. Source: Bibliothèque nationale de France.

seals and monuments and is important for understanding the artistic language pertaining to the western part of the Persian world.

4.3. The iconology of multiple-quarry hunts

In hunting depictions, special significance is afforded to the confrontation with the quarry. Each prey has its own connotation: a successful hunt thus indicates domination over the characteristics attributed to the prey and the appropriation of them by the hunter himself. For instance, the helmet that Meriones gave to Odysseus for his mission with Diomedes was a trophy decorated with boar tusks that conferred great prestige on the hunter (*Il.* 10.260–271).[63] The ostentation of the prey, or the ostentation of the act of hunting it, is therefore a self-celebration of talent.

4.3.1. Sequence of prey

In the multiple-quarry hunts of the Eastern Mediterranean dynastic monuments the prey belong to different species, all of them quadrupeds. Neither bird hunting nor fishing is depicted. In fact, prey of different species are not interchangeable, but act as complementary elements in promoting the dynasts.[64]

The most represented animal on dynastic tombs is the deer: five out of seven dynastic tombs show one or more deer in multiple-quarry representations; since the conservation state of the Mausoleum of Halicarnassus does not allow speculation on the actual composition of the hunt, one cannot exclude the original presence of a deer in this case. To this group one can associate also the ibex hunt of the Heroon of Trysa. The representation of these animals often follows the convention of the representation of pairs of specimens. A pair of fleeing ibexes is depicted on the Heroon of Trysa (A10); in Lycia this motif was already present on the sixth-century BC reliefs of Isinda (pair of deer; Fig. 26) and Gürses (perhaps a pair of ibexes on one register), which are generally assigned to dynastic tombs.[65] As discussed, a pair of deer is also depicted on the Çan Sarcophagus (Fig. 65). A sequence of two-deer hunts was additionally present on "Astarte's throne" in the 'Eshmun sanctuary in Sidon, although this was the result of a reuse.[66]

Deer hunts are often paired with boar hunts. This pairing can be detected on three dynastic tombs: the Nereid Monument, the Lycian Sarcophagus, and the Mourning Women Sarcophagus; ibex and boar hunts are paired on the Heroon of Trysa. Among other tombs, it can be detected on the Payava Sarcophagus, the Manisa Stele, the Çavuşköy Stele and the Çan Sarcophagus, thus with a marked tendency in north-western Anatolia.[67] The

[63] Atallah 1966: 68–9; Hölscher 1972: 101.

[64] Tripodi (1991: 175–8) states that these representations are symbolic bestiaries where each animal has a precise role.

[65] Marksteiner 2002: 239–41 and 242–3; Draycott 2007: 109–10 and 112–3; Hoff 2017: 446–7, cat S14.

[66] Stucky 2005: 170–2.

[67] If in Lycia, the deer hunt seems to play a major role in dynastic rather than non-dynastic multiple-quarry hunts, as already said, the Payava

recurrent pairing of deer and boar hunts should be noted as a typical practice in the Hellenized world. J. Aymard pointed out that deer and boar hunting were considered on the same level before the Roman period, when deer were instead considered weak and fearful compared to boars, bears and lions.[68] Consistently, in the *Cyropaedia* young Cyrus tells his companions of his first exhilarating experience of hunting in the open field, as opposed to that in the *paradeisoi* (Xen. *Cyr*. 1.4.11):

> So Cyrus received it and took it away and proceeded to distribute it among the boys, saying as he did so: "What tomfoolery it was, fellows, when we used to hunt the animals in the park. To me at least, it seems just like hunting animals that were tied up. For, in the first place, they were in a small space; besides, they were lean and mangy; and one of them was lame and another maimed. But the animals out on the mountains and the plains – how fine they looked, and large and sleek! And the deer leaped up skyward as if on wings, and the boars came charging at one, as they say brave men do in battle. And by reason of their bulk it was quite impossible to miss them. And to me at least," said he, "these seem really more beautiful, when dead, than those pent up creatures, when alive. But say," said he, "would not your fathers let you go out hunting, too?".[69]

On the Satrap Sarcophagus and the Nereid Monument, where the coexistence of more than one prey in a single figurative field also carries a time significance, the deer is or has been the first target of the hunters. Analogously, on the Lycian Sarcophagus, which displays three different quarry on distinct sides of the coffin, the deer is the only one that is shown already killed. These considerations raise the question of a possible precise order of the hunting scenes.

Such an order is clear on tombs of smaller scale: the Manisa Stele has a clear sequence with the deer as the first hunted prey, whereas the crest beam of the Payava Sarcophagus displays a tripartite paratactic multiple-quarry hunt with the deer hunt as the first scene from left. As A. Cohen has stressed, the reading of a long figurative field is not necessarily from left to right, since the reading direction is influenced more by narrative and compositional flows than by a fixed convention.[70] In the case of the crest beam of the Payava Sarcophagus, however, the direction of reading from left to right seems dominant, due to the marked movement to the right of the assistant and the hunter.

Moreover, it can be suggested that in some scenes without an explicit time sequence – whatever the reading direction – the deer and ibex hunts tend to occupy a precise position that – within a climax of increasing difficulty – may be interpreted as the starting episode of a multiple-quarry hunt. Among the dynastic monuments with sequences of more than two paratactic scenes, two cases in which deer and ibex hunting is present – the Heroon of Trysa and the Mourning Women Sarcophagus socle – show these prey in a marginal position.[71] In addition, on the long side of the Alexander Sarcophagus the deer occupies the right position near the edge, which can be considered a reading node of the two adjacent hunting panels.

On the basis of this analysis, it is possible to highlight a scale of difficulty with regard to prey, in which each animal has its own characteristics and represents a different level of commitment for the hunter and the other members of the expedition: scholars have underlined that the variety of pursued prey in the multiple-quarry hunts represents the many aspects of nature dominated by the ruler-hunter.[72] It is demonstrated by their reactions to the hunters: deer and ibexes normally flee; boar usually attack.

Xenophon, in a list of increasing difficulty, describes first the hunting of fawns and deer, indicating the patience and effort required in their pursuit (Xen. *Cyn*. 9). By contrast, boar hunting requires strength and strategy, since the impetuousness of the animal causes many casualties among dogs and puts the safety of the hunter at serious risk (Xen. *Cyn*. 10). In this differentiation, the use of different verbs related to dogs is significant: for deer hunting they must be able to toil (πονεῖν); for boar, they must fight the prey (πολεμεῖν). Lastly, Xenophon mentions the hunting of lions, leopards, lynxes, panthers and bears, indicated as foreign to Greece and very dangerous if a struggle with the animal ensues (Xen. *Cyn*. 11.1):

> Lions, leopards, lynxes, panthers, bears and all similar wild beasts are captured in foreign countries, about Mt. Pangaeus and Cittus beyond Macedonia, on Mysian Olympus and Pindus, on Nysa beyond Syria, and in other mountain ranges capable of supporting such animals.[73]

This convention is not followed on the Nereid Monument or on the Manisa Stele, where the deer are already dead; moreover, an unusual fleeing boar is depicted on a stele from Vezirhan, in ancient Bithynia, dating from the end of the fifth century BC (Fig. 70).[74] The reactions of the quarry, instead, is respected on the Payava Sarcophagus

Sarcophagus belonged to the local representative of the satrap, thus he could aspire to a figurative programme inspired by the dynastic tombs.

[68] For some important considerations about deer hunting in the Greek, Roman and medieval context, see Aymard 1951: 352–61.

[69] Translation from Miller 1968.

[70] Cohen 2010: 239. The case of the Parthenon frieze is exceptional, since it could lead the viewers' eye from the western to the eastern side of the building through a marked visual flow, no matter what was actually visible (see Marconi 2009).

[71] On the Mourning Women Sarcophagus the deer hunt is present only on one of the two long friezes, where it occupies a marginal position, whereas it is not present on the other one, a choice that can be explained as a *variatio*.

[72] Fornasier 2001: 249.

[73] Translation from Marchant 1971.

[74] Istanbul, Archaeological Museum 6219+71.27. *Anatolian Civilisations* 1983: 60, cat. B.146; Brixhe 2004: 42–67, cat. B–05; Karagöz 2013: 36 and 95, cat. 36. The Vezirhan Stele hosts the longest Phrygian inscription found so far, in addition to a shorter text in Greek (Gorbachov 2008; Hämmig 2013, with bibliography).

Figure 70. Stele from Vezirhan. Istanbul, Archaeological Museum 6219+71.27. D-DAI-IST-73/7 (Photo: W. Schiele 1973).

crest beam, where the sequence of prey seems to recall the passage of Xenophon's *Cynegeticus*: the deer, in first position as the easiest quarry, flees; the boar charges its attacker; the bear stands on its hind legs, facing the horseman. The lion can be detected on the so-called Hecatomnus Sarcophagus in Caria, perhaps on the Heroon of Trysa in Lycia, on the Lycian and the Alexander sarcophagi in Sidon.[75] The bear, as will be discussed below, appears on the Satrap Sarcophagus, the Mourning Women Sarcophagus and the Heroon of Trysa, whereas panthers are far more common.

Tabloid seals also provide some useful examples. On the tabloid pink agate seal in the Metropolitan Museum, New York, classified by Boardman in the "Pendant Group", the lower face depicts a hunter dressed in Persian garb and on horseback, as he takes aim at a deer fleeing to the right.[76] On the smaller sides a fallow deer, a gazelle, a wild dog and a bull move to the left; the latter is preparing to attack rather than flee. On the smallest upper side a lion sits on its hind legs, as if waiting. Once again, this sequence seems to exemplify the scale of difficulty of the prey, from the deer fleeing in the face of danger, to a series of increasingly fierce animals that react to the attack, from the bull to the lion, perhaps the last of the sequence. In addition, a tabloid seal purchased in Aleppo and now in the Bibliothèque nationale de France, shows a deer on the lowest face and a bear and a lion as quarry on the smaller sides.[77]

In conclusion, if one accepts the presence of a precise sequence, in which quadrupeds such as deer and ibex usually occupy the first position, it is possible to state a visual climax, in other words, a progression of difficulty of prey easily recognised by observers and widely shared. At any rate, the respect of conventions in depicting the animals' reactions can be interpreted as the demonstration that each prey occupies a specific role within a list of hunting deeds. Dynastic multiple-quarry hunts are, indeed, figurative lists characterised by the rhetoric of enumeration, namely the accumulation of items not synonymic; each prey often holds a specific position within a multiple-quarry hunt representation and the order of the hunting scenes thus mostly does not appear to be random.[78] Celebratory texts of the Assyrian kings' hunting that have been quoted in Chapter Three seem the most fitting literary parallels to visual prey catalogues under analysis, creating a similar effect of accumulation.[79] If those texts define the number of prey for each species, the dynastic hunting visual catalogues, however, leave room for the observer to imagine and mentally extend at leisure the sequences of hunting. In other words, multiple-quarry hunts suggest an objective infinity, an attempt to sketch something irreducible in a closed form, in this case the many prey hunted by the patron and his entourage.[80]

4.3.2. Hunting techniques

The choice of the hunting prey to be represented was an ideological matter rather than a reflection of actual practice. The case of bird hunting and fishing is enlightening. Although these activities were practised in the Eastern Mediterranean in this period, as archaeozoological analysis has demonstrated,[81] they were completely absent from the dynastic funerary monuments, and it is probable that neither nets nor traps were rendered in paint. As the

[75] On the Lycian Sarcophagus scene, see Schmidt-Dounas 1985: 65–70, and Langer-Karrenbrock 2000: 34–46, 88–95. In the sixth century BC the Lion Tomb and the Kızılbel Tomb displayed a combat with a lion and a lion hunt in Lycia (see § 2.2.2.; Mellink 1998: 37–8).

[76] New York, Metropolitan Museum of Art 49.43.7. Richter 1949: 294; 2006: 35–6, no. 138; Boardman 1970b: 316.

[77] Paris, Bibliothèque nationale de France HS 1973-1-499.

[78] "*Adiectio* through accumulation consists in the addition of semantically supplementary words; thus not – as in synonymy – in the semantic repetition of words already semantically set in the speech act" (Lausberg 1998: 298, §665). For some aspects of the genre of the list, see Eco 2009: 15–8, 133–7.

[79] *Supra*, § 3.1.2.

[80] For a definition of the list, inventory or catalogue as literary and figurative representative method, see Eco 2009: 17.

[81] For Limyra, see Galik, Forstenpointner and Weissengruber 2012.

sole exception, J. Borchhardt thought that the Muskar relief represented the trapping of a young bear using nets: if so it would be unique in Lycia.[82]

The only weapons portrayed are javelins, spears, knives, bows and stones. These weapons are handled by hunters on horseback or on foot. In other words, in Eastern Mediterranean hunts, predation occurs only by the direct act of the hunter, and the success of the weapons used depends entirely on the skill of the person who wields it. These observations seem to agree with the words of Plato, which state that the only kind of hunting valid for education is that of quadrupeds, conducted on horseback with the aid of dogs and without the use of traps, so that the hunters display their courage. Angling, trapping with nets and hunting birds were to be avoided (*Leg.* 7.823D–824B):[83]

> (823D) After these prefatory observations there will follow adequate praise and blame of hunting – praise of the kind which renders the souls of the young better, and blame of the kind which does the opposite. Our next step will be to address the young people with prayer – "O friends, would that you might never be seized with any desire or craving for hunting by sea, or for angling, (823E) or for ever pursuing water-animals with creels that do your lazy hunting for you, whether you sleep or wake. And may no longing for man-hunting by sea and piracy overtake you, and render you cruel and lawless hunters; and may the thought of committing robbery in country or city not so much as cross your minds. Neither may there seize upon any of the young the crafty craving for snaring birds – (824A) no very gentlemanly pursuit! Thus there is left for our athletes only the hunting and capture of land-animals. Of this branch of hunting, the kind called night-stalking, in which the work is intermittent, being the job of lazy men who sleep in turn, is one that deserves no praise; nor does that kind deserve praise in which there are intervals of rest from toil, when men master the wild force of beasts by nets and traps instead of doing so by the victorious might of a toil-loving soul. Accordingly, the only kind left for all, and the best kind, is the hunting of quadrupeds with horses and dogs and the hunter's own limbs, when men hunt in person, and subdue all the creatures by means of their own running, (824B) striking and shooting – all the men, that is to say, who cultivate the courage that is divine."[84]

Plato's words relate to the object, the means, the manner, the time and the place of the hunt, which, according to O. Longo, probably reveal both cultural customs and legal rules, unfortunately difficult to reconstruct for the Greek *polis*.[85]

Certainly, no direct connection can be established between Plato's indications and our monuments. Nonetheless, the words of the Athenian philosopher may help us to understand the principles governing the dynastic cycles in the Eastern Mediterranean. These criteria are tied to an aristocratic culture, which gave hunting an ethical, heroic dimension for the effort made by the hunter and the risks posed. The lack of supplementary tools – just weapons whose effectiveness depended on skill – meant that the message referring to the ability of the hunter was communicated more effectively.[86] Athenaeus, citing Hegesander, supports this interpretation (Ath. 1.18a): in Macedonia one could not recline at a feast without first hitting a boar without the use of nets, and at the age of thirty-five Cassander had not yet accomplished this feat. The hunting of these wild beasts without the use of traps and nets was not therefore common practice: it was considered an almost heroic deed and the initiation of a new phase in one's life.[87]

On a scale of values and priorities, then, only the performance of the most challenging types of quadruped hunt was represented on our monuments, whereas the simpler sorts were omitted or made explicit through the representation of dead prey.[88] For instance, hare hunting does not appear among the representative hunts but is included in those aimed at procuring food. On the Nereid Monument, architrave blocks 893 and 886 are carved with people carrying game, among which hares are depicted, perhaps with reference to the dynastic banquet,[89] but the hunting frieze shows standard representative prey such as a deer, a bear and a boar. Similarly, on the Mourning Women Sarcophagus of Sidon, the longer friezes depicting hunts in progress show only large quadrupeds as prey, but hares appear on the shorter friezes (sides C and D of the socle) representing the return from the hunt.[90]

Hunting from a chariot is found only on the Lycian Sarcophagus from Sidon and the Merehi Sarcophagus from Xanthos. In the Persian context it is often associated with a royal figure, as shown by a scaraboid seal from Kerch (Fig. 71) and the cylinder seal of Darius I from Egypt (Fig. 49).[91] On the former, the bow hunter is identifiable as the Great King due to the presence of the winged solar disc

[82] Borchhardt 1996–7: 6–7.
[83] Jaeger 1986: 178–9.
[84] Translation from Bury 1968.
[85] Longo 1987: 72–80. Vidal-Naquet (1968: 960–4), instead, distinguishes between a hoplite and an ephebic hunt model. The former was a collective hunting expedition in daytime as a dangerous confrontation with wild animals, equal to a battle. The latter was a solitary hunting of small prey, at night, through traps and nets.
[86] In the North Palace of Nineveh deer hunting with nets was placed in a hidden location on the north-western wall of Room S (Matthiae 1996: 203).
[87] On the use of traps, see Briant 1996: 310–1. An example of a multiple-quarry hunt without any dynastic traits is the collective hunt in Arabia in Xenophon's *Anabasis*, in which the Greek soldiers face gazelles, onagers and ostriches (Xen. *An.* 1.5.2–3): it is a subsistence hunting rather than heroic, since it includes birds as game (Tripodi 2000).
[88] For similar prey selectivity in the Villanovan culture, see Camporeale 1991: 57–9.
[89] London, British Museum 1848,1020.112 (Sculpture 893) and 1848,1020.111 (Sculpture 886).
[90] For hare hunting in connection with the taking of power by Cyrus, see § 3.2 (note 93).
[91] Kerch seal: St. Petersburg, The State Hermitage Museum Zh-428 (GR-19353) (Boardman 1970b: 355, pl. 928). Darius I's seal: see § 3.2. For the distinctive elements of the chariots in the Near East, see Bernard 1965: 273–6.

Figure 71. Scaraboid. St. Petersburg, The State Hermitage Museum Zh-428 (GR-19353). Photograph © The State Hermitage Museum. Photo by Vladimir Terebenin, Leonard Kheifets, Yuri Molodkovets.

and his headpiece, perhaps decorated with a crown on the top edge, as is more clearly seen on the seal from Egypt.[92] On this seal, already described in Chapter Three, the Great King attacks a lion by shooting arrows from the chariot.[93] Another cylinder seal shows a figure, perhaps the king, sitting on the back of a chariot driven by a charioteer, while he strikes at a lion with a mace.[94] By analogy the damaged part of the Kerch scaraboid seal probably depicted a lion about to pounce upon the chariot.

The chariot was an important attribute when the Persian king appeared in public. Within the context of the discussion of the luxurious lifestyle of the Persians, Athenaeus mentions the first book of Heracleides of Cyme's *Persica*, which explains that the Persian king, in the Court of the Immortals, walked on a Sardis carpet intended only for him, but when he reached the far end of the palace, he rode in a chariot or sometimes on horseback, so he was never seen walking out of the building.[95] Beyond the use of the chariot during parades (Xen. *Cyr*. 8.3.14) or in battle, as in the case of Darius III on the Alexander Mosaic, the examples just mentioned do not exclude the use of this vehicle in other situations, such as in a representative kind of hunt.[96] This issue is relevant to this topic, as on the Lycian Sarcophagus the lion hunt from a chariot makes it possible to interpret the scene as a dynastic hunt.[97]

4.3.3. The bear hunt

Bear hunting is one of the elements particular to dynastic hunt representations in the Eastern Mediterranean during the fifth and fourth centuries BC.[98] Bear hunts are represented on the hunt frieze of the Nereid Monument (Sculpture 889; Fig. 58b), on the northern inner wall of the Heroon of Trysa (block A15; Fig. 59) and on the socle of the Mourning Women Sarcophagus (Fig. 55); they are also present on the crest beam of the Payava Sarcophagus (Fig. 27), on the fragmentary block relating to the tomb in Islamlar and on the Muskar rock tomb relief.[99] Seal impressions from Dascylium, the Anatolian satrapal capital, show bear hunts as well, where hunters on foot and on horseback face the prey.[100] Bears appear on tabloid seals too, potentially in hunting contexts.

Lycia and Anatolia in general seem to provide the most conspicuous corpus of bear hunting representations in the Eastern Mediterranean under Persian rule. The first reason for the numerous occurrences in this area is certainly geographical, as testified by Xenophon (Xen. *Cyn*. 11.1): for instance, bear hunts were practised in Anatolia even in recent times. In the context under investigation they can be traced back to the Hittite period, when the bear was associated with more dangerous animals like lions and leopards.[101] Later, they were shown on the monumental cycles of the Syro-Anatolian region. For example, at least two bears appear on the "small orthostats" at Tell Halaf, probably as hunt prey. It is likely that a bear hunt is also depicted on the North Gate at Karatepe, despite the fact that the quarry is smaller in size than the archer.[102] In Phoenicia there appear to be examples earlier than the Mourning Women Sarcophagus, such as the Ghineh relief, near Byblos, where a man strikes a bear with a dagger; the scene is accompanied by the representation of a man with two dogs and a woman in mourning, which led to the erroneous assumption that it depicted the death of Adonis.[103]

[92] For a discussion of the crowns of the Achaemenid kings, see von Gall 1974: 157. *Contra* Root 1979: 92–3.

[93] Miller 2003: 28. See § 3.2.

[94] Oxford, Ashmolean Museum 1889.370. Buchanan 1966: 122, no. 685. The seal was acquired in Izmir. The identification of the king on this example is supported by the hunt technique, with the hunter striking the prey from the back of a chariot. This is the same adopted by Ashurbanipal when he strikes with a spear the lion bounding towards the royal chariot: the Assyrians also conducted the hunt in this way, alongside the traditional pursuit of prey, shown on Darius' seal (Matthiae 1998: 178). The identification of the king on the Oxford seal is therefore likely, even if the presence of a dog is not usual in Achaemenid representations of royal hunting.

[95] Ath. 12.514c = *FGrH* 689 F 1. See Lenfant 2009: 267–75, esp. 274–5.

[96] For hunt images with chariot as unrealistic, instead, see Briant 1996: 244.

[97] Fischer-Bossert 2003: 196. Another hunt with chariot, but free of royal attributes such as the charioteer and the lion as prey, is represented in the context of a crowded multiple-quarry hunt on the lekythos signed by the Athenian Xenophantos. *Infra*, § 4.3.4. See Miller 2003: 21–3 and Franks 2009, with bibliography.

[98] See also Étienne 2000: 69–70; Eichinger 2005: 67–8.

[99] Islamlar: Zahle 1979: 344–5, no. 69; Benda-Weber 2005: 109, no. 3. Muskar: Zahle 1979: 306–9 and 319; Benda-Weber 2005: 109, no. 7.

[100] Ankara University, Erg. 274 and 325; Kaptan 1996: 89–91. See also Carstens 2006: 127–8.

[101] Ehelolf 1938: 27–33. For more details on the presence of the bear in Hittite texts, see Archi 1988: 32 and note 36, 33 and note 37.

[102] On Tell Halaf, see § 3.1.1.2. On the "small orthostats", see von Oppenheim [n.d.]: 141–85; Orthmann 1971: 120–2. On the relief of Karatepe, see Matthiae 1963: 116–7; Çambel and Özyar 2003: 58–9. The Karatepe relief may also confirm the association at Tell Halaf of the bear with an archer.

[103] Seyrig 1940: 113–4; Atallah 1966: 75–6; Eichinger 2005: 152, no. 2OR.

The second reason is that bear hunts may carry a specific meaning. Literary evidence pertaining to the Eastern Mediterranean associates bears and lions as the preferred prey for those who covet the rank of king, in addition to those who already hold it. David obtains Saul's permission to confront Goliath after relating his exploits with a lion and a bear (1 *Sam*. 17.34–37):

> (34) But David said to Saul, "Your servant used to keep sheep for his father; and when there came a lion, or a bear, and took a lamb from the flock, (35) I went after him and smote him and delivered it out of his mouth; and if he arose against me, I caught him by his beard, and smote him and killed him. (36) Your servant has killed both lions and bears; and this uncircumcised Philistine shall be like one of them, seeing he has defied the armies of the living God." (37) And David said, "The Lord who delivered me from the paw of the lion and from the paw of the bear, will deliver me from the hand of this Philistine." And Saul said to David, "Go, and the Lord be with you!"[104]

This passage not only establishes a relationship between hunting and war, but the killing of a lion and a bear also seems to guarantee for David the role of liberator, and indeed he later became the king of his people.

In this context one should reconsider a couple of Xenophon's descriptions. On the one hand, as mentioned in Chapter Three, the passage referring to Cyrus the Younger, which seems to be inspired by a proper encomium, stresses the role of bear hunting in the aspiration to the throne of a figure that Xenophon believed to be legitimate (Xen. *An*. 1.9.6).[105] Moreover, in a passage of *Cyropaedia*, Gobryas complains to Cyrus about the killing of his own son by the new king of Assyria. This had occurred long before, when the latter was still the crown prince. Unlike his young hunting partner, the prince had not succeeded in killing a bear or a lion during a hunting trip, and so murdered Gobryas' son out of jealousy (Xen. *Cyr*. 4.6.3–4). His reaction may be explained by the fact that he should have killed the beasts, since he was destined for the throne. Gobryas' son was probably not just the target of the prince's jealousy: he also committed a breach of royal etiquette, since, as will be explained, lion killing was a royal privilege.[106]

Literary evidence not only shows that the bear was placed among the most dangerous prey, but that its association with the lion reveals its great representative significance in connection with royalty. In Europe is should be considered that the bear was the pre-eminent animal until the twelfth or thirteenth century AD, when it gave way to the lion.[107] The significant presence of the bear in dynastic hunts can therefore be explained by the relationship with the local contexts, it being rooted in earlier figurative traditions and is certainly significant as a symbol of power.[108] Moreover, with reference to bear-hunting scenes, the monuments represent a continuity with the earlier phases.

4.3.4. Mythological hunts

The multiple-quarry hunts on the dynastic monuments should be interpreted as real or historical events; in other words, as far as is known, there is no evidence that these hunting scenes were mythological. In Lycia, however, mythological animals are also depicted alongside the most dangerous prey.

On the Merehi Tomb the Chimaera is one of the two prey depicted on the curved sides of the lid (Fig. 64b). The beast appeared in funerary contexts in Lycia, on the inner southern wall of the Heroon of Trysa (Fig. 15), on the relief of a rock tomb at Tlos (the so-called Tomb of Bellerophon) and maybe as an acroterion of the Heroon of Limyra. This wide presence of Chimaera has a link with the Lycian origin of this mythological beast.[109]

Alternatively, a mythological prey may be depicted as the climax of a paratactic multiple-quarry hunt. One of the sides of the crest beam of the Caeneus Sarcophagus of Limyra is occupied by the hunt of a panther and a boar (Fig. 63). In a fragment discovered in the 1980s, a rider looms over a winged griffin attacking a semi-prone man on the ground.[110] The subject is taken from the saga of the Arimaspians, a mythical people according to the Greeks, who lived north of the Black Sea and were in permanent conflict with the griffins, who wanted to steal their gold.[111] A similar association between wild animal hunts and griffins is present on the Xenophantos lekythos, which was found in 1836 at Pantikapaion in Crimea, present-day Kerch (Fig. 73).[112] Its imagery combines Greek and Persian themes and among the prey of the hunting representation, a deer, a boar and griffins are recognisable.

It is plausible that these mythical episodes were considered part of hunt imagery and that the combination of real and mythological marked the climax of the level of prey danger and at the same time constituted the mythological parallel that conveyed a message of celebration for the hunter.[113] For instance, inside the Heroon of Trysa two hunting representations face one another: on the northern wall, as noted, is the longest sequence of hunting scenes in this

[104] Translation from May and Metzger 1962.
[105] *Supra*, § 3.2.
[106] *Infra*, § 5.3.1.
[107] Pastoureau 2008: 161.

[108] See also Eichinger 2005: 69–70.
[109] On Chimaera, see now Cianferoni, Iozzo and Setari 2012.
[110] Borchhardt 1983.
[111] *Götter, Heroen, Herrscher* 1990: 122–3. For Arimaspians in literary tradition, see *LIMC* VIII.1: 529; D'Ercole 2009: 203–9. This depiction is comparable with other works of the fourth century BC, such as the Attic crater with tall rim, now in the Louvre, with riders coming to the rescue of a fellow attacked by two griffins (Paris, Musée du Louvre G 530. *LIMC* VIII.1: 532, no. 39); this pattern is seen on other vessels with variations.
[112] St. Petersburg, The State Hermitage Museum P.1837-2.
[113] For the combination or fusion of real and mythical hunts, we can refer to Persian production (seals and jambs in Persepolis).

context, whereas on the southern wall was a depiction of the Calydonian Boar Hunt, recognisable by the presence of Atalanta among the hunters. These two representations follow different conventions and compositional strategies, whereas the state of conservation does not allow analysis of the style in detail; however, they form part of the same message and imagery of power.[114]

4.3.5. Geography

Vegetation is the only element of spatial localisation in dynastic multiple-quarry hunts, notably trees. On the Mourning Women Sarcophagus they always appear behind the prey or a riderless horse (for instance, Fig. 75). The sculptor thus regarded trees as useful compositional elements for creating verticality and directing the gaze to the quarry, rather than on a naturalistic level. As has been mentioned, on the Heroon of Trysa the trees conceal the joints of the slabs, moreover, the third ibex on B9 flees into a mountainous landscape, an element that enlivens the depiction of the hunt.[115]

If on the Nereid Monument there seems to be a lack of interest in landscapes, it is noteworthy that this may be reflected on a late source on the Mausoleum of Halicarnassus. Gregory of Tours' reference to sculpted trees may fit well with the hunting scenes, enriching the reconstruction of this part of the Mausoleum.[116]

An interest in the representation of vegetation may be detected also on the monuments from north-western Anatolia: in the aforementioned stele from Çavuşköy the tree plays an important visual role in highlighting the two prey (Fig. 67). A tree separating two distinct hunts, can be found on the Çan Sarcophagus (Fig. 65). Here, the presence of different colours for the two scenes – blue for the deer hunt and green for the boar hunt – may remind us that the use of painting could differentiate the settings of hunting also on other monuments being analysed.[117] On these two monuments, therefore, trees were elements of spatial localisation of hunts, but also formal devices for organising the narrative and the structure of the scenes.

The spatial context of these hunting representations raises the issue of the real practice in the Eastern Mediterranean. Combination of prey of more than one species living in different habitats has led scholars to propose the *paraideisoi* as settings of these dynastic multiple-quarry hunts, since there different species could be hunted in a short time, kept in substantial captivity.[118] Due to the information about a *paradeisos* in Sidon, for instance, such a setting has been evoked for many multiple-quarry hunts represented on the marble sarcophagi.[119]

There is nothing to indicate, however, that the hunts represented on the most impressive monuments of this area were conducted in *paradeisoi.*[120] Moreover one cannot prove that *paradeisoi* existed at all Eastern Mediterranean dynastic sites. For instance, nothing is known about Xanthos, whereas J. Borchhardt hypothesised that the ruler of Trysa owned a *paradeisos*.[121] Even the case of the Aramaic rock inscription in Rough Cilicia, mentioned earlier, could attest that a figure of high rank was in the habit of hunting outdoors, unless one assumes a hunting park in that area, as has been suggested.[122] In addition, it is not necessary to locate in *paradeisoi* those hunting scenes present on the Graeco-Persian stelae, since these may refer to characters below royal rank and therefore unlikely to be associated with hunts in reserves.[123]

In addition, the occurrence of a wide variety of prey living in different habitats could convey a celebratory theme regarding the extension and diversification of the dynast's possessions, from the plains to the mountains.[124] The celebration of different parts of the dynastic possession would correspond to the Persian Achaemenid imperial ideology on a smaller scale. In Chapter Three lists of quarry chased by the Assyrian king organised by geography have been discussed: hunting meant control over a precise territory.[125] In the Persian Achaemenid ideology individual areas of the empire had a precise role, and this was particularly evident at the royal table, to which the first fruits were sent from every region of the empire, as indicated by Athenaeus, following Deinon.[126] As stressed by P. Briant, the variety of food at the royal table was only one of the elements that emphasised the vastness of Persian possessions.[127] Similarly, the ancient sources explain that the Great King's nomadism was stimulated by his desire to live in an "eternal spring" (Xen. *Cyr*. 8.6.22), as if he took the best of the climate of each region.[128] Indeed, the Great King granted the Athenian general Themistocles, who took refuge in Persian territory, annuities from various cities in Anatolia, if not the cities

[114] See Fornasier 2001: 238.

[115] For this expedient, see Gschwantler 1993. On the depiction and the meaning of trees in these representations, see also Franks 2012: 84.

[116] Gregory of Tours *De cursu stellarum ratio* 12.

[117] Sevinç *et al.* 2001: 393.

[118] *Supra*, § 3.2.

[119] Fornasier (2001: 249) for the Satrap Sarcophagus; Martin (2017: 147) for the Alexander Sarcophagus. *Contra* Fleischer (1983: 32), who does not believe that the hunt on the socle of the Mourning Women Sarcophagus is set in a *paradeisos*.

[120] Cohen (2010: 87) says that the Sidonian hunts do not "allow true geographical specificity".

[121] Borchhardt 1996–7: 6–7. Also Demargne believes that the setting of the hunt of the Nereid Monument is a *paradeisos* (Childs and Demargne 1989: 355).

[122] Lemaire and Lozachmeur 1990: 153. *Supra*, § 4.1.

[123] Borchhardt, instead, defines the hunt of the Çavuşköy Stele "im Paradeisos" (1968: 206). Cremer (1984: 91) believes that the hunting representations of the Graeco-Persian stelae from north-western Anatolia had the hunting frieze of an Achaemenid palace as a model.

[124] For the hunting dynast as a figure ruling over nature, see Fornasier 2001: 249.

[125] See § 3.1.2.

[126] Ath. 14.652b–c = *FGrH* 690 F 12a. See also Xen. *Cyr*. 8.6.6. Capdetrey 2013: 175–8; Tolini 2013: 145–6.

[127] Briant 1989: 37.

[128] For a critical analysis of this aspect of Achaemenid regality, see Briant 1988.

themselves, to ensure that his supplies were complete.[129]

The variety of territories and, consequently, the variety of the fruits produced for the benefit of the ruler were essential elements of the imperial ideology: according to Xenophon, Cyrus wanted this ideological fundament reproduced even at the furthest boundaries of the empire (Xen. *Cyr.* 8.6.10–13), and this could be reflected on the monuments through the multiple-quarry hunt.[130] The territories of the main Lycian cities such as Xanthos were characterised by a great variety of landscape. Phoenician cities enjoyed a specific relationship between the urban administrative centre and the rural environment that provided the main resources. At Sidon – the place where the greatest concentration of dynastic multiple-quarry hunt images has been found – epigraphic sources attest to a precise distinction between the coastal district and the mainland.[131] Such a variety of environments would fit very well with the different prey represented on our multiple-quarry hunts.

4.3.6. Timeframe

Timeframes in the multiple-quarry hunt concern different aspects. First, if present, scenes depicting preparations for the hunt and the return give an account of different phases of the activity, an aspect that will be discussed in the following chapter.[132]

Second, the coexistence of different prey in the same figurative field may imply a timeline of the various types of hunt. This is the case with the hypotactic multiple-quarry hunts, since the same hunter faces first one prey then another. As demonstrated, a time sequence may be implied by the hunting relief of the Satrap Sarcophagus. This is more explicit on slab 889 of the Nereid Monument frieze, where the lifeless body of the deer emphasises a temporal sequence, since this hunting episode is presented as over (Fig. 58b). Similarly, some of the tabloid seals show a hunter with a different species of prey, which one assumes are pursued by the same character. Von Gall questioned the association of deer and boar hunting in Graeco-Persian representations, assigning these two prey to different habitats.[133] A combination of prey of different species living in different habitats, however, does not exclude the possibility that a hunting event could take place in a limited span of time out of *paradeisoi*. Yet boar can and do live in lowlands and marshes, as well as on high ground, so there is some overlap with deer habitats, while deer, in turn, seek higher altitudes during hotter weather, sharing the space with bears. Bearing in mind the time taken to pursue an animal in the open field, it is possible that animals of different species could be hunted at the same time at specific times of the year, if the hunt lasted more than a day.

In paratactic hunts, however, the timeline sequence is not clear and, indeed, B. Tripodi speaks of separate, simultaneous scenes.[134] This interpretation may be correct if one considers the literary evidence describing collective hunts with a large number of participants, such as the expedition of Cyrus the Elder against the king of Armenia (Xen. *Cyr.* 2.4.19–20). This is not the case, however, for our entire corpus of monuments. If one considers the hunting frieze of the Payava Sarcophagus of Xanthos, it is easy to interpret the repeated figure of hunter in each scene as the same character, the protagonist, who represents the deceased (Fig. 27).[135] Moreover, the composition of the bear and boar hunts on the Nereid Monument is similar: for instance, in both representations an attendant appears on the left (Figs. 58b-c). It cannot be ruled out that in both scenes the characters in action represent the same people, while taking into account the modular composition of the two scenes, linked to the practice of serial production and the function of architectural decoration.

Due to their celebratory intent these images are not necessarily accurate reports of real events: it cannot be ruled out thus that the representations served to catalogue the kinds of prey that could be hunted throughout the year.[136] The idea of multiple-quarry hunts as the celebration of the patron's deeds in different moments and contexts does not therefore exclude that certain paratactic multiple-quarry hunt scenes may repeat the same protagonists. In this historical and geographical context, the use of continuous narrative – an artistic convention whereby a figure is repeated in one figurative field to indicate different moments in time – is not common, although it was suggested previously for the sixth-century BC Lion Tomb from Xanthos (Fig. 72).[137] Cases such as the Satrap Sarcophagus, the Nereid Monument and the external wall of the Heroon of Trysa, however, show that the practice of repeating the same figure in the same figurative cycle was quite normal.[138] This appears evident also on the Manisa Stele, where the deceased appears both in the upper register and in the lower one (Fig. 66). The technique of continuous narrative, widely used in the neo-Assyrian period, may be a legacy of Near Eastern civilisations, but is more likely to be a consequence of the way paratactic hunts are expressed, in which each independent scene is

[129] Thuc. 1.138.5 and Plut. *Them.* 29.11. See Gomme 1945: 292 and 445; Frost 1980: 219–23; Carena, Manfredini and Piccirilli 1983: 278–80; Briant 1985: 58–9; Hornblower 1991: 224.

[130] See also the observations on the representation of the vastity of domains in the Vergina hunting frieze (D'Onofrio 2018: 46). On the Vergina frieze, see § 6.2.

[131] Oggiano and Xella 2009: 72; Oggiano and Pedrazzi 2013: 60–3. For Phoenician urban territories, see Elayi 1987: 11–20.

[132] See § 5.1.2.

[133] Von Gall 1989: 152.

[134] Tripodi 1991: 153.

[135] The repetition of the deceased's inscribed name in several scenes of this tomb – the name may have been present also in the audience scene – may confirm the need to identify a specific figure, who does not appear with particular attributes. For the inscriptions, see *TAM* I: 34–6, no. 40; Demargne and Laroche 1974: 137–9.

[136] For hunt images as seasonal activities in the late imperial age, see Calcani 1996–7: 198.

[137] For definition of continuous narrative in art, von Blanckenhagen 1957: 78–9; Small 1999: 568. See also Tomasi Velli 2007: 8. On the Lion Tomb, Marksteiner 2002: 237.

[138] See Ridgway 1997: 81–2.

Figure 72. A warrior holding two shields, an attendant and an equestrian on the Lion Tomb of Xanthos. Drawing. After Boardman 1995: fig. 208.3. Courtesy of Sir John Boardman.

centred around a single prey.[139] The presence of such a technique in the areas concerned here is a phenomenon to be highlighted.

4.4. Conclusion

From a figurative point of view, multiple-quarry hunts may be defined more precisely. Royal or aristocratic hunt representations in the Eastern Mediterranean may show a variety of hunts that took place simultaneously with several hunters involved, or in a time sequence, perhaps by the same characters.

Like the reworked roundels on the Arch of Constantine in Rome, which originally represented hunts performed by Hadrian in person in different areas of the empire, without intending to give an account of specific events, the multiple-quarry hunts of the Eastern Mediterranean do not necessarily capture specific events in certain places, but perpetuate the picture of complex hunts, probably repeated in the dynast's life, while also celebrating the skills of the hunter and the richness of his possessions.[140] F. Queyrel, by describing the hunting representation of the long side of the Alexander Sarcophagus, has defined this scene as "paradigmatic".[141] Accordingly, H.M. Franks, investigating the hunting frieze of Tomb II in Vergina, has drawn attention to the permeability of mythological and non-mythological spheres in the wake of Greek vase painting.[142]

Accordingly, multiple-quarry hunts do not necessarily depict historical events, but their symbolic status – conveyed by the accumulation of different prey – does not project them onto an entirely unreal dimension: they could be the celebratory image of the hunting deeds, ideally carried out by the dynast during his lifetime.

These multiple-quarry hunts followed a well-defined structure and precise principles, as elucidated in the present chapter. These features constitute a unique narrative aspect that identifies dynastic artistic language in the Eastern Mediterranean during the fifth and fourth centuries BC.

[139] For continuous narrative in the ancient Near East, see Güterbock 1957: 64–5, 70.

[140] For the Hadrianic roundels, see Aymard 1951: 530–5, and more recently Oppermann 1991; Schmidt-Colinet 1996; Calcani 1996–7; 2000; Martini and Schernig 2000; Faust 2011: 386–92. The roundels, together with the medallions minted in AD 129–137, are the most ancient figurative evidence representing a Roman emperor as a hunter (Tuck 2005: 236–40). See also Le Roux 2009.

[141] Queyrel 2011: 39–40.

[142] Franks 2012: 24.

Figure 73. (following page) Lekythos by Xenophantos. St. Petersburg, The State Hermitage Museum P.1837-2. Photograph © The State Hermitage Museum. Photo by Vladimir Terebenin, Leonard Kheifets, Yuri Molodkovets.

5

The Hunt as Mirror of Social Structure

This chapter will focus on the protagonists of dynastic multiple-quarry hunt representations in order to obtain more information about the social message of these images. Given the lack of literary sources, Eastern Mediterranean hunting scenes constitute an exceptional tool for decoding the structure of local courts and, more generally, of dynastic societies within the Persian Empire.

5.1. Number of participants

Dynastic funerary monuments generally show hunts with several figures. On the one hand this is connected to the increased availability of surface areas to be decorated. On the other, these crowded images convey complex messages related to the dynast's power and the management of a large retinue.

5.1.1. Hunting scenes

More modest figurative schemes show one man in action. On the Manisa Stele, the horseman in the upper register is likely the deceased, accompanied on the lower register by his squire, on foot, and his dog (Fig. 66). Similarly, on the Çavuşköy Stele (Fig. 67) and on the Payava Sarcophagus (Fig. 27) of Xanthos the hunter is followed by an aide and is assisted by one or more dogs.

On the dynastic monuments the prevailing technique shown is that of encirclement, which, by definition, requires the prey to be surrounded by a number of participants. The patron is without doubt the protagonist of the hunt but he is not always isolated, and often appears flanked by companions and servants, in varying numbers. The most crowded multiple-quarry hunts are those on the two long sides of the socle of the Mourning Women Sarcophagus of Sidon: twenty-three hunters are depicted on frieze A and twenty-four on frieze B. There are four hunting scenes on each of these friezes, all with a group of five to seven hunters arranged around one or two prey. If the sequence organised around two quarry of the same species at the end of each side (deer on side A and panthers on side B) is considered as one hunting scene, the number of hunters involved in a hunting scene with a double quarry is equivalent to other groups. Similarly, the Lycian Sarcophagus shows five horsemen around a boar (Fig. 57).[1] Conversely, in Lycia it is the Nereid Monument that presents the largest hunting group and again the hunt is by encirclement, specifically, four horsemen and a man on foot, both in the bear and the boar hunting scenes (Figs. 58b-c). Then, on block 888 (Fig. 58d), there are three hunters on horseback and four on foot (nevertheless, the first two figures on the left belong to the previous scene, which thus makes a total of seven hunters). None of the nine hunting scenes on the northern wall of the Heroon of Trysa are crowded (Fig. 59), but on the opposite wall the representation of the Calydonian Boar Hunt with numerous participants seems to be inspired by the dynastic hunts genre.[2] There is no doubt that the visual impact determined by the number of hunters indicates the precise status of the deceased. At a political level, this implies a well-structured system.

5.1.2. Preparation and return scenes

The large number of participants in the scenes depicting preparations for the hunt and the return from it deserve close attention. These scenes act as pendants to the hunts themselves, not only extending the timeframe, but also clearly showing the dynast's large retinue; they contribute to the image of a large, well-organised hunting group, and in the case of the return scenes show the successful outcome of the activity.

Within this corpus the Mourning Women Sarcophagus affords ample space for this subject, with the transport of hunted prey and some deer still alive depicted on both short sides of the socle. It shows a hierarchy of the different figures, because some (C1, C3, C9, D4, D14, D15, D16) seem to have a commanding role (Fig. 74).[3] This theme – present on Anatolian stelae – can also be found on the Nereid Monument, as has been mentioned. On slab 895, for instance, one of the figures leads a horse by its bridle, perhaps as part of a preparatory scene.[4] It is a less lively and varied depiction than that on the socle of the Mourning Women Sarcophagus, however, due to the repeated use of patterns for the figures.[5] As already discussed in Chapter Two, according to J. Borchhardt, one of the friezes of the Heroon of Limyra also depicted the dynast setting off for the hunt, an attractive hypothesis, since this scene would complement the war theme of the other frieze.[6] Nevertheless, unlike Limyra (if J. Borchhardt's theory were accepted), the aforementioned departure and return scenes on the Mourning Women Sarcophagus and on

[1] Schmidt-Dounas 1985: 18–21; Langer-Karrenbrock 2000: 24–34, 85–8.

[2] Nollé 2001: 27–31; Poggio 2019a: 138–49.

[3] According to Fleischer (1983: 32), these scenes indicate that the hunt takes place outdoors. The presence of trees establishes a connection with the setting of the longer hunt friezes.

[4] London, British Museum 1848,1020.118 (Sculpture 895). For the relation of this slab with the hunt scenes, see Childs and Demargne 1989: 283.

[5] *Supra*, § 2.3.2. (note 139).

[6] Borchhardt 1976: 75. *Contra* Şare 2013: 65–70. See § 2.1.2.

C1 C2 C3 C4 C5 C6 C7

Figure 74. Detail of the return from the hunt on the Mourning Women Sarcophagus from Sidon. Istanbul, Archaeological Museum 368. D-DAI-IST-R19.741 (Photo: W. Schiele 1981).

the Nereid Monument represent the retinue and not the dynast himself. Similarly, in the Palace of Ashurbanipal in Nineveh, the departure and return (Room R) were combined with hunting scenes (Room S), but the main hunter was present only in the hunting scenes.[7]

5.2. Main hunters

The question of how recognisable the dynast and members of his family were in the carved representations and, more specifically, in hunting scenes is an important one. This question needs to take into account the visibility of monumental decorations. The reliefs and free-standing sculptures of many of the tombs analysed were designed in close association with the architecture. The architrave of the Nereid Monument and the socle of the Mourning Women Sarcophagus, for example, differ in size, but the carvings on both are difficult to see. The first task of these representations, therefore, was to create an overall impression in which the structural and figurative components were in harmony. Since close examination of the dynastic monuments was rarely possible, the portrayal of attributes and *schemata* prevailed over attempts to define individual features.[8]

5.2.1. The dynast

Rulers were the main protagonists of the figurative cycles on the dynastic tombs. Attributes, iconographic schemes and composition all played a significant part in their identification.

Coinage was the only privileged field for the characterisation of the facial traits of satraps and dynasts in the Eastern Mediterranean. The first appearance of "dynastic portraits" seems to have been in Lycia, characterised not only by traditional attributes, but also by inscriptions bearing the name of the dynast – identifying the effigy – and some individual traits. A telling case is that of the issue by Kherẽi, a dynast at the end of the fifth century BC (Fig. 4). The faces of Kherẽi on the reverse of the coins are evidence of recurring traits and physical characteristics, such as the large, aquiline nose, together with a typified depiction of the beard, and accompanied by the inscription of the name of the dynast.[9] In Phoenicia direct reference to rulers began to appear in the last quarter of the fifth century BC, when King Ba'lshallim I of Sidon was the first to place his initials on the coin types in the region, but the first to add a dynastic "portrait"

[7] See Miller 2003: 29; Matthiae 1998: 144–5. See also Barnett 1976: 48.
[8] On *schemata*, see Catoni 2008.

[9] Mørkholm and Zahle 1976: 79–85; see also Babelon 1910: § LIII. On the importance of legend for the recognition of dynasts, see Schwabacher 1968: 117. On different interpretations about local coinage, see Dusinberre 2000 and Mildenberg 2000.

on Phoenician coinage was King ʻAbdʻastart I of Sidon (372–362/1 BC). The use of dynastic "portrait" on coinage lies in the character of the medium: the circulation of coins marked the boundaries of influence of an individual ruler, and his portrayal was an emblem of authority.

As for attributes on the dynastic monuments, the main character on the Satrap Sarcophagus of Sidon can be recognised in all the scenes, including the hunt, thanks to his beard and tiara (Figs. 17–18 and 56). This headgear, a typical Persian one, was one of the main signs of authority in the Eastern Mediterranean.[10] Elsewhere, the ruler is identified mainly by compositional strategy and iconographic layout. The hunting scenes of the Nereid Monument, for example, lack significant iconographic attributes.[11] Indeed, the geometrical fulcra of BM 889 and BM 887 are not the bear and the boar, the narrative focuses as targets of the action, but the two riders facing the prey (Figs. 58b-c). It may be assumed that both the figures on horseback in front of the bear and the boar should be interpreted as the ruler. According to the sequence of slabs proposed by W.A.P. Childs and P. Demargne, the rider's position on BM 887 would have been in line with the eastern pediment, which is unequivocally carved with the dynast and his family.[12] The presence of the dynast as main hunter also on BM 889 could be assumed on the basis of the repetition of the main hunter on the crest beam of the Payava Sarcophagus.[13] Here, an inscription indicates in the audience scene the name of an important historical character, the satrap Autophradates. He is shown with the most familiar attributes: he wears Persian clothing and a tiara; he is armed with a dagger (*akinakes*), has a pointed beard and sits on a draped stool, in a manner similar to that previously observed on block 879 of the Nereid Monument (Fig. 6).[14]

As noted in the preceding chapter, the hunting technique may also be used to identify the rank of the hunter, such as the use of a chariot, as shown on the Lycian Sarcophagus and on Persian seals.[15]

5.2.2. The dynast's family

Due to the hereditary nature of power in the Eastern Mediterranean, the definition of the dynast's image on Eastern Mediterranean funerary monuments would be incomplete without a reference to the role of his family. The following brief analysis will therefore venture beyond hunt representations.

In Lycia there is a consistent emphasis on the circle of members of the dynastic family in intimate representations. Two examples are significant. On the famous fifth-century BC Harpy Tomb from Xanthos, the reliefs show a clear separation between the male and female spheres, and there are no hunting and battle episodes to highlight the exploits of an individual.[16] At the beginning of the fourth century BC the east pediment of the Nereid Monument celebrated the dynastic family alongside dignitaries and servants.[17]

The importance of the figure of the heir to the throne is certainly traceable in the Achaemenid figurative tradition, but the older Anatolian context – such as the Syro-Hittite context discussed in Chapter Three – is worth mentioning here. In Karkemish, on the reliefs of the so-called Royal Buttress, dating back to the mid-eighth century BC, an intimate scene within the royal household, emphasising the inheritance of power, appeared in a public setting. Here the king is presented by the regent, and is followed by younger siblings, the smallest in the arms of a nurse.[18] It is hard to identify members of the dynastic family in Lycian hunting representations, however, although their presence is likely. More considerations will follow below.

In Phoenicia, on the contrary, there is a lack of family images, except for the banquet scene on the Satrap Sarcophagus, but the presence of the heir in hunting representations has been hypothesised. Considering the hereditary character of Phoenician kingship, it is plausible that the scenes of the dynast's self-representation, including the hunt, stress his relationship with the younger generation, a guarantee of the authority being handed down.[19] On the Lycian Sarcophagus an alternation between old and young generations in the hunting scenes has been noticed.[20] One horseman in the boar hunt belongs to an older generation, being bearded, whereas the other hunters in this scene and all the figures in the lion hunt relief are clean-shaven. Such a prevalence of young hunters may convey a precise meaning on the new generations of the ruling family. The alternation mature/young may recall Xenophon's story of the young Cyrus the Elder's first outdoor hunt (Xen. *Cyr*. 1.4.7–9), indicating the importance of the heir's hunt as initiation to power within monarchical ideology. It is not easy to identify precisely the main protagonists on the Mourning Women Sarcophagus as well: G. Mendel recognised the "maître de chasse" in figures A4, A10, A14, A19, B5, B8, B21 and B23; F. Studniczka suggested identifying the deceased as one of the bearded huntsmen

[10] On the Persian tiara, see Hdt. 3.12. There were two styles of tiara: the τιάρα ἀπαγή, the soft, which was more widespread (Hdt. 7.61), and the τιάρα ὀρθή, the rigid, a prerogative of the Great King, his family members and dignitaries (e.g.: Xen. *An*. 2.5.23; Xen. *Cyr*. 8.3.13; Hsch. τ 836). The τιάρα ὀρθή would be the equivalent of Greek *kidaris* (Ar. *Av*. 486–487; Pfrommer 1998: 56). Similarly, the head found at Heraclea, in Bithynia, dated to the third quarter of the sixth century BC, is not characterised by personal traits, but the tiara helped to establish his identity (Ankara, Museum of Anatolian Civilisations 19367. Akurgal 1986: 9–14; Summerer 2005).

[11] P. Demargne highlights that the rider facing the boar, whom he identifies with the dynast, does not show any specific treatment compared to the other riders (Childs and Demargne 1989: 188).

[12] Borchhardt and Bleibtreu 2008: 61–2; see also Childs and Demargne 1989: 280.

[13] *Supra*, § 4.3.6.

[14] Demargne and Laroche 1974: 78–9; Jenkins 2006: 180–1.

[15] See § 4.3.2.

[16] See § 2.2.2.

[17] Poggio 2016b: 212–6, with bibliography.

[18] Orthmann 1971: 35, 509–10.

[19] For the nature of inheriting Phoenician royal power, see Elayi 1987: 25–8.

[20] Fischer-Bossert 2003: 195.

on horseback on each side (A10 and B21).[21] An alternation of older and younger hunters can be observed here. In the first series of hunts each quarry is approached by a bearded man wearing the common τιάρα ἀπαγή (A4, A10, A14, A19). In the second series, instead, the frontline generally shows a clean-shaven man: figure B19 grabs a panther by the neck, a gesture that has heroicising connotations (Fig. 75). The will of alternating mature and young hunters in frontline is reflected by the use of models. If one considers for instance the scene of the deer hunt on both the long sides of the socle, the position of B15 and B16 towards the deer mirrors that of A19 and A20 (Fig. 82), but the direction of the deer is reversed: hence, there is an inversion of the role between the mature and the young hunter towards the prey. One can observe that on side A there is always a mature man – riding a horse or on foot – who directly faces the prey, whereas on side B the presence of younger hunters facing the quarry, in addition to the bare-hand grip of B19, is prevalent.

Similarly, on the Satrap Sarcophagus a young figure is recognisable both in the panther hunt scene, assisting the main hunter, and in the departure with the chariot (Figs. 17 and 56).

This distinction between the hunts conducted by the dynast and by the heir may relate to the neo-Assyrian context. Both at Nimrud, in the Northwest Palace of Ashurnasirpal II, and at Nineveh, in the North Palace of Ashurbanipal, the hunt is the only activity in which the heir to the throne enjoys any independence. In both palaces the representation of the king's hunt and that of the heir are found in distinct settings. At Nimrud, Ashurnasirpal's hunts were shown on reliefs in Room B (the Throne Room; Figs. 38-39), while the crown prince's ones were found in the west wing of the palace. At Nineveh, royal lion hunts decorated rooms C and S'; those of lions, onagers and gazelles carried out by the heir occupied the walls of room S (Fig. 41).[22] The crown prince's independence in hunting points to the ideological meaning of the activity, the only one that would allow the future monarch to show and apply his skills without the supervision of the sovereign. The variety of prey and species both at Nimrud and Nineveh suggests the repeatability of the action, with the possibility of improvement, while battle – for obvious reasons – was unique.

In conclusion, there are some differences in dynastic family iconography in the Eastern Mediterranean. In Lycia there is more emphasis on an intimate atmosphere, with the dynastic couple depicted together with their offspring. This feature may have its roots in the local tradition that attributes much importance to the theme of family in official imagery as in the Syro-Hittite context. In Phoenicia, on the contrary, there is a lack of family images, except for the banquet scene on the Satrap Sarcophagus, while it may be assumed that the heir is depicted carrying out a representative activity like hunting, as seen in the neo-Assyrian context in Chapter Three. This is significant given that Phoenicia had been under neo-Assyrian control. If this theory is correct, one might speculate that in Sidon, in the absence of military and intimate representations in the royal imagery, hunting was the privileged iconography for emphasising the link between the dynast and his heir.

5.3. Hunting and hierarchies: the dynast's retinue

5.3.1. Friends and dignitaries

As noted above, the chase groups are composed of several hunters, as on the Nereid Monument and the Mourning Women Sarcophagus. Apart from the Satrap and the Alexander sarcophagi, however, the identification of distinct characters within a large group is not certain. This means that the main hunter is surrounded by friends and dignitaries distinguishable from him by compositional devices rather than dress and attributes. They belonged to the restricted circle of the ruler's close coterie and assisted the main hunter in various ways. Figure B18 on the socle of the Mourning Women Sarcophagus of Sidon, for instance, is shown behind B19 (the dynast's heir?), who faces a panther and grabs its neck, presumably using a short sword (Fig. 75). With the right he is ready to hurl a stone, while with his left hand B18 holds a scabbard in mid-air, so perhaps he has promptly provided his companion (B19) with the weapon in order to fight the feline. In the hunt scenes in the Throne Room of Ashurnasirpal's palace in Nimrud, the king is assisted by attendants ready to intervene in the case of danger: neo-Assyrian art, again, seems to provide a pattern for the detailed representation in Sidon.[23]

Senior dignitaries and friends of the ruler must have complied with a precise hierarchy according to court hunt etiquette.[24] Xenophon reports that Cyrus the Elder, when still a boy, declined the right to be the first to strike the prey, a right assigned by his grandfather Astyages (Xen. *Cyr.* 1.4.14). The episode is not necessarily historically reliable – Xenophon's work had moralistic intent, praising the benevolence of the future sovereign toward his peers. However, there is little doubt regarding the royal prerogative to strike a wild beast first. This principle was especially applicable to lions, even if they are attacking. Ctesias, a contemporary of Xenophon, records an episode involving Artaxerxes I (465/4–424/3 BC) and Megabyzus:[25]

[21] Mendel 1912: 64–6; Studniczka 1905: 36. It is unclear, however, whether Mendel meant the "maître de chasse" of each scene to be identified with the same person.

[22] For royal hunts at Nimrud, see Meuszyński 1981: 23, nos. B-20 and B-19; for those of the prince, see Paley and Sobolewski 1987: 76. For Nineveh hunts, see Matthiae 1996: 195–212. See § 3.1.2. (note 57).

[23] For hunting accidents, see § 5.5.

[24] Briant 1996: 243–4.

[25] Phot. *Bibl.* 72.41a.31–36 = *FGrH* 688 F 14 (§ 43). Hermolaus, one of Alexander the Great's pages, anticipated the Macedonian king in bringing down a boar – according to Arrian in a situation of danger – and for this he was punished (Arr. *Anab.* 4.13.2; Curt. 8.6.7). See also Heckel 2009: 138–9, *s.v.* Hermolaus.

B13 B14 B15 B16 B17 B18 B19 B20 B21

Figure 75. Detail of the hunting socle frieze of the Mourning Women Sarcophagus from Sidon. Istanbul, Archaeological Museum 368. D-DAI-IST-R19.732 (Photo: W. Schiele 1981).

> The King went out hunting and was attacked by a lion. Megabyzus struck the beast with a javelin as it was flying through the air and killed it. And Artaxerxes was annoyed because Megabyzus had struck it before he could hit it himself. And he ordered that Megabyzus should be beheaded.[26]

According to Plutarch, in apparent contradiction to Ctesias' account, Artaxerxes I was the first to allow hunt companions to go into action without waiting for the monarch (Plut. *Mor.* 173d). P. Briant, in this respect, believes that innovations associated with Artaxerxes I should be attributed instead to Artaxerxes II (405/4–359 BC), since at his time the right of the king to strike lions first was no longer in force (Diod. Sic. 15.10.3):[27]

> It is related that Tiribazus pointed out many services to the King, and one very great one, as a result of which he was highly regarded and became a very great friend. Once during a hunt, while the King was riding in a chariot, two lions came at him, tore to pieces two of the four horses belonging to the chariot, and then charged upon the King himself; but at that very moment Tiribazus appeared, slew the lions, and rescued the King from the danger.[28]

However, it would be difficult to attribute the confusion over the two Artaxerxes to Plutarch, since he declared that he had drawn upon Ctesias to write the biography of Artaxerxes II.[29] E. Almagor, instead, refers this divergence to the fact that Plutarch's anecdote was altered by an editor who ignored Ctesias' version.[30] One can observe that the information provided by Ctesias and Plutarch about Artaxerxes I may refer to different episodes in the life of the king. Moreover, Ctesias mentions a lion hunt, the quintessential royal hunt, which may have had specific rules, whereas Plutarch does not specify the chased prey.[31]

As to Diodorus Siculus' passage on Artaxerxes II, Plutarch confirms that the satrap Tiribazus had an exceptional position at the Persian court, since in the account of the battle of Cunaxa he points out that he had the privilege of helping the Great King to mount a horse (Plut. *Artax.* 10.1). This sheds light on the importance of friends and dignitaries during royal hunts, allowing us to hypothesise something similar for the Eastern Mediterranean.

5.3.2. Servants

People of lower rank obviously played an important part in the hunt group. Both in literary and in figurative language, the greater the number of participants, the more explicit the power of the ruler and the more detailed the description of the entourage. Xenophon relates how servants were trained by Cyrus, mentioning a hierarchy within the retinue, the members of which carried out precise tasks (Xen. *Cyr.* 8.1.44):

[26] Translation from Llewellyn-Jones and Robson 2010: 190.
[27] Briant 1996: 588.
[28] Translation from Oldfather 1954. On this passage, see Almagor 2018: 218–9.
[29] For the sources of Plutarch, see Manfredini, Orsi and Antelami 1987: xxviii–xxxvi.
[30] Almagor 2018: 275–6.
[31] Seyer (2007: 59–61) suggests that the hunt described by Ctesias allegorically indicated the attempt by Megabyzus to subvert order in Persia.

> And he managed it in this way: whenever they were to drive the animals down into the plains for the horsemen, he allowed those of the lower classes, but none of the freemen, to take food with them on the hunt [...].[32]

The most frequently depicted figure in scenes from the Eastern Mediterranean is a squire on foot, following the hunter on horseback to help him in various ways. His presence emphasises compliance with prescribed hunt etiquette, and thus adds realism to the scene. There are clear examples on several Graeco-Persian stelae in the Dascylium area. One of these, found in 1981 in Sultaniye Köy, dates to the late sixth century BC and is divided into three registers, showing a banquet, a funerary procession and a fallow deer hunt.[33] In the latter, the horseman chases the prey with two dogs.[34] Then a man on foot carries a javelin. In the hunting scene of the Çavuşköy Stele, on the left edge, set back from the horseman, a walking figure carries two javelins or spears (Fig. 67).[35] M.C. Miller associates this representation with Xenophon, since the historian, among other weapons, mentions two spears, ready for any contingency (Xen. *Cyr.* 1.2.9):[36]

> But when the king goes out hunting, he takes out half the garrison; and this he does many times a month. Those who go must take bow and arrows and, in addition to the quiver, a sabre or bill in its scabbard; they carry along also a light shield and two spears, one to throw, the other to use in case of necessity in a hand-to-hand encounter.[37]

As to the weapons used in hunts, the use of javelins, lighter than spears, made it possible to face animals from varying distances.[38] The presence of two javelins is also indicated in Oppian (Opp. *Cyn.* 1.91–92).

On the stele from Vezirhan, in ancient Bithynia, dating from the end of the fifth century BC, the mention in the inscription of a sacred place with trees dedicated to the Mother Goddess, equated with Artemis, is accompanied by figurative scenes that include, significantly, a hunting scene in the lower register.[39] A man dashes in pursuit of a boar that is already wounded, and he lifts his right arm, ready to strike the final blow. The prey, targeted by a dog, escapes and does not confront its attacker. A squire assists the rider, carrying one or two spears (Fig. 70).[40]

Servants may have had the further task of transporting slain prey, as on block 889 of the Nereid Monument (Fig. 58b) and another servant carrying a javelin appears on block 887 (Fig. 58c). On the crest beam of the Payava Sarcophagus the servant, a clear status symbol, and the dog are reduced to a single unit, on the left (Fig. 27).

Addressing another typology of evidence, a Graeco-Persian-type scaraboid seal from Ithome, in Messenia, shows a similar iconography: the victorious hunter waits for his squire to recover the body of the animal and the trident used to kill it.[41]

In the *Onomasticon*, a lexicographical work of the second century AD, the rhetorician Julius Pollux provided a list of helpers in hunts (Poll. *Onom.* 5.17). Alongside the dogs and the horses, he mentions two tasks connected with these animals, the κυναγωγός, the keeper of the hounds, and the ἱππαγωγός, the keeper of the horses, necessary for the proper conduct of hunts.

With regard to the κυναγωγός, Xenophon wrote that dogs were essential for hunting, and the success depended on their characteristics, proper training and care.[42] He outlines the role of κυναγωγός (Xen. *Cyn.* 9.1–2):

> (1) For hunting fawns and deer use Indian hounds; for they are strong, big, speedy and plucky, and these qualities render them capable of hard work. Hunt the calves in spring, since they are born at that season. (2) First go to the meadows and reconnoitre, to discover where hinds are most plentiful. Wherever they are, let the keeper of the hounds go with the hounds and javelins to this place before daybreak and tie up the dogs to trees some distance off, so that they may not catch sight of the hinds and bark, and let him watch from a coign of vantage.[43]

Among the funerary monuments under review, the κυναγωγός is present twice (A7 and B1) on the Mourning Women Sarcophagus. The figure is distinguished by a direct relationship with the dog, since he bends over the animal, touching it with one hand and, at least in the case of A7, pointing with the other in the direction in which to run (Figs. 32 and 76). As attested by Arrian, dogs should be obedient to the man who leads them in the hunt, in the same way that subjects obey the sovereign, almost intuiting his intentions (Arr. *Cyn.* 7.5–6). It is reasonable that the man on relief A20 on the north wall of the Heroon of Trysa (Fig. 59) is a dog handler, as is the other, on the far left of the hunting scene on the Payava Sarcophagus, although here the relationship to the dog is less clear (Fig. 27).[44] In the upper register of Xenophantos' lekythos, on

[32] Translation from Miller 1968.
[33] Bursa, Archaeological Museum 8500. Altheim-Stiehl, Metzler and Schwertheim 1983; *Anatolian Civilisations* 1983: 56, cat. B.141; Nollé 1992: 19–22, cat. S3.
[34] As an artistic device, these two animals, as on Archaic East Greek representations, are depicted under the horse, in a space that would otherwise have remained empty.
[35] Pfuhl and Möbius 1977: 30–1, no. 73. *Supra*, § 4.2.2.2.
[36] Miller 2003: 26 and 30.
[37] Translation from Miller 1968.
[38] See also Marconi 1997: 1077.
[39] See § 4.3.1. for bibliography.
[40] *Anatolian Civilisations* 1983: 60, cat. B.146.
[41] Berlin, Staatlische Museen, Antikensammlung 8250. Furtwängler 1900: II, 56, no. 13; Boardman 1970b: 353, pl. 890. For the use of trident spears in hunting, see Opp. *Cyn.* 1.154.
[42] Briant (1996: 947) on hunts mentions the ἵππων καὶ κυνῶν ἐπιμεληταί (Xen. *Cyr.* 8.1.9). See also Tripodi 1994: 507.
[43] Translation from Marchant 1971.
[44] Otherwise, this figure may be a squire. For Trysa, see Benndorf and Niemann 1889: 169. The importance of the subject in this area is also seen in the figure to the left of the marble relief from the region of Troy, possibly early Hellenistic (Cohen 2010: 36 and fig. 6).

A6 A7 A8 A9 A10 A11 A12 A13

Figure 76. Detail of the hunting socle frieze on the Mourning Women Sarcophagus from Sidon. Istanbul, Archaeological Museum 368. D-DAI-IST-R19.737 (Photo: W. Schiele 1981).

the left of the central axis formed by the two hunters on horseback and chariot, a character represented in Persian dress struggles to restrain a nervous dog on a leash (Fig. 73). This κυναγωγός, as pointed out by H.M. Franks, is the only relief figure to be unnamed:[45] therefore, his rank is to be considered equivalent to that of the other anonymous figures on the red-figure vase. On a smaller lekythos created by Xenophantos or his workshop, found at Kerch in the Zmeinoi Kurgan, there is an iconographic compendium of the larger vase with similar models of relief figures (Fig. 77).[46] Again, on the left of the scene is a κυναγωγός. Although relegated to anonymity like the other attendants, the κυναγωγός of Xenophantos' large lekythos played a significant role due to his skills and tasks, as confirmed by literary sources. It is probable that the importance of this figure, despite his anonymity, in the characterisation of the hunting scenes made it necessary to use the same model to facilitate its replication on different vases. Thus there emerges a constant positioning of the figure of the dog attendant at the edge of the scene, dictated by his special responsibilities, which did not overlap with those of the hunters.[47]

According to Pollux, the horses also needed staff to care for them, but the term ἱππαγωγός, in the tradition prior to this author, does not seem to indicate a person, but rather more frequently the ships carrying these animals.[48] Pollux gives the term an unmistakable meaning, however, and, irrespective of terminology, one or more persons were needed for the care of the horses. On the Mourning Women Sarcophagus, character C13 leads a recalcitrant horse by the bridle; perhaps C2 performed the same function.[49] The hunter would not always face his quarry on horseback: sometimes he would dismount and proceed on foot, so someone in the retinue would be needed to restrain the horse, which might be startled by a dangerous situation, as depicted on one of the short sides of the Alexander Sarcophagus (Fig. 62).[50] Horses also required great care in feeding and grooming.[51]

Another crucial figure was the man who alerted the hunters to the sighting of prey using a wind instrument, as mentioned in the second century BC by Agatharchides of Cnidus, who indicated the presence of trumpet players during hunts (Diod. Sic. 3.37.3).[52] On an iconographic level, on the architrave of the Nereid Monument a wind

[45] Franks 2009: 461.

[46] St. Petersburg, The State Hermitage Museum, ZM-3. Zervoudaki 1968: 26–7, no. 36. The association between the two vases is also confirmed by the names: the two hunters on the smaller lekythos are Atramis and Darius, who also appear on the larger vase hunting respectively a griffin and a boar, whereas on the smaller example the prey are two deer. The position of the artist's signature is also analogous. On the mixed technique used by the artist, see Skrzhinskaya 2000: 281.

[47] On this figure, see also Anderson 1985: 37.

[48] See, for instance, Hdt. 6.48, 6.95 and 7.97; Thuc. 4.42.1; Ar. *Eq.* 599.

[49] The bridle must have been rendered through painting. Frieze C depicts the return from the hunt (*supra*, § 5.1.2.).

[50] Poggio 2011: 482–5.

[51] We know from the Persepolis tablets that feed for horses was distributed in the Persian capital (Gabrielli 2006: 39–45).

[52] Jacobson 2007: 27, 36 note 10.

instrument player gives a signal, perhaps the *halali*, which indicates when the prey, exhausted, is surrounded by dogs (Fig. 58d).[53] A character with a similar function was painted in the Marisa Tomb, dated to the mid-third century BC (Fig. 89).[54] The connection of this particular iconography to this funerary testimony further strengthens the link with the Eastern Mediterranean tradition, and confirms that the hunting depictions of the Persian era portray well-codified practices.

So in the Eastern Mediterranean from the fifth to the fourth century BC significant attention was paid to the hunt participants. The well-structured organisation of hunting is traceable in different historical contexts. Although distant in time and space, one can compare the hunting organisation with that of the dukes of Burgundy. Here, starting from the second half of the fourteenth century AD, there was a remarkable hierarchic arrangement of the participants, divided into four categories: hunter, assistant hunter, valet and the page for the dogs. The total number of employees increased progressively until it reached a maximum of thirty-seven in the years 1401–1403, numbering even more than the French king's retinue. In later years, however, due to the high cost of maintenance, the number was gradually reduced. An interesting element is the social composition and method for entering the duke's hunting corps, because members came from different classes of society, depending on their role. For example, the hunt masters belonged to the local aristocracy, which also occupied important administrative positions. This role within the hunt was considered so prestigious that it was passed down through the same family, while valets and pages came from lower social classes.[55]

This example may help to better understand the mechanism of the management of hunting groups even in antiquity. Indeed, Xenophon describes several tasks of participants in a collective and multiple-quarry hunt that took place during Cyrus the Elder's expedition against the king of Armenia (Xen. *Cyr*. 2.4.19–20):

> (19) And as he proceeded on his way, in the very first field a hare started up. And an eagle flying up from the east caught sight of the hare as it ran and swooping down struck it, seized it, and carried it up, then bore it away to a hill not far off and disposed of his prey at his pleasure. Then Cyrus, observing the omen, was delighted and did homage to Sovereign Zeus and said to those who were by: 'Our hunt, comrades, please God, will be successful.' (20) When they arrived at the frontier, he at once proceeded to hunt, as he used to do; and the most of his men, on foot and on horseback, were marching in a straight line before him, in order to start up the game as they approached. But the best of his foot and horse stood at intervals and lay in wait for what was started up, and pursued it in relays. And they took many boars, deer, antelope, and wild asses; for many wild asses breed in those regions even unto this day.[56]

In conclusion, as at the Burgundian court, one may infer that hunt groups were managed by a miniature government, whose functioning reflects the ways in which the dynast exercised power.[57]

5.4. Horses

Among the elements that distinguish the rank of the hunters shown on the monuments studied here is the use of horses. On the architrave with hunt scenes on the Nereid Monument, the main participants are on horseback, while the figures on foot are attendants, including one carrying lifeless prey and a wind instrument player. Consistently, the celebration of the military feats of Arbinas of Xanthos – to whom the Nereid Monument is generally referred – in the inscription from the sanctuary of Letoon includes physical abilities and moral qualities, such as mastery of the bow, valour and the equestrian arts.[58] Hierarchisation conveyed by the use of the horse is also visible on those stelae where a squire follows the hunter on horseback: the aforementioned stelae from Manisa (Fig. 66), Çavuşköy (Fig. 67), Vezirhan (Fig. 70) and Sultaniye Köy. On the long side of the Alexander Sarcophagus, there is a clear distinction between hunters on horseback and hunters on foot, since the former are grouped around the lion, which is the most important prey from the point of view of both composition and meaning (Fig. 61).

In Sidon there are representations in which all participants hunt on horseback, as in the hunting scene on the Satrap Sarcophagus and the boar hunt on the Lycian Sarcophagus.[59] The Mourning Women Sarcophagus is a unique case, since each of the crowded hunt scenes shows only one of the characters on horseback. The boar hunt on side B, framed by two hunters on horseback (B7 and B12), is an exception. Of all the riders, only A10 is in the front line against the quarry, standing out from the surrounding hunt group, so it is plausible to identify him as the main hunter of that scene.[60] The absence of mounted hunters in the deer hunt – as shown on the A and B sides of the Mourning Women Sarcophagus – is more usual; this is also found on the Heroon of Trysa ibex relief (A10; Fig. 59). The preference for pursuing these prey on foot can be

[53] Nollé 2001: 24; Borchhardt and Bleibtreu 2008: 62. Nieswandt (1995: 120), instead, connects the presence of the trumpeter to battle scenes.

[54] In the animal frieze behind the hunter facing a feline, a figure holds a wind instrument in his right hand. For the Marisa Tomb, see Peters and Thiersch 1905; Erlich 2009: 62–77; Jacobson 2007; see § 6.2.

[55] For a study on hunt practices and entourage in the Duchy of Burgundy, see Beck 2000.

[56] Translation from Miller 1968.

[57] See also [Arist.] *Mund*. 398a.

[58] Through the comparison of literary passages, J. Bousquet showed that the expression ἵππων τε διώγματα εἰδ[ώς] (see l. 15) indicates the practice of riding horses rather than chasing them, as suggested, conversely, by P. Demargne (Bousquet 1975: 147 note 23; for the observations of Demargne, see Bousquet 1975: 150). See also Poggio 2011: 480–1, 485. For further considerations on the inscription from the Letoon and its relationship with Iranian culture, see Robert 1975: 329–30.

[59] See Apicella 2010: 73.

[60] Studniczka 1905: 36.

traced back to the earliest hunt representations, such as the relief on the Tomb at Isinda, as has been noted.[61]

Horse riding, along with archery and speaking the truth, was part of the so-called "trivium" of the Persian "paideia", formulated by Herodotus (Hdt. 1.136) and mentioned often by Xenophon in the *Cyropaedia* (Xen. *Cyr.* 1.3.15–18; 1.6.6; 8.3.25). Herodotus' formulation of the "trivium" has rightly been traced back to forms of self-celebration by Near Eastern monarchs.[62]

The link between royalty and the use of the horse, which descends from an Indo-European tradition, finds confirmation in the Persian context, as demonstrated by the episode of Darius seizing power. According to Herodotus, for the choice of the new king to succeed Cambyses, the six who contended for the title after the elimination of usurpers had to ride through the city's suburbs at dawn: he whose horse whinnied first would become the new king. Darius, son of Hystaspes, won the throne thanks to a stratagem thought up by his squire Oebares (Hdt. 3.84–87).[63] The anecdote was popular and, importantly, was shared by Ctesias of Cnidus: since Ctesias sometimes diverges from Herodotus, D. Lenfant has argued that in this case the episode descends directly from Persian sources.[64]

According to Plutarch, Cyrus the Younger, while scheming to seize the Persian throne from his brother Artaxerxes, boasts of his own qualities and said that his brother "was too effeminate and cowardly either to sit his horse in a hunt, or his throne in a time of peril" (Plut. *Artax.* 6.3).[65] Plutarch's association between royalty and horseback hunting thus seems utterly credible. Moreover, it seems to me that the Persian concept of "paideia" could match the Late Persian issue of a tetradrachm, whose obverse shows the kneeling king with crown and quiver drawing his bow, often accompanied by the legend BA (namely ΒΑΣΙΛΕΩΣ). On the reverse, the type shows a Persian horseman who – on the basis of Graeco-Persian art – may be interpreted as a hunter, given the position of the arm stretched out behind his shoulder, normally used in hunting rather than battle scenes.[66]

It is therefore no coincidence that horseback hunts on red-figure vases of the fifth century BC are associated with distant worlds, generically classified as "Eastern" contexts. This is anomalous, since hunting on horseback was more usual in earlier black-figure production. As pointed out by A. Schnapp, in black-figure production this iconography was the hallmark of the upper class in post-Solonic Athens.[67] With the use of the red-figure technique, depictions of collective and horseback hunting gradually gave way to hunts with fewer participants, often only one, and identifiable as part of specific myths, where the polis as a whole could be identified.[68] Horses in hunts of the Classical period, then, seem to be traced back to the "Eastern" context. In this respect the Basel cup, which shows a doe surrounded by four hunters, including two on horseback (Fig. 79), is exemplary.[69] Significantly, the setting is non-Greek, seen in the clothing of at least three of the characters and the presence of a palm tree.[70] At the same time, the mounted multiple-quarry hunt on the lekythos from Kerch should be interpreted as an exceptional testimony of the meeting of Greek and Persian artistic languages, of which the artist had a thorough understanding.[71]

5.5. Hunt participants in action: accidents

In the hunting scenes concerned here no attempt is made to conceal the challenges of the hunt. Indeed, literary sources attest that royal hunts could be dangerous. Herodotus is the only one to speak of physical injury to a Persian ruler during a multiple-quarry hunt: Darius seriously dislocated his foot while dismounting from his horse (Hdt. 3.129).[72] One could speculate that Darius was going to proceed on foot and face a wild animal, with the combined technique of hunting on horseback and on foot. Cyrus the Younger, a royal aspirant to the throne, moreover, was unseated and injured during a bear hunt (Xen. *An.* 1.9.6).[73] Those accompanying Cyrus the Elder warn the young enthusiast with these words (Xen. *Cyr.* 1.4.7):

> And they told him that bears and boars and lions and leopards had killed many who came close to them, but that deer and gazelles and wild sheep and wild asses were harmless. And they said this also, that one must be on one's guard against dangerous places no less than

[61] *Supra*, § 4.3.1. See also Poggio 2010: 236.

[62] Asheri, Lloyd and Corcella 2007: 170.

[63] For some considerations on the episode, see Asheri, Lloyd and Corcella 2007: 477; Rollinger 2018. On the rise to power of Darius, see Cook 1983: 54–5.

[64] Phot. *Bibl.* 72.38a.32–35 = *FGrH* 688 F 13 (§ 17). Lenfant 2004: lxxx–lxxxi. It is worth noting that the connection of Herodotus' passage with Persian sources would be confirmed by the fact that Herodotus also describes the mutilation of the heads of the Magi to be shown to the people (Hdt. 3.79), a common practice in the ancient Near East. For this practice, see Minunno 2008; Dolce 2018. In Herodotus (1.101) the Magi were one of the Median tribes and were members of the hereditary priestly clan; according to Darius' inscription of Behistun the usurper Gaumāta was a Magus (Asheri, Lloyd and Corcella 2007: 171–2; Dandamayev 2012).

[65] Translation from Perrin 1962. On this passage, Almagor 2018: 218.

[66] See, for example, Boardman 1970b: pls 881–3. Babelon (1910: 159–66, nos. 117–122) connects this issue to Evagoras II of Cyprus. See also Mildenberg 1993: 72.

[67] Schnapp 1997: 242–3.

[68] Schnapp 1997: 400–1; Barringer 2001: 42–6.

[69] Basel, Antikenmuseum BS 438.

[70] *ARV*²: 351, no. 8. Barringer 2001: 27 and 214 note 62. Schauenburg (1969: 17–18) reconnected this particular setting to the artist or the patron spending time abroad. A. Schnapp interpreted the hunter on horseback in Eastern garb first as an Amazon (1979b: 57, no. 46), then as a Scythian, while the second figure on foot should be identified as an Amazon (Schnapp 1997: 357–8). For a mounted deer hunt on a *phiale mesomphalos* dating back to the first quarter of the fifth century BC, see *CVA* Berlin, Staatliche Museen zu Berlin, Antikensammlung 1 [Deutsche Demokratische Republik 3]: 79, no. 6 and pl. 52.4; Schauenburg 1969: 33, no. 72).

[71] *Supra*, § 4.3.4.

[72] *Supra*, § 3.2.

[73] *Supra*, § 3.2. See also the onset of hunting outside the *paradeisos* of Cyrus the Elder, who was almost thrown from his horse during the chase of a deer (Xen. *Cyr.* 1.4.8); for this passage, § 3.2. For a riding accident during the expedition of Xerxes, see Hdt. 7.88.

against wild beasts; for many riders had been thrown over precipices, horses and all.[74]

Different types of accidents can be identified on the monuments with horses as the primary victims. The horses are sometimes attacked by wild animals: on the long side of the Alexander Sarcophagus, the lion mauls the horse of the hunter in Persian dress (Fig. 80).[75] Similarly, in Room S of the North Palace of Nineveh, the prince on horseback kills a lion that jumps in front of him, while another feline attacks a second horse that he keeps tied behind him (Fig. 41).[76] Diodorus Siculus highlights the vulnerability of the horses facing lions in the story of a hunt of Artaxerxes II (Diod. Sic. 15.10.3).[77]

A similar representation is to be found on an Attic oinochoe of the late fifth century BC, where a man in Persian garb throws open his arms helplessly as a lion mauls his horse, rearing up on its hind legs (Fig. 78).[78] The full-face representation of the lion is similar to reliefs at Persepolis on which a lion mauls a bull, but this scene recalls those of a feline attacking a horse present in Assyrian art and in Sidon. Once again, Attic pottery seems to follow iconographies from "Eastern" areas, easily identifiable as such. A new element in the Attic context, however, is the disorientation of the unhorsed hunter: M.C. Miller rightly suggests that the scene should be identified as a lion hunt that ends with the hunter in flight; indeed, the horse's bridle suggests that the animal belongs to the man.[79] In Nineveh and Sidon, however, the context makes it clear that the lion is destined to succumb, since the hunter remains firmly in the saddle and seems willing to persevere with the hunt.[80]

As on the Paris oinochoe, block 888 of the Nereid Monument shows a man who appears to be helpless as he deals with his runaway horse: this interpretation seems more plausible than a wild horse hunt because it is unlikely that the capture or killing of a fast and agile prey would be done on foot (Fig. 58d).[81] In the overall reading of the architrave the runaway horse episode is counterbalanced by the celebration of the dynast as a hunter on blocks 889 and 887. On the Paris oinochoe, instead, the helplessness of the Persian figure and the ferocity of the lion are the crucial aspects of the illustration, with an almost ironic outcome, suitable for the use of the vase in a symposium context.

In Attic production, horses attacked by griffins are found in representations of the mythical conflict between griffins and Arimaspians; the context, in an Athenian perspective, is again "Eastern" or exotic. This cultural horizon is evoked in manifold ways in a cup with a ram-head vessel, dating back to 430 BC (Fig. 81).[82] Both the shape and the iconography reveal the source of inspiration. On one hand, the vase shape echoes precious rhyta, which are typical of the Persian world.[83] On the other, hand the Arimaspian on the tall rim of the vessel is dressed and equipped in the Eastern style. The man is armed with a bow and faces the griffin, which is attacking the horse.[84]

A second type of hunting accident on the monuments consists of horses startled by wild beasts.[85] On Phoenician funerary monuments of the Achaemenid age, horses are depicted as vulnerable animals, whether mounted by riders of non-dynastic rank or unmounted during a hunt. The hunting scene on the Satrap Sarcophagus is a unique case here. On the right a horse drags away its rider, who still clutches the reins (Fig. 56). This iconography, as I. Kleemann notes, is found only in one other likely hunt scene, an ivory artefact from Kul-Oba, near Kerch in Crimea, which is carved with a man being dragged along the ground by his horse. Generally, however, similar images are encountered in depictions of battles or horse races.[86] I. Kleemann has attributed a functional character to this representation, since the marked movement of the startled horse would lead the viewer's eyes to the right, round the corner of the coffin.[87] This explanation has been criticised by J.K. Anderson, who has rightly given more importance to the accident.[88] As already pointed out, the theme of difficulties in the hunt may pervade the whole scene: it is likely that the first rider to the left of the hunting representation is facing a similar situation with his horse.[89] Therefore, the hunting accident theme emerges as an integral part of the hunting imagery and the visual celebration of the dynastic deeds.

However, the startled horse usually appears without a rider, while the hunter confronts his quarry on foot. The panther hunt on the Alexander Sarcophagus of Sidon shows the main hunter facing the wild animal and about to strike it with a majestic gesture. Behind him, a startled horse seems to flee from the scene, but is held back with great effort by a member of the hunting expedition (Fig. 62).[90] This is an elaborate variation of the basic composition consisting of a hunter on foot followed by his horse, found both in monumental art – see the two startled horses on the socle frieze of the Mourning Women Sarcophagus (for instance, Fig. 82) – and on other media. On a cylinder seal with an engraved Aramaic name, a horse is carved behind a hunter

[74] Translation from Miller 1968.
[75] Von Graeve 1970: 58–60.
[76] Matthiae 1996: 201.
[77] *Supra*, § 5.3.1.
[78] Paris, Bibliothèque Nationale de France 473. Raeck 1981: 328, P 588.
[79] Miller 2003: 34–6.
[80] For "Eastern" iconographies on Attic pottery, see § 5.4.
[81] Poggio 2011: 485.

[82] St. Petersburg, The State Hermitage Museum B-1819 (GR-4753). Hoffmann 1962: 36, no. 99; *LIMC* VIII.1: 532, no. 42; Miller 2003: 36.
[83] See Miller 1997: 141–4. For rhyta on the Nereid Monument, see § 2.2.2.
[84] See also an Attic crater dated to the mid-fourth century BC (Paris, Musée du Louvre G 529. *LIMC* VIII.1: 532, no. 40).
[85] On this particular reaction when facing felines, see Tuck 2005: 236–7.
[86] Of the comparisons offered by I. Kleemann, I mention the Chertomlyk scabbard, now in St. Petersburg, and an amphora from Ruvo. On both, the unhorsed rider hangs on to the reins and occupies the space under the horse (Kleemann 1958: 142–4).
[87] Kleemann 1958: 144.
[88] Anderson 1985: 75 and 166 note 40. See also Poggio 2011: 486.
[89] *Supra*, § 4.2.1.
[90] Von Graeve 1970: 60–1. See also Poggio 2011: 484.

Figure 77. Smaller lekythos by Xenophantos. St. Petersburg, The State Hermitage Museum ZM-3. Photograph © The State Hermitage Museum. Photo by Vladimir Terebenin, Leonard Kheifets, Yuri Molodkovets.

a

Figure 78a. Lion mauling a horse on a red-figure oinochoe. Paris, Bibliothèque nationale de France 473. Source: Bibliothèque nationale de France.

b

Figure 78b. Lion mauling a horse on a red-figure oinochoe. Paris, Bibliothèque nationale de France 473. Source: Bibliothèque nationale de France.

Figure 79. Doe hunt on a red-figure cup. Basel, Antikenmuseum BS 438. Antikenmuseum Basel und Sammlung Ludwig / Andreas F. Voegelin.

on foot in Persian garb who is spearing his prey.[91] On a Graeco-Persian cylinder seal, on the other hand, a skittish horse is seen drawing back from the clash in the centre, striking the ground with one front hoof and lifting the other, while pulling back (Fig. 83).[92]

Again, the reference to the Eastern Mediterranean context may help in assessing images on Greek vases. Cup G 623 in the Louvre, dating back to 420 BC, from Etruria, shows the same scene on both sides, with the hunter on foot confronting a boar, while holding the reins of his horse (Fig. 84).[93] According to J.-L. Durand and A. Schnapp, in the Attic context the cup testifies to the transition from the iconography of the horseback chase to the hunt on foot. In their view, therefore, the horse is part of a scene in which the focus is on the heroism of the individual hunter.[94] As J.M. Barringer points out, however, the hunter in the two scenes is distinguished by his "Eastern" dress: the tunic, headgear and boots.[95] Such characterisation of the hunter as an "Eastern" figure may offer the key to explaining the iconography – the hunter on foot with his horse behind – that is anomalous in the Attic context, but more common in the Eastern Mediterranean and in Graeco-Persian art.

In conclusion, on dynastic funerary monuments only one case of a violent accident involving a hunter is found, represented on slab A17 of the hunt sequence at Trysa. Here a kneeling man is attacked by a feline, perhaps a lion, while his companion attempts to rescue him (Fig. 85). This unusual representation was probably influenced by the mythical model of the Meleager hunt, depicted on another wall of the same monument, which include more wounded victims than any other representations of the Calydonian

[91] London, British Museum 89144 (Wiseman [1960]: no. 111; Tallis 2005: 228, no. 417).

[92] Boston, Museum of Fine Arts 03.1011 (Boardman 1970b: 352, pl. 850). According to Boardman, the figuration on a stamp seal with the hunter striking a wild boar with a spear and his horse in the second line derives from cylinder seal representations (Boardman 1970a: 36; 44, no. 170).

[93] Paris, Musée du Louvre G 623. *ARV*[2] 1294; *BAdd*[2] 359. The cup dates to approximately 440 BC according to Barringer (2001: 27). Pottier (1922: 295–6) rightly initially highlights that the scene is more generic than mythological, but then assumes that it represents the myth of Theseus killing the Crommyonian Sow or of Meleager fighting the Calydonian Boar. In the Classical Age, with the spread of hunt scenes with one or two hunters, there was often duplication, with or without variation, of a representation on both sides of the vases, as on two red-figure cups in the Louvre (G 22: *ARV*[2] 151, no. 52; *BAdd*[2] 180; G 637: *ARV*[2] 770, no. 5; *BAdd*[2] 287); see also *CVA* Castle Ashby [Great Britain 15]: 23, no. 58 and pl. 37.

[94] Durand and Schnapp 1984: 62. The idea of the horse as a filler and no longer a distinctive element of the hunt was already expressed in Schnapp (1979b: 57, no. 46). For further considerations on "Eastern" iconography in Attic pottery, see § 5.4.

[95] Barringer 2001: 27.

Figure 80. Attacking lion on the Alexander Sarcophagus from Sidon, detail of the long side with hunt. Istanbul, Archaeological Museum 370. D-DAI-IST-8120 (Photo: Sébah & Joaillier about 1900).

Boar in the Greek world, where only Ancaeus is generally depicted as a victim of the beast.[96]

Hence, in the Greek tradition hunting accidents were not uncommon. Herodotus' episode on Atys, son of Croesus, killed by the Phrygian Adrastus during a boar hunt in Mysia (Hdt. 1.43), would reconnect with a similar tradition handed down by Pausanias (7.17.9–10). In it, Zeus, infuriated by the favour of the Mother Goddess granted to Attis, who was celebrating her rites, sent a boar to ravage Lydian crops; Attis and other Lydians were killed by the wild animal.[97] The tale of the wounding of the young Odysseus (*Od.* 19.392–466) plays a special role in the plot: the wound left a scar that enabled his faithful nurse Eurycleia, by then blind, to recognise him many years later, when he returned in disguise. The scar caused by hunting accidents is a visible sign of the bravery of the hunter, as in the case of Cyrus the Younger.[98] Moreover, in the fourth century BC the boar hunt was introduced into

[96] Poggio 2019a.

[97] See Moggi and Osanna 2000: 284–5; Asheri, Lloyd and Corcella 2007: 104. For a survey of the victims of boars in mythological tales, see Atallah 1966: 63.

[98] *Supra* § 3.2.

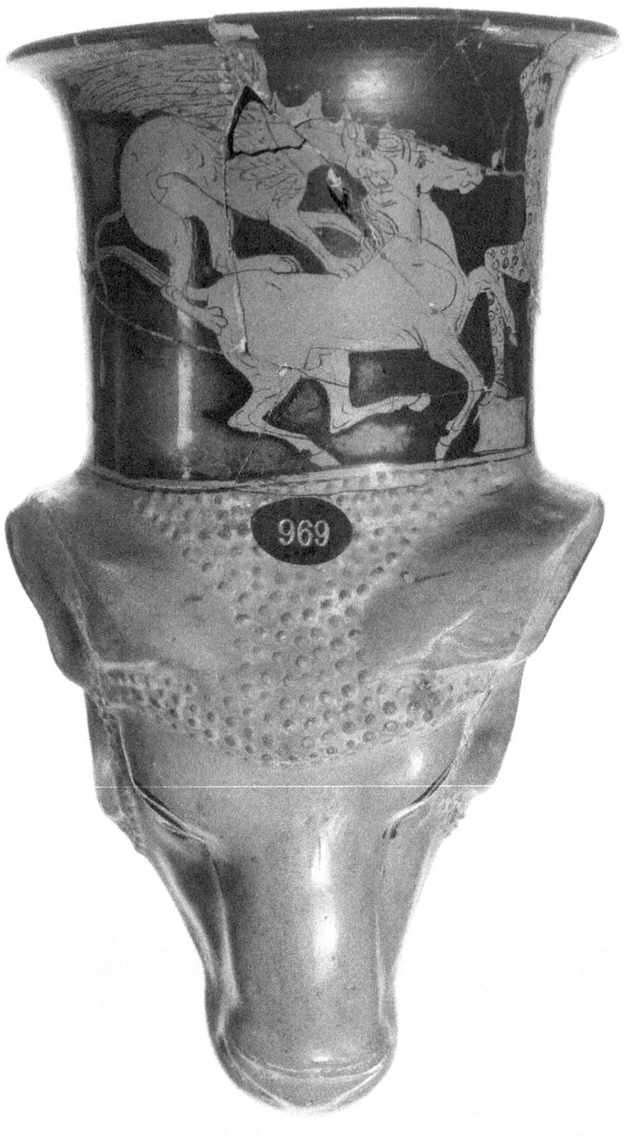

Figure 81. Red-figure ram-head rhyton. St. Petersburg, The State Hermitage Museum B-1819 (GR-4753). Photograph © The State Hermitage Museum. Photo by Vladimir Terebenin, Leonard Kheifets, Yuri Molodkovets.

the myth of Adonis, a character of Eastern origin, and this is also the period of tales of heroic deaths inflicted by wild animals.[99]

These examples show that in the Greek tradition hunting accidents were present but projected to the mythical plane or to a cultural context other than their own, such as the "Eastern". Similarly, in Greek battle images from the Classical period violence expresses itself mainly when the enemy is the "Other" – a Giant, an Amazon, or a Persian. Instead in this dynastic environment, the dangers of hunting expeditions are shown decisively and explicitly. The analysis conducted on Eastern Mediterranean funerary monuments suggests a tendency to represent the dangers of the hunt as part of the ideological framework of royalty, since this theme is absent on more modest monuments such as stelae.

The image of the hunter in distress is impressed on the mind of the observer, as in the case of the Paris oinochoe, while in texts it is possible to contextualise and explain falls and accidents. This means that in the dynastic contexts the representations of accidents could undermine the message of celebration. Thus these monuments focus on accidents affecting the entourage, merely alluding to those involving the main hunter. Philostratus' *Hunters* scene is useful to reflect on these accidents, such as that on the Satrap Sarcophagus (Philostr. *Imag.* 1.28.8):

> Thereupon the dogs drag the boar to the ground, and the lovers on the bank shout as if in rivalry to see who will outshout is neighbour; and one [of the hunters] is thrown from his horse which he excited beyond control instead of holding it in check; and he weaves for the youth a crown of flowers from the meadow in the marsh. The lad is still in the pool, still in the attitude in which he hurled his javelin, while the youths stand in astonishment and gaze at him as though he were a picture.[100]

The writer describes the painting in a narrative form (*ekphrasis*): in this intellectual device he transposes the scheme of the victorious hunter (the man in the act of hurling a javelin), before the eyes of the narrator, into crystallised pose, a source of admiration for the protagonist's companions, although a participant falls from his horse.[101] This "painting in a painting" not only evokes works now lost and reiterates the spread of iconography of the hunter falling from a horse on multiple media, but also shows the combination of a successful hunt and an accident in one picture that does not undermine the celebratory meaning of the image.[102]

One may conclude by mentioning a particular type of hunting accident, handed down by literary sources in association with Persian royal hunts. Due to their hazardous nature, hunts were appropriate scenarios for eliminating people who displeased the king, and were therefore plausible settings for a narrative of court intrigue. The episode related by Herodotus falls into the first case, in which the envious Cambyses sent his brother Smerdis away from Egypt. After the departure of his relative for Persia, a messenger appeared to the Persian king in a dream, bearing the news of Smerdis sitting on the royal throne (Hdt. 3.30):

> Fearing therefore for himself, lest his brother might slay him and so be king, he sent to Persia Prexaspes, the

[99] On Adonis, see Atallah 1966: 77; *LIMC* I.1: 228–9.

[100] Translation from Fairbanks 1960.

[101] For the *Hunters* scene, see Elsner 1995: 33–6. For the *schema* concept, see Catoni 2008; see also Anguissola 2018: 218–9.

[102] For representations of multiple-quarry hunts in painting, see the Vergina and Marisa tombs in the following chapter (§ 6.2.).

Figure 82. Startled horse on the socle frieze of the Mourning Women Sarcophagus from Sidon. Istanbul, Archaeological Museum 368. D-DAI-IST-R19.745 (Photo: W. Schiele 1981).

Figure 83. Cylinder seal. Boston, Museum of Fine Arts 03.1011. Photograph © 2019 Museum of Fine Arts, Boston.

> trustiest of his Persians, to kill Smerdis. Prexaspes went up to Susa and so did; some say that he took Smerdis out a-hunting, others that he brought him to the Red Sea and there drowned him.[103]

Conversely, the designated victim of a conspiracy in the episode narrated by Aelian (*VH* 6.14) is the king:

> I learn of this very kind act of Darius the son of Hystaspes. Aribazus the Hyrcanian plotted against him in alliance with other Persians of note. The plot was timed for a hunt. Darius learned of it in advance, but was not deterred; he ordered the men to make ready their equipment and horses and instructed them to hold their weapons at the ready. Looking at them severely he said: "Why don't you do what you set out to do?" Seeing his unflinching gaze they abandoned their plan; fear gripped them to such an extent that they dropped their spears, jumped off their horses and knelt before Darius, surrendering unconditionally. He despatched them in various directions, sending some to the Indian frontier, others to the Scythian. They remained loyal to him, remembering his kindness.[104]

These examples use a *topos*, but the choice of hunting is significant because it corresponded to a real situation, of the vulnerability of participants, including the ruler. This type of accident does not find a place in the decoration of the monuments, but it helps clarify the danger presented by hunting, requiring a wide range of skills and abilities.

5.6. Conclusion

The visual sphere is part of the social discourse.[105] Therefore, it is useful to make some conclusive

[103] Translation from Godley 1971. In the Behistun inscription Bardiya – the Persian name of which Smerdis is the Greek version – was killed by his brother Cambyses before the start of the Egyptian campaign (Asheri, Lloyd and Corcella 2007: 429).
[104] Translation from Wilson 1997.
[105] See also Zanker 2002: 133–4.

Figure 84. Boar hunt scenes on a red-figure cup. Paris, Musée du Louvre G 623. Photo © RMN-Grand Palais (Musée du Louvre) / Hervé Lewandowski.

Figure 85. A hunter attacked by a feline on a relief from the Heroon of Trysa. Vienna, Kunsthistorisches Museum ANSA I 569. © KHM-Museumsverband.

observations on the social structure and the ideology of power emerging from the images of the participants in dynastic multiple-quarry hunts. In particular, the different messages conveyed by multiple-quarry hunts is of interest here.

The first point to emerge in this chapter is the fact that dynastic multiple-quarry hunts are generally group hunts that use the encirclement technique, although there are regional peculiarities as to the overall organisation of the scene.

As for Lycian dynastic monuments, it is evident that multiple-quarry hunts show a different treatment in comparison with other themes, as the case of the Nereid Monument can clarify. As considered already in Chapter Four, the figurative programme of this tomb displays the repeated figure of the dynast in different situations.[106] On the small frieze of the socle (Sculpture 879) he is depicted as a leader performing his military duties (Fig. 6). The identification of the dynast is conveyed less by physiognomic traits – the current state of conservation would hinder recognition – than by the attributes and compositional dynamics, in which the focus is on symbols to draw the observer's attention: the bearded man, larger than those around him, seated on a richly decorated and draped throne with a footrest, in the shade of a parasol.[107] In his right hand, in a majestic gesture, the dynast holds a sceptre (now missing). Clothing also played a primary role: anatomical armour and a tiara.[108]

The presence of the dynast in the banquet scene of the cella frieze is again characterised by a cluster of attributes and highlighted by compositional devices. In a series of ten *klinai*, eight accommodate two guests, while two show only one each (Sculptures 902 and 903). The dynast is easily recognised on block 903, and it is no coincidence that this occupied the centre of the frieze (Fig. 24). The figure stands out for its majesty, for its larger size, for its central role in the actions of the other characters, such as the servants and the counsellor, and for its specific attributes: a long beard falling vertically down the chest and combed into well-defined sections; a diadem encircling the head; the decorated rhyton; the cushioned footrest, and the crouched dog like that of the east pediment of the monument. This means that the elements of a true Greek symposium, with a crater on the left and the guests sitting in pairs, are combined with a very dynastic message in which the ruler enjoys majestic solitude. Such a distinct hierarchy is not only applied to the participants but also to the servants. Among them, two "butlers" organise the other servants on block 900, near the crater, and on block 903 near the dynast; these are the two focal points of the frieze and of the coordination of service.[109] The primary goal of this scene is the self-representation of the dynast, with many guests in his home, efficient and well-organised serving staff, and precious furnishings including rhyta. Similarly, the ruler, his family and the members of the court – dignitaries and serving staff – are proudly displayed in a well-structured "group picture" on the eastern pediment of the Nereid Monument.[110]

It may appear therefore surprising that the hunting scenes of the architrave frieze do not show relevant elements that can recall the dominant role of the dynast, unless one considers the compositional strategy and iconographic layout, as already mentioned in this chapter. Since in the other situations – which are group scenes as well – the dynast is well identified, it should be considered that the different treatment of the dynast according to the themes was intentional.

At Trysa, analogously, the identification of dynastic figures is assured by attributes and specific postures in the battle scenes (in the battle frieze of the exterior façade), in the banquet (on the south inner wall) and on the outer side of the architrave, whereas in the multiple-quarry hunt the only distinction might be the use of the horse.[111] It could be questioned whether the mounted hunt is a sign of distinction, and in the boar hunt (A16) whether the hunter mounting the horse is more important than that on foot. In the case of more than one hunter riding a horse, as in the case of the panther hunt (A11-12), can a distinction be made? Apart from those figures who are clearly part of the staff, the absence of clear signs of hierarchy among the hunters may refer to a specific meaning of the hunt within court life.

In Persia, the Great King did not hunt alone: the whole court was involved and during longer hunts even concubines were present.[112] Nevertheless, only his closest companions and courtiers had the honour of accompanying him on the actual hunt. Indeed, Plutarch lists the exceptional privileges that Themistocles enjoyed at the Persian court, and mentions attendance at the royal hunts (Plut. *Them.* 29.4).[113] Hunts took place outdoors and – although there were privileges reserved for the king that we have already considered – the participants were on the same level, as the exposure to danger demonstrates. On the other side of the coin – as discussed – was the vulnerability of the ruler during the hunts: the possibility of staying armed with the Great King made it easier for court nobles to conspire during a hunt.[114]

[106] *Supra*, § 4.3.6.
[107] Borchhardt and Bleibtreu 2007.
[108] For the tiara, see Childs and Demargne 1989: 265; *Götter, Heroen, Herrscher* 1990: 167, no. 55 (with a different interpretation of the main figure). See also § 5.2.1. (note 10).

[109] From a technical point of view the two "butlers" seem to have been created using the same model, in mirror image. For the definition of "butlers" or servants of the "type ordonnateur", see Childs and Demargne 1989: 206–7. On this frieze and its meaning, see Poggio 2017b.
[110] Demargne 1983: 169.
[111] Of course in the case of the Trysa reliefs the state of conservation may prevent further considerations. For the identification of the dynast and his son in the banquet frieze, see Landskron 2017: 214–6.
[112] Ath. 12.514c = *FGrH* 689 F 1.
[113] Briant 1996: 311.
[114] *Supra*, § 5.5.

Therefore, the theme of the group hunt seems to project this activity into a dimension in which the ruler interacts and collaborates with his fellows – relatives and friends – rather than simply dominating as in other activities such as war. Present-day team building activities may help us to understand how group hunts could help to strengthen the ties between the ruler and his circle in a collaborative deed. This means that the group hunt was the ideal visual theme to render such a situation and the presence of the Calydonian Boar Hunt at Trysa – the collaborative hunt *par excellence*, with different hunters of various provenance – is perhaps the best heroic counterpart of the dynastic hunt on the same monument.[115]

The fact that many of the dynastic multiple-quarry hunts are group hunts may be explained through this collaborative aspect. Returning to the Nereid Monument and the presence of mounted hunters without distinctive features, one should consider the organisation of the power in this region. Lycia was characterised by an aristocratic society in which the dynastic power was hereditary and legitimised by family ties.[116] On the one hand, epigraphic evidence shows the importance of ancestors in dynastic self-representation.[117] On the other hand, the relationship with the other living members of the family was also important. Lycian dynastic tombs in fact show that the immediate family – wife and children – was part of the dynastic self-representation, as shown by the aforementioned eastern pediment of the Nereid Monument and the local appropriation of the myth of the slaughter of the suitors at Trysa.[118] Moreover, it is known that there was a practice of power-sharing among members of the dynastic family:[119] the dynast of the Inscribed Pillar of Xanthos – a fifth-century BC funerary monument mentioned in Chapter Two – declares that he shared the power with his kinsmen (l. 8: συνγενέσιν δῶκε μέρος βασιλέας, literally: "[he] gave part of the kingdom to his kinsmen"), presumably by maintaining a prominent position.[120]

Even Xenophon's "epitaph" of Cyrus the Younger, satrap and *karanos* in western Anatolia, mentions the collaborative dimension of friendship (Xen. *An.* 1.9.21):

> For, just as the precise object for which he thought he needed friends himself was that he might have co-workers (συνεργοὺς), so he tried on his own part to be a most vigorous co-worker with his friends (συνεργὸς τοῖς φίλοις κράτιστος) to secure that which he found each one of them desired.[121]

[115] For the Calydonian Hunt as an emblematic group hunt, see Franks 2012: 68; Poggio 2019a: 141.
[116] Keen 1992.
[117] Domingo Gygax 2001: 72–3.
[118] Poggio 2007; 2016b.
[119] Domingo Gygax 2001: 72–3, 83; Thonemann 2009: 169–71.
[120] On the Greek inscription of the Inscribed Pillar and – more specifically – on this passage, see Bousquet 1975: 140–1; Asheri 1983: 91–3; Savalli 1988: 110–2; Ceccarelli 1996: 64 note 17.
[121] Translation from Brownson 1961. See also Lendle 1995: 82–4. On Xenophon's portrait of Cyrus the Younger, see § 3.2.

Therefore, the representation of the multiple-quarry hunt on the Nereid Monument, the only scene of the monument in which the dynast is not clearly recognisable, may visually embody this collaborative management of the dynastic power; hunts, much more than battle and banquet scenes, appear as the ideal setting to render the collaborative dimension of rulership.

In addition, the existence of such a relationship between dynasts and a group of people associated with power might be suggested by the practice of honouring deceased rulers. As considered in Chapter Two, south-western Anatolian dynastic tombs are characterised by enclosures aimed at regulating the access to these monuments, which were the setting of commemorative rituals, as it has been deduced by the presence of a roofed space decorated with a banquet scene in the Heroon of Trysa; moreover, these rituals are sometimes archaeologically documented in periods long after the time of burial, as the Heroon of Trysa, the Mausoleum of Halicarnassus and the Heroon of Limyra show.[122] These practices, aimed at perpetuating the memory of the deceased, also played a meaningful role in strengthening family and social ties by defining the social structure.[123]

In Phoenicia the situation is uneven. On the Satrap Sarcophagus the dynast is highly recognisable not only for the royal attributes but also for the majestic way he is carrying out the hunt, in contrast with the hunters in difficulty. This situation seems to recall the hunting representation on the Hecatomnus Sarcophagus, although it does not belong to the multiple-quarry hunt iconography: in Mylasa there is a clear hierarchical distinction, with the dynast recognisable through his facial traits and the fact that he is mounting the horse – the only figure doing so – and facing the lion, which has royal connotations.

On the Lycian Sarcophagus, there is no distinct sign that clearly distinguishes between the hunters and, at the same time, there is a pronounced element of collaboration among participants; the fact that this sarcophagus is the one that shows a clear connection with the Anatolian milieu, as outlined in Chapter Two, does not appear to be coincidence. The low density of hunters' distinctive features and a marked collaborative dimension are detectable on the Mourning Women Sarcophagus, which also shows a direct relationship with the Anatolian context.

In the hunting representations of the Alexander Sarcophagus the aforementioned aspects are coexistent and at the same time they have been overcome: in the lion hunt the mounted hunters are acting in a collaborative dimension but there is a high degree of individuality; there is a marked emphasis on hierarchy within the hunting team. It is the expression of shared hunting deeds which distinguishes the Hellenistic-Macedonian tradition (for example, Arr. *Anab.* 4.13.1; Curt. 8.6.4), and which

[122] *Supra*, § 2.2.1.
[123] On the importance of rituals see Morris 1996.

will be transmitted to the Roman tradition: in the *Historia Augusta* the portrayal of Hadrian is enriched by an account of his passion for the hunt, and in that regard it should be pointed out that his hunting exploits occurred in the presence of friends: "Venationem semper cum amicis participavit".[124]

[124] SHA *Hadr.* 26.3.

Figure 86. (following page) The façade of the Tomb II in Vergina with the hunt frieze, reconstruction by G. Miltsakakis. Courtesy of Ch. Saatsoglou-Paliadeli and the Aristotle University Excavation Archive.

6

Conclusion: Hunting, Politics, and Tradition

The present study has focused on the importance and the meaning of a specific hunting iconography, the multiple-quarry hunt, as the one favoured in dynastic funerary imagery during the fifth- and fourth-century BC Eastern Mediterranean.

In spite of scattered information, the Eastern Mediterranean in this period appears as an interconnected world, with an extensive movement of people including rulers, artists, intellectuals, merchants, ambassadors, slaves, as well as materials and ideas. In this context the multiple-quarry hunt is the most common iconography that can be referred to as the celebration of figures of dynastic rank.

The present analysis has revealed a number of relevant points that can explain the success of this iconography. First, the universal value of the hunt in dynastic societies made its use possible in different political entities: as considered, if Lycian dynasts appear very active as military leaders, Phoenician rulers' authority in this field was limited. The hunt, however, allowed the expression of dynastic skills without overriding the limited spheres of power within the Persian Achaemenid Empire.

Second, preceding cases in the area under analysis – considered in Chapter Three – have revealed that the multiple-quarry hunt did not come out of the blue, but was rooted in the older tradition of combining different species of prey; in particular, the narrative language that developed in the Cypro-Levantine area also thanks to Hellenic craftsmanship, might have played a relevant role in the elaboration of the paratactic multiple-quarry hunts, whereas the presence of hunting images on a monumental scale can be traced back to Hittite, Syro-Hittite and neo-Assyrian contexts. At the same time, it is not possible to identify any specific role of Persian imagery, which appears quite poor in this respect. This observation allows us to outline a more detailed picture than the generic characterisation of these representations as inspired by "oriental" models.[1]

Third, the combination of different species of prey in one single figurative field conveys a more structured message by juxtaposing animals with different characteristics. The analysis of these sequences – represented by different kinds of evidence – has highlighted a possible criterion in building the sequence of prey, which required different strategies and abilities in the hunters, as shown in Chapter Four.

[1] See Fornasier (2001: 235 and note 910) for the debate on the "gestreckter" and "versammelter Galopp".

Finally, the meaning of these representations is not focused only on prey, but also on the hunters; the privileged scheme of the group hunt for these representations is closely connected to the possibility of showing a well-structured organisation around the dynast. More than in other themes, multiple-quarry hunts in this context include a variety of social roles, as demonstrated in Chapter Five.

6.1. Competition

If these considerations speak about the messages conveyed by the multiple-quarry hunt and the reasons for its success, the next step is to reflect on the broader dynamics that favoured the adoption of a shared iconography in different regions in a limited time span.

The case of Straton of Sidon and Nicocles of Salamis discussed in Chapter One, seems to suggest that the quest for prestige fuelled a competitive struggle between dynasts in the Eastern Mediterranean in the fourth century BC.[2] This dynamic may be inserted into the "competitive viewpoint" that M. Weiskopf has suggested for the Persian administrative system, since it was based on the principle that "great deeds proved one worthy of post and promotion".[3]

Such a competitive dynamic among Eastern Mediterranean dynasts triggered a "horizontal" emulation, an imitative attitude aimed at equalling or outdoing the artistic achievements, such as the tombs, of the other rulers. This "horizontal" emulation was complementary to the "vertical" emulation of central Persian power by peripheral entities. This vertical emulation has a literary ground in Xenophon's passage on Cyrus the Elder's instructions on the peripheral organisation of the Persian Achaemenid Empire (Xen. *Cyr.* 8.6.10–13) and has been widely explored in recent decades. From an artistic point of view, some scholars have proposed that the *imitatio regis* in western Anatolian art is a direct link to central imperial power; in recent years this task has been extended to many fields of the material culture (e.g. the so-called Achaemenid bowls) in order to look for the "Achaemenid impact" in the peripheries.[4]

Horizontal competition, instead, would deserve more attention in order to better understand artistic and cultural dynamics, closely connected with political and military

[2] Briant 1996: 690–1. *Supra*, § 1.2.

[3] Weiskopf 1989: 14.

[4] Fornasier 2001: 234; Miller 2007; Nieswandt 2011: 323. On the "Achaemenid impact", see also Khatchadourian 2012: 964–5; Poggio 2019b. For Lycia Jacobs (1987) proposes an Anatolian horizon rather than a Near Eastern one.

events, in the western part of the Persian Achaemenid Empire. Already the monumentalisation of the Lycian Acropolis of Xanthos at the beginning of the fifth century BC has been interpreted within a competitive perspective with other western Anatolian cities.[5] This process would have taken place after the Persian Wars and this fits with those direct contacts among Eastern Mediterranean dynasts embodied by the dynasts' direct participation in the Second Persian War according to the Herodotean account I mentioned in Chapter One. The participation in the Persian fleet has been interpreted as an experience that favoured the interaction between the Phoenician cities and shared trends in the funerary context.[6] The fifth century BC appears as a crucial turning point for this competitive dynamic that was progressively consolidated, leading to the competition through monuments and images I have described in the previous chapters.[7] Moreover, the occurrence of turmoil in the first half of the fourth century BC – generally known as the "Great Satraps' Revolt" – in the western part of the Persian Empire (Diod. Sic. 15.90.2–4) may reveal an increasingly competitive strengthening of the local powers. In the last decades of the twentieth century the scholarly debate attempted to demonstrate that these were actually a series of revolts generated by the rivalries between western satraps rather than a coordinated rebellion against the Great King.[8] This horizontal concurrential process could have alternative trajectories and dynamics in comparison with the vertical one. The case of the multiple-quarry hunt shows that the *imitatio regis* might have a role only in ideological terms, whereas on an iconographic level the process appears to be entirely Eastern Mediterranean.

A good example of this long wave of competition and emulation in the coastal regions of the Eastern Mediterranean is numismatic evidence. Alongside the unvarying nature of the coins emanating from the central Persian power (Fig. 87) – four unvaried types on the obverse with the figure of the Persian king with a long beard, crenellated crown and a Persian-style tunic[9] – were local coins bearing different "dynastic portraits", from the second half of the fifth century BC, which were the signs of an increasingly structured ideology of power (Fig. 4). In particular, Anatolia stands out for coins with reference to local rulers.[10] As noted in Chapter Five, the first appearance of the "dynastic portraits" seems to have been in Lycia, where the dynasts were characterised by traditional attributes, legends with names and some individual traits; in this context an explicit reference to the central

Figure 87. Obverse of an alloy coin with the Great King drawing bow. London, British Museum 1852,1027.2. © Trustees of the British Museum.

Persian authority seems to be lacking.[11] This practice additionally had repercussions in the intervening decades in other coastal areas of the Eastern Mediterranean such as Phoenicia.[12] The spread and the small scale, allowing close observation, was no doubt a spur to competition among the different power situations within the Persian Empire.

Horizontal competition was a real engine for the cultural and artistic developments in the Eastern Mediterranean in the fifth and fourth centuries BC. "Competition" was a well-established concept in twentieth-century sociology. According to M. Weber, "a peaceful conflict is ' competition' in so far as it consists in a formally peaceful attempt to attain control over opportunities and advantages which are also desired by others".[13] The shaping of landscapes and cityscapes, the quest for prestigious material such as white marble, and the engagement of Greek and Greek-trained artists who had to deal with a set of iconographies connected to power such as the multiple-quarry hunt, all these elements fall into this competitive dynamic.

Such a climate recalls another "transitional phase", that between the end of the Republic and the beginning of the Empire in Rome in the first century BC. Here, competition in the artistic and architectural fields, fuelled by wealthy individuals such as aristocrats and freedmen, marked

[5] Draycott 2015.

[6] Martin 2017: 132 and 136; Quinn 2018: 77.

[7] For Lycia see Lucchese 2009: 77. As for the inter-satrapal competitions, see Briant 1996: 611. For the production of stone monuments as indicator of political rivalry far from urban centres in the Late Bronze Age, see Glatz and Plourde 2011.

[8] See discussion in Weiskopf 1989; Hornblower 1990; Moysey 1992; Briant 1996: 675–94, 1018–24.

[9] Briant 1996: 420–1, 959–60; Dusinberre 2000: 165; for slightly different considerations, see Carradice 1987. See also Root 1979: 116–8.

[10] Saladino 2017.

[11] For an overview of the interpretation of heads on Lycian coins, see Vismara 2005. See also § 5.2.1.

[12] See Betlyon 1982: 7 and, on the impact of Lycian coinage on Phoenician coinage, 127 note 23.

[13] Weber 1947: 132–3. See also Bourdieu 1993.

changes and innovation in Roman visual language: "The compelling need to outdo the competition led to the use of every imaginable form of pretension or novelty of design".[14]

Our dynastic tombs thus should be inserted into a sort of artistic market, generated by that atmosphere of competition among dynasts I have described; if the reasons listed at the beginning of this chapter may explain the widespread occurrence of the multiple-quarry hunt in the Eastern Mediterranean, the competition/emulation dynamic at work in this context constituted an engine of this recurring presence in dynastic figurative programmes. The multiple-quarry hunt, therefore, meets the local rulers' need of displaying their own skills and exhibiting a complex social structure; such needs are the expressions of both the vertical emulation – with the central Persian structures undoubtedly representing a reference point – and the horizontal emulation, which fuelled artistic dynamics and favoured the use of shared iconographic schemes, rooted in the Eastern Mediterranean horizon.

6.2. Spread

The multiple-quarry hunt theme can additionally be found in regions outside the geographic scope of the present study, but contemporary to or slightly later than the dynastic tombs under consideration. These are cases that demonstrate the spread and the transmediality of this iconography.

The first case is Tomb II at Vergina. Since 1977 M. Andronikos has been excavating the tombs in the Great Tumulus of Vergina, a site identified as Aegae, the ancient royal capital of Macedonia.[15] The wealth of the tombs of the Great Tumulus, alongside the identification of the site as the ancient Macedonian capital, has led scholars to support the identification of this complex as royal, attributing it to the Argead dynasty.[16] Among these graves, Tomb II displays a painted frieze depicting a multiple-quarry hunt above the entrance to the burial chamber as an architraval decoration (Fig. 86).[17] This extraordinary artistic evidence has been at the centre of scholarly debate for many reasons. Iconographic peculiarities, antiquarian details, and its similarity to evidence from the Persian Empire, such as the dynastic tombs being studied, raised many questions.[18] Moreover, the possibility of analysing this evidence against a well-known context has reinforced the investigation of the social and political values of the hunting theme.

There are at least four scenes, all with different species of prey: two deer, a boar, a lion and a bear. Scholars have proposed different readings of this sequence: on the one hand a hypothesis begins with the central boar–lion syntagma.[19] The deer and bear episodes are almost to be considered secondary; on the other hand, the deer-boar and lion-bear hunts have been read respectively as unheroic and heroic/royal hunts.[20] In light of the analysis in Chapter Four, this sequence seems to correspond to the order of many paratactic multiple-quarry hunts. In the recurring deer–boar syntagma the prey are arranged in order of difficulty, with the deer coming first. Lastly come the toughest hunts, with the lion, probably having royal significance, and a bear.

Since the Persian political centre did not elaborate bear hunting iconography, the reference model for Tomb II at Vergina has been attributed to the Homeric tradition.[21] Instead, however, this prey may invoke the dynastic context of the Eastern Mediterranean, which presented bear hunting as a specificity with respect to the figurative language of the Persian centre of power, as seen in Chapter Four.[22] Moreover, the presence of two deer in the first scene invokes the long-lasting convention that has already been mentioned for the Heroon of Trysa and the Çan Sarcophagus.[23] Obviously there are some peculiarities, such as the presence at the far right of the frieze of the man leaning forward with a net, an element missing from the corpus of monuments.[24] The inclusion of the lion hunt at Vergina could be a local element, although lion hunting scenes were also present in the Eastern Mediterranean, as has been demonstrated.

Therefore it should be considered that the Vergina hunt was the result of contacts between Macedonia and the western Persian Achaemenid Empire with consequent adaptations to the local context.[25] The scholarly debate around the iconography in Vergina also involves chronological issues. Andronikos, followed by other scholars, suggested attributing the tomb to Philip II (*ca.* 382-336 BC), but a second trend of opinion assigns it to Philip III Arrhidaeus (*ca.* 358-317 BC).[26] One of the problematic aspects of the dating, indeed, is whether Macedonian contacts with Eastern contexts should be limited to the period after the death of Alexander the Great.

[14] Zanker 1988: 17. See also the competition among cities of the Eastern Roman Empire (Campanile 2016).
[15] Andronikos 1978.
[16] Palagia 2017: 157.
[17] For some considerations on the Vergina frieze, see Tripodi 1991: 192–3; Miller 2014: 192–4. For the discussion, see Franks 2012: 116–26; Hall 2014: 97–117; D'Onofrio 2018. In general, for the role of hunting in Macedonian society, see the studies collected in Tripodi 1998. See also Palagia 2000.
[18] Tripodi 1991; Briant 1991; Prestianni Giallombardo 1991.
[19] Franks 2012: 16–17. See also Hall 2014: 111.
[20] Fornasier 2001: 221–2.
[21] Étienne 2000: 74–5. On the bear hunt scene, see also D'Onofrio 2018: 41.
[22] See § 4.3.3.
[23] See § 4.3.1.
[24] Borza and Palagia (2007: 99) propose that this hunter has captured another bear for reasons of symmetry with respect to the two deer. Fornasier (2001: 224–5), conversely, has connected this scene with a dynastic meaning. See § 4.3.2 for a hypothetical use of nets in the bear hunt in Muskar.
[25] See Briant 1991: 240–43; Fornasier 2001: 218. On Macedonia in the Eastern Mediterranean context, including also relationship with the Persian Achaemenid Empire, see now Müller *et al.* 2017.
[26] Attribution to Philip II: Andronikos (1987), and more recently Saatsoglou–Paliadeli (2004: 167–9; 2007: 52) and Adornato (2012: 264). Attribution to Philip III Arrhidaeus: Borza and Palagia 2007: 102–3; Arena 2013. For a dating after Alexander the Great: Tripodi 1991.

To answer this question it is useful to consider the historical and social framework outlined in Chapter One. First of all, personalities such as Theopompus of Chios travelled extensively: he participated in the funerary contest in honour of Mausolus, and was at the court of Philip II, from whom he received a pension.[27] As mentioned in the first chapter, Pixodarus of Caria suggested to Philip II of Macedonia that a marriage should be arranged between the Carian ruler's daughter, Ada II, and Philip's son Philip Arrhidaeus. Therefore, regardless of the identification of the owner of Tomb II at Vergina, contacts between the two shores of the Aegean must be dated to the reign of Philip II.[28]

Furthermore, the Vergina Tomb is not the only occurrence of a multiple-quarry hunt in the northern Aegean. In ancient Thrace the Alexandrovo Tomb, dating back to the late fourth to early third century BC, was discovered in a tumulus in south-eastern Bulgaria at the end of 2000. It consists of a long *dromos* and two chambers, one with a domed and painted ceiling (Fig. 88).[29] A sequence of four episodes is distributed within the circular figurative field in a paratactic arrangement, each hunting scene having a prey consisting of two boars and two deer. Thrace, previously under Persian control, was characterised by a strongly hierarchical society, much like that of the dynastic system in the Eastern Mediterranean. It is hardly surprising, therefore, that a multiple-quarry hunting example has been found in this area, almost certainly due to direct contact with the Anatolian-Persian world.[30]

These two cases, very different from a stylistic point of view, witness the impact of the multiple-quarry hunt iconography outside its probable cradle, the Eastern Mediterranean. The affected regions were in contact with the Persian Achaemenid Empire: concerning the widespread occurrence of the multiple-quarry hunt the area under analysis in the present research appears as the most immediate interface of the Persian Achaemenid world with other Aegean regions.

However, the multiple-quarry hunt remained in the imagery of the Eastern Mediterranean beyond the Persian Achaemenid period. Alongside some innovations such as the balance of war and hunt themes on the coffin, as already outlined in Chapter Two, the Alexander Sarcophagus – the last of the series of marble sarcophagi from Sidon, dated to the last quarter of the fourth century BC – testifies to the permanence of the multiple-quarry hunt alongside complementary themes such as the startled horse, in spite of the political and dynastic change determined by Alexander the Great's conquest.

It is therefore not surprising that a possible Hellenistic interpretation of the theme can be found in the Marisa Tomb with a precise link to Sidon: the tomb is attributed by an inscription to Apollophanes, head of the local Sidonian colony.[31] The main chamber of this tomb, dating back to the mid-third century BC, displayed a continuous frieze on the north and south walls with elements found on these monuments, such as a trumpet player and a hunter on horseback facing his prey with a spear according to Graeco-Persian patterns (Figs. 89).[32] The particularity of the frieze is that a series of animals both real and fantastic fills the frieze alongside the hunting scene.[33] This frieze fits with the Hellenistic desire for classification, thanks to the presence of Greek labels, and the result is an encyclopaedic representation of wildlife.[34] However, the combination of this sequence of animals with the hunting scenes, jointly with the aforementioned observations, may recall the tendency of associating real and mythological hunts in the Persian Achaemenid period. The attribution of the tomb to the head of the Sidonian colony may reveal a long-lasting memory of the hunting imagery used for the royal tombs in Sidon between the fifth and fourth centuries BC.

Further evidence of the long-lasting importance of rulers as hunters pursuing multiple quarry in the Eastern Mediterranean can be offered by Flavius Josephus' passage about Herod the Great (Joseph. *BJ* 1.429–430):

> Herod's genius was matched by his physical constitution. Always foremost in the chase, in which he distinguished himself above all by his skill in horsemanship, he on one occasion brought down forty wild beasts in a single day; for the country breeds boars and, in greater abundance, stags and wild asses. As a fighter he was irresistible; and at practice spectators were often struck with astonishment at the precision with which he threw the javelin, the unerring aim with which he bent the bow.[35]

According to Josephus, in just one day Herod had the upper hand over forty different species of prey: the killing of various animal species in a limited period of time belongs to the same ideology as our dynastic context.

In conclusion, this research has focused on a specific iconography developed during a very limited timespan (the end of the fifth – fourth century BC) and within

[27] Euseb. *Praep. evang.* 10.3.5 = *FGrH* 115 F 345. *RE* V: 2176–2223; Ferretto 1984: 11–22; Flower 1994: 11–25. On his participation in the Carian contest, see Ottone 2009: 142–5. On Theopompus and Philip II, see Santi Amantini 2011. On the chronological debate over the life of Theopompus, see Ottone 2010 and Carlucci 2013.

[28] See § 1.2. See also Briant 1991; Fornasier 2001: 218; Cohen 2010: 88–9; Adornato 2012; Franks 2012: 116–9. On contacts between the two shores of the Aegean, see Poggio 2019a.

[29] Kitov 2001. On the tomb, see also Kitov 2005; Barov *et al.* 2006; Vassileva 2010: 40–4; Todorov 2011; Miller 2014: 194–5. On mound tombs in Thracian culture, see Hoddinott 1975: 28–9.

[30] Vassileva 2010: 44.

[31] Jacobson 2007: 14–5; Erlich 2009: 62. See also Miller 2014: 195–6.

[32] See Mellink's opinion in Özgüç 1971: 30–1, 92–3; Held 2008–9. For the figure of the hunter see also the amphora from the Anatolian site of Kültepe (Ankara, Museum of Anatolian Civilisations 19072; *Anatolian Civilisations* 1983: 93, cat. B.227).

[33] For an explanatory summary table, see Erlich 2009: 82–5.

[34] For the animal-themed frieze, see Adornato 2008: 228–39.

[35] Translation from Thackeray 1967.

Figure 88. The domed ceiling of the Alexandrovo Tomb. Courtesy of K. Kitanov, NAIM – BAS, Sofia.

a defined geographic scope (the coastal regions of the Eastern Mediterranean). The compact nature of the topic offered an exemplary case study. As already mentioned, the competition fuelled within the western Persian Achaemenid Empire favoured the elaboration of the multiple-quarry hunt on a monumental scale, in particular in funerary contexts.

The success of this iconography can be detected along three interdependent trajectories. The first one is geographic, since it affected areas beyond the borders of the Persian Achaemenid Empire, such as Macedonia. The second one is chronological, since this iconography is still discernible after the end of the political framework that allowed this artistic phenomenon. Finally, the transmediality of the multiple-quarry hunt – present in sculpture, painting, glyptic, and literary texts – made this success more stable.

Rooted in the preceding period, the multiple-quarry hunt became the "political hunt" *par excellence* in the Eastern Mediterranean under Persian rule, shaping and innovating the tradition of hunting imagery in this area at the intersection of the Mediterranean world and the Near East.

Figure 89. (following page) Detail of the decoration of the Marisa Tomb. After Peters and Thiersch 1905: pl. VI.

Bibliography

ABV

J.D. Beazley, *Attic Black-Figure Vase-Painters*, Oxford, 1956.

Adams, J.N.

2003 *Bilingualism and the Latin Language*, Cambridge – New York.

Adams, J.N., Janse, M. and Swain, S. (eds.)

2002 *Bilingualism in Ancient Society: Language Contact and the Written Text*, Oxford – New York.

Adornato, G.

2008 Didascalie, disegni e zoologia sul Papiro di Artemidoro, in «Archiv für Papyrusforschung und verwandte Gebiete», 54, 224–45.

2012 Skopas alla corte macedone? Motivi stilistici skopadei tra Grecia e Macedonia, in M. Castiglione and A. Poggio (eds.), *Arte-Potere. Forme artistiche, istituzioni, paradigmi interpretativi*, Atti del convegno (Pisa, 2010), Milan, 259–72.

Akurgal, E.

1941 *Griechische Reliefs des VI. Jahrhunderts aus Lykien*, Berlin.

1986 *Neue archaische Skulpturen aus Anatolien*, in H. Kyrieleis (ed.), *Archaische und klassische griechische Plastik*, Akten des internationalen Kolloquiums (Athen, 1985), Vol. 1. *Archaische griechische Plastik*, Mainz, 1–14.

Alexiou, E.

2010 *Der Euagoras des Isokrates. Ein Kommentar* (Untersuchungen zur antiken Literatur und Geschichte; 101), Berlin – New York.

Allsen, T.T.

2006 *The Royal Hunt in Eurasian History*, Philadelphia.

Almagor, E.

2018 *Plutarch and the Persica*, Edinburgh.

Altheim-Stiehl, R., Metzler, D. and Schwertheim, E.

1983 Eine neue gräko-persische Grabstele aus Sultaniye Köy und ihre Bedeutung für die Geschichte und Topographie von Daskyleion, in «Epigraphica Anatolica», 1, 1–23.

Álvarez-Mon, J.

2010 *The Arjān Tomb. At the Crossroad of the Elamite and the Persian Empires* (Acta Iranica; 49), Leuven – Paris – Walpole, MA.

Anatolian Civilisations

1983 *The Anatolian Civilisations*, Vol. 2. *Greek, Roman, Byzantine* (exhibition catalogue), Istanbul.

Anderson, J.K.

1985 *Hunting in the Ancient World*, Berkeley – Los Angeles – London.

Andronikos, M.

1978 *The Royal Graves at Vergina*, Athens.

1987 *Vergina. The Royal Tombs and the Ancient City*, Athens.

Anguissola, A.

2018 *Supports in Roman Marble Sculpture. Workshop Practice and Modes of Viewing*, Cambridge – New York.

Apicella, C.

2010 La représentation du roi à la fin de la période achéménide à Sidon, entre modèle grec et modèle oriental, in L. Capdetrey and Y. Lafond (eds.), *La cité et ses élites. Pratiques et représentation des formes de domination et de contrôle social dans les cités grecques*, Actes du colloque (Poitiers, 2006) (Études 25), Bordeaux, 69–79.

Archi, A.

1988 Société des hommes et société des animaux, in F. Imparati (ed.), *Studi di storia e di filologia anatolica dedicati a Giovanni Pugliese Carratelli*, Florence, 25–37.

Arena, E.

2013 Alessandro IV e la tomba III del "Grande Tumulo" di Vergina: per un riesame storico, in «Athenaeum», 101, 71–101.

ARV

J.D. Beazley, *Attic Red-Figure Vase-Painters*, Oxford, 1942.

ARV^2

J.D. Beazley, *Attic Red-Figure Vase-Painters*, 3 vols, 2nd ed., Oxford, 1963.

Asheri, D.

1983 *Fra ellenismo e iranismo. Studi sulla società e cultura di Xanthos nella età achemenide*, Bologna.

Asheri, D., Lloyd, A. and Corcella, A.

2007 *A Commentary on Herodotus Books I-IV*, ed. by O. Murray and A. Moreno, with a contribution by M. Brosius, Oxford – New York.

Assmann, J.Chr.

1963 Zur Baugeschichte der Königsgruft von Sidon, in «Archäologischer Anzeiger», 690–716.

Ataç, M.-A.

2010 *The Mythology of Kingship in Neo-Assyrian Art*, Cambridge – New York.

Atallah, W.

1966 *Adonis dans la littérature et l'art grecs*, Paris.

Aymard, J.

1951 *Essai sur les chasses romaines des origines à la fin du siècle des Antonins* (Cynegetica), Paris.

Babelon, E.

1910 *Traité des monnaies grecques et romaines*, Vol. 2.II, Paris.

BAdd^2

T.H. Carpenter, Beazley Addenda: Additional References to ABV, ARV^2 & Paralipomena, 2nd ed., Oxford, 1989.

Bahrani, Z., Çelik, Z. and Eldem, E. (eds.)

2011 *Scramble for the Past: a Story of Archaeology in the Ottoman Empire, 1753-1914* (exhibition catalogue), Istanbul.

Barberi Squarotti, G., Colturato, A. and Goria, C. (eds.)

2018 *Il mito di Diana nella cultura delle corti: arte, letteratura, musica* (Centro Studi delle Residenze Reali Sabaude. La civiltà delle corti; 2), Florence.

Bardelli, G.

2012 Lumi vulcenti. Riflessioni sullo stile pittorico della Tomba François, in M. Harari and S. Paltineri (eds.), *Segni e colore. Dialoghi sulla pittura tardoclassica ed ellenistica*, Atti del Convegno (Pavia, 2012), Rome, 129–34.

Barnard, A. (ed.)

2004 *Hunter-Gatherers in History, Archaeology and Anthropology*, Oxford – New York.

Barnett, R.D.

1976 *Sculptures from the North Palace of Ashurbanipal at Nineveh* (668–627 B.C.), London.

Barov, Z. *et al.*

2006 The Preservation and Display of a Fourth-Century BCE Painted Thracian Tomb in Bulgaria, in D. Saunders, J.H. Townsend and S. Woodcock (eds.), *The Object in Context: Crossing Conservation Boundaries*, (Studies in Conservation 51. Suppl.; 2), London, 211–6.

Barringer, J.M.

1995 *Divine Escorts. Nereids in Archaic and Classical Greek Art*, Ann Arbor.

2001 *The Hunt in Ancient Greece*, Baltimore – London.

2008 *Art, Myth, and Ritual in Classical Greece*, New York.

Baughan, E.P.

2002–4 Rev. Dusinberre 2003, in «Journal of Field Archaeology», 29, 1/2, 225–8.

2011 Sculpted Symposiasts of Ionia, in «American Journal of Archaeology», 115, 19–53.

2013 *Couched in Death: Klinai and Identity in Anatolia and Beyond*, Madison.

Baxandall, M.

1980 *The Limewood Sculptors of Renaissance Germany*, New Haven – London.

Beck, C.

2000 Chasses et équipages de chasse en Bourgogne ducale (vers 1360-1420), in A. Paravicini Bagliani and B. Van den Abeele (eds.), *La Chasse au Moyen Âge: Société, traités, symboles*, Florence, 151–74.

Benda-Weber, I.

2005 *Lykier und Karer: zwei autochthone Ethnien Kleinasiens zwischen Orient und Okzident* (Asia Minor Studien; 56), Bonn.

Benndorf, O. and Niemann, G.

1889 *Das Heroon von Gjölbaschi-Trysa*, Vienna.

Bérard, C.

1988 La Grèce en barbarie. L'apostrophe et le bon usage des mythes, in C. Calame (ed.), *Métamorphoses du mythe en Grèce antique*, Geneva, 187–99.

Bernard, P.

1965 Remarques sur le décor sculpté d'un édifice de Xanthos, in «Syria», 42, 261–88.

Berthon, R.

2017 Herding for the Kingdom, Herding for the Empire. The Contribution of Zooarchaeology to the Knowledge of Hittite Economy, in A. Schachner (ed.), *Innovation versus Beharrung: Was macht den Unterschied des hethitischen Reichs im Anatolien des 2. Jahrtausends v. Ch.?*, Internationaler Workshop zu Ehren von Jürgen Seeher (Istanbul, 2014) (Byzas; 23), Istanbul, 175–84.

Betlyon, J.W.

1982 *The Coinage and Mints of Phoenicia. The Pre-Alexandrine Period* (Harvard Semitic Monographs; 26), Chico.

Bevilacqua, F. (ed.)

2002 *Anabasi di Senofonte*, Turin.

Bianchi Bandinelli, R.

1939 *Clusium*, 1. *Le pitture delle tombe arcaiche* (Monumenti della pittura antica scoperti in Italia. Sezione prima: La pittura etrusca), Rome.

Bienkowski, P. and Millard, A. (eds.)

2000 *Dictionary of the Ancient Near East*, London.

Biffi, N. (ed., transl. and comm.)

2005 *L'Estremo Oriente di Strabone. Libro XV della Geografia. Introduzione, traduzione e commento* (Quaderni di «Invigilata Lucernis»; 26), S. Spirito.

Bittel, K.

1976 *Die Hethiter: Die Kunst Anatoliens vom Ende des 3. bis zum Anfang des 1. Jahrtausends vor Chr.*, Munich.

Blanchard, V. (ed.)

2019a *Royaumes oubliés. De l'Empire Hittite aux Araméens* (exhibition catalogue), Paris.

Blanchard, V.

2019b L'art des royaumes néo-hittites et araméens, in V. Blanchard (ed.), *Royaumes oubliés. De l'Empire Hittite aux Araméens* (exhibition catalogue), Paris, 133–45.

Blanck, H.

1982 Die Malereien des sogenannten Priester-Sarkophages in Tarquinia, in H. Blanck and S. Steingräber (eds.), *Miscellanea Archaeologica Tobias Dohrn dedicata* (Archaeologica; 26), Rome, 11–28.

Blümel, C.

1969 *Greek Sculptors at Work*, 2nd ed., London (Transl. of: *Griechische Bildhauerarbeit*, Berlin – Leipzig, 1927).

Boardman, J.

1970a Pyramidal Stamp Seals in the Persian Empire, in «Iran», 8, 19–45.

1970b *Greek Gems and Finger Rings. Early Bronze Age to Late Classical*, London.

1995 *Greek Sculpture. The Late Classical Period and Sculpture in Colonies and Overseas. A Handbook*, London.

2000 *Persia and the West. An Archaeological Investigation of the Genesis of Achaemenid Art*, London.

Boffo, L.

2008 L'Asia Minore tra Greci e Persiani, in M. Giangiulio (ed.), *Storia d'Europa e del Mediterraneo*, Vol. 4, Rome, 41–68.

Bökönyi, S.

1993 Hunting in Arslantepe, Anatolia, in M. Frangipane *et al.* (eds.), *Between the Rivers and over the Mountains. Archaeologica Anatolica et Mesopotamica Alba Palmieri Dedicata*, Rome, 341–59.

Bonatz, D.

2000 *Das syro-hethitische Grabdenkmal. Untersuchungen zur Entstehung einer neuen Bildgattung in der Eisenzeit im nordsyrisch-südostanatolischen Raum*, Mainz.

Borchhardt, J.

1968 Epichorische, gräko-persisch beeinflußte Reliefs in Kilikien, in «Istanbuler Mitteilungen», 18, 161–211.

1976 *Die Bauskulptur des Heroons von Limyra. Das Grabmal des lykischen Königs Perikles* (Istanbuler Forschungen; 32), Berlin.

1983 Limyra, in «Antike Welt», 14.2, 59.

1985 Die Dependenztheorie, erläutert an der Tumba des Grafen Niclas zu Salm, in *Lebendige Altertumswissenschaft. Festgabe zur Vollendung des 70. Lebensjahres von Hermann Vetters dargebracht von Freunden, Schülern und Kollegen*, Vienna, 357–361.

1993 Zum Ostfries des Heroons von Zemuri/Limyra, in «Istanbuler Mitteilungen», 43, 351–9.

1996–7 Zur Politik der Dynasten Trbbênimi und Perikle von Zêmuri, in «Lykia», 3, 1–23.

Borchhardt, J. and Bleibtreu, E.

2007 Der Sonnenschirm als Zeichen der Herrschaft, in E. Christof *et al.* (eds.), *Πότνια Θηρών: Festschrift für Gerda Schwarz zum 65. Geburtstag* (Veröffentlichungen des Instituts für Archäologie der Karl-Franzens-Universität Graz; 8), Vienna, 29–67.

2008 Wildschweinjagd zwischen Ost und West, in E. Winter (ed.), *Vom Euphrat bis zum Bosporus. Kleinasien in der Antike. Festschrift für Elmar Schwertheim zum 65. Geburtstag* (Asia Minor Studien; 65), Vol. 1, Bonn, 61–101.

Bordenache Battaglia, G. and Emiliozzi, A.

1990 *Le ciste prenestine*, Vol. 1.2, Rome.

Börker-Klähn, J.

1982 *Altvorderasiatische Bildstelen und vergleichbare Felsreliefs, Mit einem Beitrag von Adelheid Shunnar-Misera* (Baghdader Forschungen; 4), Mainz.

Borza, E.N. and Palagia, O.

2007 The Chronology of the Macedonian Royal Tombs at Vergina, in «Jahrbuch des Deutschen Archäologischen Instituts», 122, 81–125.

Bossert, H.Th.

1950 Reisen in Kilikien, in «Orientalia», 19, 122–5.

Boucharlat, R.

2015 Rev. Dusinberre 2013, in «Topoi», 20, 507–10.

Bourdieu, P.

1993 *The Field of Cultural Production: Essays on Art and Literature*, New York.

Bousquet, J.

1975 Arbinas, fils de Gergis, dynaste de Xanthos, in «Comptes rendus des séances de l'Académie des Inscriptions et Belles-Lettres», 138–50.

Brecoulaki, H.

2006 *La peinture funéraire de Macédoine. Emplois et fonctions de la couleur. IVe-IIe s. av. J.-C.* (Meletemata; 48), Athens.

Brereton, G.

2018 I am Ashurbanipal, King of the World, King of Assyria, in G. Brereton (ed.), *I am Ashurbanipal: King of the World, King of Assyria* (exhibition catalogue), London, 10–9.

Briant, P.

1982 *Rois, tributs et paysans. Études sur les formations tributaires du Moyen-Orient ancien* (Centre de Recherches d'Histoire Ancienne; 43), Paris.

1985 Dons de terres et de villes: l'Asie Mineure dans le contexte achéménide, in «Révue des Études Anciennes», 87, 53–72.

1987 *Pouvoir central et polycentrisme culturel dans l'Empire Achéménide. Quelques réflexions et suggestions*, in H. Sancisi-Weerdenburg (ed.), *Sources, Structures and Synthesis*, Proceedings of the workshop (Groningen, 1983) (Achaemenid History; 1), Leiden, 1–31.

1988 Le nomadisme du Grand Roi, in «Iranica Antiqua» 23, 253–73.

1989 Table du roi, tribut et redistribution chez les Achéménides, in P. Briant and C. Herrenschmidt (eds.), *Le tribut dans l'Empire Perse*, Actes de la table ronde (Paris, 1986) (Travaux de l'Institut d'Études Iraniennes de l'Université de la Sorbonne Nouvelle; 13), Paris, 35–44.

1991 Chasses royales macédoniennes et chasses royales perses: le thème de la chasse au lion sur "La chasse de Vergina", in «Dialogues d'histoire ancienne», 17, 1, 211–55.

1996 *Histoire de l'empire perse. De Cyrus à Alexandre*, Paris.

1998 Cités et satrapies dans l'Empire achéménide: Xanthos et Pixôdaros, in «Comptes rendus des séances de l'Académie des Inscriptions et Belles-Lettres», 305–47.

2000 *Leçon inaugurale, Collège de France*, published online at https://www.college-de-france.fr/media/pierre-briant/UPL24864_UPL51738_LI.Briant_1_.pdf [28 October 2018].

2003 *Darius dans l'ombre d'Alexandre*, Paris.

Briant, P. and Boucharlat, R.

2005 Introduction, in P. Briant and R. Boucharlat (eds.), *L'archéologie de l'empire achéménide: nouvelles recherches* (Persika; 6), Paris, 17–25.

Brixhe, C.

2004 Corpus des inscriptions paléo-phrygiennes. Supplément II, in «Kadmos», 43, 1–130.

Brosius, M.

2007 New Out of Old? Court and Court Ceremonies in Achaemenid Persia, in A.J.S. Spawforth (ed.), *The Court and Court Society in Ancient Monarchies*, Cambridge – New York, 17–57.

Brownson, C.L. (ed. and transl.)

1961 *Xenophon. Hellenica, Books VI & VII. Anabasis, Books I-III.* Cambridge, MA – London (Reprint. Original edition: 1921).

Bruns-Özgan, Chr.

1987 *Lykische Grabreliefs des 5. und 4. Jahrhunderts v. Chr.* (Istanbuler Mitteilungen. Beiheft; 33), Tübingen.

Bryce, T.

2002 *Life and Society in the Hittite World*, Oxford – New York.

2012 *The World of the Neo-Hittite Kingdoms: A Political and Military History*, Oxford.

Bryce, T.R. and Zahle, J.

1986 *The Lycians in Literary and Epigraphic Sources*, Vol. 1. *A Study of Lycian History and Civilisation to the Conquest of Alexander the Great I-II*, Copenhagen.

Buchanan, B.

1966 *Catalogue of Ancient Near Eastern Seals in the Ashmolean Museum*, Vol. 1, Oxford.

Buchholz, H.-G., Jöhrens, G. and Maull, I.

1973 *Jagd und Fischfang* (Archaeologia Homerica; 2, Kapitel J), Göttingen.

Buranelli, F. (ed.)

1987 *La Tomba François di Vulci* (exhibition catalogue), Rome.

Burgin, J.

2011 A Geographical Note on the Xanthos Stele, in «Kadmos», 49, 181–6.

Bury, R.G. (ed. and transl.)

1968 *Plato*, Vol. 11. *Laws*, 2. *Books VII-XII.* London – Cambridge, MA (Reprint. Original edition: 1926).

Calcani, G.

1996–7 I tondi adrianei e l'Arco di Costantino, in «Rivista dell'Istituto Nazionale di Archeologia e Storia dell'Arte», s. III, 19-20, 175–201.

2000 I Tondi dell'Arco: Adriano e Costantino, in *Adriano. Architettura e progetto* (exhibition catalogue), Milan, 137–47.

Caliò, L.M.

2006 Rev. Zahle and Kjeldsen 2004, in «Archeologia Classica», 57, 594–6.

2007–8 Tombe e culto dinastico nelle città carie, in G. Bartoloni and M.G. Benedettini (eds.), *Sepolti tra i vivi / Buried Among the Living: Evidenza ed interpretazione di contesti funerari in abitato*, Atti del Convegno (Rome, 2006), in «Scienze dell'Antichità», 14, 497–535.

Caliò, L.M. and Interdonato, E.

2005 *Theatri curvaturae similis*. Note sull'urbanistica delle città a forma di teatro, in «Archeologia Classica», 56, 49–130.

Çambel, H. and Özyar, A.

2003 *Karatepe – Aslantaş. Azatiwataya. Die Bildwerke*, Mainz.

Campanile, D.

2016 Stoicismo e propensione evergetica in età romana, in «Mediterraneo Antico », 19, 1-2, 145–56.

Camporeale, G.

1991 Eroi e signori nelle prime scene narrative etrusche, in «Mélanges de l'École française de Rome. Antiquité», 103, 57–69.

Capdetrey, L.

2013 La "Table du Roi": une institution hellénistique?, in C. Grandjean, C. Hugoniot and B. Lion (eds.), *Le banquet du monarque dans le monde antique*, Tours – Rennes, 173–98.

Carena, C., Manfredini, M. and Piccirilli, L. (ed., transl. and comm.)

1983 *Plutarco. Le Vite di Temistocle e Camillo*, Milan.

Carlucci, G.

2013 Vita di Teopompo di Chio. Una ipotesi di ricostruzione, in L. Canfora and R. Otranto (eds.), *Teopompo. Elleniche, libro II. PSI 1304*, Bari, 7–24.

Carradice, I.

1987 The "Regal" Coinage of the Persian Empire, in I. Carradice (ed.), *Coinage and Administration in the Athenian and Persian Empires*, Symposium (Oxford, 1986) (BAR International Series; 343), Oxford, 73–108.

Carroll, M.

2003 *Earthly Paradises. Ancient Gardens in History and Archaeology*, London.

Carstens, A.M.

2006 Cultural Contact and Cultural Change: Colonialism and Empire, in T. Bekker-Nielsen (ed.), *Rome and the Black Sea Region. Domination, Romanisation, Resistance* (Black Sea Studies; 5), Aarhus, 119–31.

2009 *Karia and the Hekatomnids. The Creation of a Dynasty* (BAR International Series; 1943), Oxford.

Casabonne, O.

1996 Notes Ciliciennes, in «Anatolia Antiqua», 4, 111–9.

1999 Local Powers and Persian Model in Achaemenid Cilicia: a Reassessment, in S. Durugönül and M. Durukan (eds.), *I. Uluslararası Kilikia Arkeolojisi Sempozyumu Bildirileri* (Mersin, 1998), Vol. 1, in «Olba», 2, 57–66.

2000 Notes Ciliciennes, in «Anatolia Antiqua», 8, 89–103.

2004 *La Cilicie à l'époque achéménide* (Persika; 3), Paris.

Cassin, E.

1981 Le roi et le lion, in «Revue de l'histoire des religions», 198, 355–401. (= *Le semblable et le différent. Symbolismes du pouvoir dans le Proche-Orient ancien*, Paris, 1987, 167–213).

Càssola, F. (ed., transl. and comm.)

1991 *Inni omerici*, Milan (Reprint. Original edition: 1975).

Catoni, M.L.

2008 *La comunicazione non verbale nella Grecia antica. Gli schemata nella danza, nell'arte, nella vita*, Turin.

2010 *Bere vino puro. Immagini del simposio*, Milan.

Cau, N.

1999 La spedizione di Melesandro in Licia nel racconto della Stele di Xanthos (TL 44a, 34 ss.): un tentativo di interpretazione, in B. Virgilio (ed.), *Studi Ellenistici XII*, Pisa – Rome, 19–40.

2003 Note sulla Stele di Xanthos: TL 44b, 11-23 e 47-57, in «Kadmos», 42, 50–64.

Caubet, A. (ed.)

1995 *Khorsabad, le palais de Sargon II, roi d'Assyrie*, Actes du colloque (Paris, 1994), Paris.

Ceccarelli, P.

1996 La struttura dell'epigramma del Pilastro Iscritto di Xanthos (TAM I 44 = CEG 177), in A. Dell'Era and A. Russi (eds.), *Vir bonus docendi peritus. Omaggio dell'Università dell'Aquila a Giovanni Garuti*, Foggia, 47–69.

Chamoux, F.

1958 *Observations sur la survivance des thèmes helléniques dans la sculpture provençale*, in *Actes du colloque sur les influences helléniques en Gaule (Dijon, 1957)*, Dijon, 31–41.

Childs, W.A.P.

1973a Prolegomena to a Lycian Chronology: the Nereid Monument from Xanthos, in «Opuscula Romana», 9, 105–16.

1973b The Date of the Heroon from Gölbaşi-Trysa, in «American Journal of Archaeology», 77, 210.

1976 Prolegomena to a Lycian Chronology, II: the Heroon from Trysa, in «Revue Archéologique», 281–316.

1978 *The City-Reliefs of Lycia* (Princeton Monographs in Art and Archaeology; 42), Princeton.

1991 Rev. Jacobs 1987, in «Gnomon», 63, 244–7.

Childs, W.A.P. and Demargne, P.

1989 *Le monument des Néréides. Le décor sculpté* (Fouilles de Xanthos; 8), Paris.

Cholidis, N. and Martin, L. (eds.)

2010 *Tell Halaf. Im Krieg zerstörte Denkmäler und ihre Restaurierung. Für die Max Freiherr von Oppenheim-Stiftung und das Vorderasiatische Museum der Staatlichen Museen zu Berlin* (Tell Halaf; 5), Berlin – New York.

Cianferoni, G.C., Iozzo, M. and Setari, E. (eds.)

2012 *Myth, Allegory, Emblem. The Many Lives of the Chimaera of Arezzo*, Proceedings of the International Colloquium (Malibu, 2009), Rome.

Cohen, A.

2010 *Art in the Era of Alexander the Great. Paradigms of Manhood and Their Cultural Traditions*, New York.

Colas-Rannou, F.

2009 Images et société en Lycie au VIe siècle avant J.-C.: le pilier d'Isinda et son progamme iconographique, in «Revue des Études Anciennes», 111, 453–74.

Colburn, H.P.

2013 Connectivity and Communication in the Achaemenid Empire, in «Journal of the Economic and Social History of the Orient», 56, 29–52.

Cook, B.F.

2005 *Relief Sculpture of the Mausoleum at Halicarnassus*, with contributions by B. Ashmole and D. Strong (Oxford Monographs on Classical Archaeology), Oxford.

Cook, J.M.

1983 *The Persian Empire*, London – Melbourne – Toronto.

Corso, A.

2019 The Masters of the Mausoleum of Halicarnassus, in «Quaderni ticinesi. Numismatica e antichità classiche», 48, 45–62.

Coupel, P. and Demargne, P.

1969 *Le monument des Néréides. L'architecture* (Fouilles de Xanthos; 3), Paris.

Cremer, M.

1984 Zwei neue graeco-persische Stelen, in «Epigraphica Anatolica», 3, 87–100.

Crepon, P.

1981 Le thème du cerf dans l'iconographie anatolienne des origines à l'époque hittite, in *Hethitica IV* (Bibliothèque des Cahiers de l'Institut de Linguistique de Louvain; 21), Louvain-la-Neuve, 117–55.

Crivello, F.

2004 L'immagine ripetuta: filiazione e creazione nell'arte del Medioevo, in E. Castelnuovo and G. Sergi (eds.), *Arti e storia nel Medioevo*, Vol. 3. *Del vedere: pubblici, forme e funzioni*, Turin, 567–92.

Curtis, J.

2012 *The Oxus Treasure*, London.

2013 *An Examination of Late Assyrian Metalwork with Special Reference to Nimrud*, With an Appendix on Scientific Analysis by Matthew J. Ponting, Oxford – Oakville.

Curtis, J.E. and Tallis, N.

2008 The Arrangement of the Bands and Content Matter, in J.E. Curtis and N. Tallis (eds.), *The Balawat Gates of Ashurnasirpal II*, London, 26–9.

CVA

Corpus Vasorum Antiquorum.

Czichon, R.M.

1992 *Die Gestaltungsprinzipien der neuassyrischen Flachbildkunst und ihre Entwicklung vom 9. zum 7. Jahrhundert v. Chr.* (Münchener Universitäts-Schriften. Philosophische Fakultät; 12. Münchener vorderasiatische Studien; 13), Munich – Vienna.

1995 Zur Komposition der Taprammi-Schale, in «Istanbuler Mitteilungen», 45, 5–12.

DaCosta Kaufmann, T., Dossin, C. and Joyeux-Prunel, B. (eds.)

2016 *Circulations in the Global History of Art* (Studies in Art Historiography), London – New York.

Dalton, O.M.

1964 *The Treasure of the Oxus: With Other Examples of Early Oriental Metal-Work*, London.

Daltrop, G.

1966 *Die Kalydonische Jagd in der Antike* (Die Jagd in der Kunst), Hamburg – Berlin.

1969 *Die Jagdmosaiken der römischen Villa bei Piazza Armerina* (Die Jagd in der Kunst), Hamburg – Berlin.

Dandamayev, M.A.

2012 *Magi*, published online at http://www.iranicaonline.org/articles/magi [15 July 2019].

Davesne, A.

1998 *Les reliefs perses*, in A. Davesne and F. Laroche-Traunecker, *Gülnar I. Le site de Meydancıkkale:*

Recherches entreprises sous la direction d'Emmanuel Laroche (1971-1982), Paris, 293–306.

Davesne, A. and Laroche-Traunecker, F.

1998 *Gülnar I. Le site de Meydancıkkale: Recherches entreprises sous la direction d'Emmanuel Laroche (1971-1982)*, Paris.

Davies, L.G. *et al.*

2008 Description of the Palace Gates, in J.E. Curtis and N. Tallis (eds.), *The Balawat Gates of Ashurnasirpal II*, London, 30–45.

De Angelis, F.

1996 La battaglia di Maratona nella Stoa Poikile, in «Annali della Scuola Normale Superiore di Pisa. Classe di Lettere e Filosofia», s. IV, 1, 119–71.

Delaporte, L.

1923 *Catalogue des cylindres, cachets et pierres gravées de style oriental*, Vol. 2. *Acquisitions*, Paris.

1940 *Malatya. Fouilles de la mission archéologique française dirigées par M. Louis Delaporte. Arslantepe*, Vol. 1. *La Porte des Lions* (Mémoires de l'Istitut Français d'Archéologie de Stamboul; 5), Paris.

Delivorrias, A.

2009 The Throne of Apollo at the Amyklaion: Old Proposals, New Perspectives, in W.G. Cavanagh, C. Gallou and M. Georgiadis (eds.), *Sparta and Laconia: From Prehistory to Pre-Modern*, Proceedings of the Conference (Sparta, 2005), London, 133–5.

Deltour-Levie, C.

1982 *Les piliers funéraires de Lycie*, Louvain-la-Neuve.

Demargne, P.

1958 *Les piliers funéraires* (Fouilles de Xanthos; 1), Paris.

1962 À propos d'un sarcophage de Xanthos. Essai de reconstitution et d'interprétation, in «Revue des Études Anciennes», 64, 35–42.

1974 Profil et frontalité au sarcophage de Payava (Xanthos de Lycie), in *Mansel'e Armağan / Mélanges Mansel*, Vol. 1, Ankara, 527–35.

1983 Serviteurs orientaux sur deux monuments funéraires de Xanthos, in R. M. Boehmer and H. Hauptmann (eds.), *Beiträge zur Altertumskunde Kleinasiens. Festschrift für Kurt Bittel*, Mainz, 167–70.

Demargne, P. and Laroche, E.

1974 *Tombes-maisons, tombes rupestres et sarcophages. Les épitaphes lyciennes* (Fouilles de Xanthos; 5), Paris.

De Mérode, R. and Damblon-Willemaers, N.

1983 Essai sur l'iconographie des cervides chez les Hittites, in R. Donceel and R. Lebrun (eds.), *Archéologie et religions de l'Anatolie ancienne. Mélanges en l'honneur du Professeur Paul Naster*, Louvain-la-Neuve, 173–86.

Dentzer, J.-M.

1982 *Le motif du banquet couché dans le Proche-Orient et le monde grec du VIIe au IVe siècle avant J.-C.*, Rome.

D'Ercole, M.C.

2009 Arimaspes et griffons, de la Mer Noire à l'Adriatique via Athènes, in «Mètis», n.s., 7, 203–25.

Des Courtils, J.

2003 *The Guide to Xanthos and Letoon* (Ancient Cities of Anatolia; 4), Istanbul.

2007 Nouvelles découvertes à Xanthos, in «Revue Archéologique», 159–61.

2012 Xanthos: état des questions, in M. Seyer, (ed.), *40 Jahre Grabung Limyra*, Akten des internationalen Symposions (Wien, 2009) (Forschungen in Limyra; 6), Vienna, 155–62.

Di Paolo, S.

2009 What Production Model can be Deduced for First-Millennium BC Syro-Phoenician Ivories?, in S.M. Cecchini *et al.* (eds.), *Syrian and Phoenician Ivories of the Early First Millennium BCE: Chronology, Regional Styles and Iconographic Repertories, Patterns of Inter-Regional Distribution*, Acts of the International Workshop (Pisa, 2004), Pisa, 133–53.

Dolce, R.

2018 *"Losing One's Head" in the Ancient Near East. Interpretation and Meaning of Decapitation*, London – New York.

Domingo Gygax, M.

2001 *Untersuchungen zu den lykischen Gemeinwesen in klassischer und hellenistischer Zeit* (Antiquitas: Reihe 1, Abhandlungen zur alten Geschichte; 49), Bonn.

Domingo Gygax, M. and Tietz, W.

2005 "He who of all mankind set up the most numerous trophies to Zeus". The Inscribed Pillar of Xanthos Reconsidered, in «Anatolian Studies», 55, 89–98.

Donner, H. and Röllig, W.

1973 *Kanaanäische und aramäische Inschriften*, Vol. 2. *Kommentar*, 3rd ed., Wiesbaden.

Dönmez, A. and Schürr, D.

2015 Zum Agora-Pfeiler in Xanthos IV. Finding a new fragment of the inscription and evidence pointing to a temenos tomb, in «Kadmos», 54, 119–49.

D'Onofrio, A.M.

2018 La metafora della caccia nel fregio della Tomba II del Grande Tumulo di Vergina: dalla *hybris* dei Persiani alla *andragathia* dei re macedoni, in «Ostraka», 27, 35–48.

Draycott, C.M.

2007 Dynastic Definitions: Differentiating Status Claims in the Archaic Pillar Tomb Reliefs of Lycia, in A. Çilingiroğlu and A. Sagona (eds.), *Anatolian Iron Ages 6*, Proceedings of the Colloquium (Eskişehir, 2004) (Ancient Near Eastern Studies. Suppl.; 20), Leuven – Paris – Dudley, MA, 103–34.

2010 What Does "Being 'Graeco-Persian'" Mean? An Introduction to the Papers, in «Bollettino di Archeologia On Line», published online at http://bollettinodiarcheologiaonline.beniculturali.it/edizione-speciale-congresso-di-archeologia-a-i-a-c-2008/ [3 December 2019].

2011 Funerary or Military Convoy? Thoughts on the Tatarlı Convoy Painting and Meanings of 'Greco-Persian' Convoys, in L. Summerer, A. Ivantchik and A. von Kienlin (eds.), *Kelainai – Apameia Kibotos: Développement urbain dans le contexte anatolien / Stadtentwicklung im anatolischen Kontext*, Actes du colloque international / Akten des internationalen Kolloquiums (Munich, 2009) (Kelainai; 1), Bordeaux, 55–61.

2014 Rev. Dusinberre 2013, in «American Journal of Archaeology», 118.3, published online at www.ajaonline.org/online-review-book/1836 [15 July 2019].

2015 'Heroa' and the city. Kuprlli's new architecture and the making of the 'Lycian acropolis' of Xanthus in the early Classical period, in «Anatolian Studies», 65, 97–142.

2016 Drinking to Death: the 'Totenmahl', Drinking Culture and Funerary Representation in Late Archaic and Achaemenid Western Anatolia, in C.M. Draycott and M. Stamatopoulou (eds.), *Dining and Death: Interdisciplinary Perspectives on the 'Funerary Banquet' in Ancient Art, Burial and Belief* (Colloquia Antiqua; 16), Leuven – Paris – Bristol, CT, 219–98.

Duindam, J.

2011 Royal Courts in Dynastic States and Empires, in Duindam, J., Artan, T., and Kunt, M. (eds.), *Royal Courts in Dynastic States and Empires. A Global Perspective*, Leiden – Boston, 1–23.

Duindam, J., Artan, T., and Kunt, M. (eds.)

2011 *Royal Courts in Dynastic States and Empires. A Global Perspective*, Leiden – Boston.

Dupont-Sommer, A.

1950 Deux nouvelles inscriptions sémitiques trouvées en Cilicie, in «Jahrbuch für Kleinasiatische Forschung», 1, 43–7.

Durand, J.-L. and Schnapp, A.

1984 Boucherie sacrificielle et chasses initiatiques, in *La Cité des images. Religion et société en Grèce antique* (exhibition catalogue), Paris, 49–66.

Dusinberre, E.R.M.

1999 Satrapal Sardis: Achaemenid Bowls in an Achaemenid Capital, in «American Journal of Archaeology», 103, 73–102.

2000 King or God? Imperial Iconography and The "Tiarate Head" Coins of Achaemenid Anatolia, in D.C. Hopkins (ed.), *Across the Anatolian Plateau. Readings in the Archaeology of Ancient Turkey* (The Annual of the American Schools of Oriental Research; 57), Boston, 157–71.

2003 *Aspects of Empire in Achaemenid Sardis*, Cambridge – New York.

2013 *Empire, Authority, and Autonomy in Achaemenid Anatolia*, Cambridge – New York.

EAA

Enciclopedia dell'Arte Antica Classica e Orientale, 7 vols, Rome, 1958–66.

Ebbinghaus, S. (ed.)

2018 *Animal-Shaped Vessels from the Ancient World. Feasting with Gods, Heroes, and Kings* (exhibition catalogue), Cambridge, MA.

Ebbinghaus, S.

2000 A Banquet at Xanthos. Seven Rhyta on the Northern Cella Frieze of the "Nereid" Monument, in G.R. Tsetskhladze, A.J.N.W. Prag and A.M. Snodgrass (eds.), *Periplous. Papers on Classical Art and Archaeology Presented to Sir John Boardman*, London, 99–109.

Eco, U.

2009 *Vertigine della lista*, Milan.

Ehelolf, H.

1938 *Texte verschiedenen Inhalts: vorwiegend aus den Grabungen seit 1931* (Keilschrifturkunden aus Boghazköi; 29), Vol. 1, Berlin.

Eichinger, W.

2005 *Der Bär und seine Darstellung in der Antike* (Antiquitates. Archäologische Forschungsergebnisse; 32), Hamburg.

Eichler, F.

1950 *Die Reliefs des Heroon von Gjölbaschi-Trysa*, Vienna.

Elayi, J.

1987 *Recherches sur les cités phéniciennes à l'époque perse* (AION. Supplemento; 51), Naples.

1988 Les sarcophages phéniciens d'époque perse, in «Iranica Antiqua», 23, 275-322.

Elias, N.

1983 *The Court Society*, New York (Transl. of: *Die höfische Gesellschaft*, Darmstadt – Neuwied, 1969).

Elsner, J.

1995 *Art and the Roman Viewer. The Transformation of Art from the Pagan World to Christianity*, Cambridge – New York.

Emre, K.

2002 Felsreliefs, Stelen, Orthostaten. Großplastik als monumentale Form staatlicher und religiöser Repräsentation, in *Die Hethiter und ihr Reich. Das Volk der 1000 Götter* (exhibition catalogue), Stuttgart, 218–33.

Emre, K. and Çınaroğlu, A.

1993 A Group of Metal Hittite Vessels from Kınık - Kastamonu, in M.J. Mellink, E. Porada and T. Özgüç (eds.), *Aspects of Art and Iconography: Anatolia and its Neighbors. Studies in Honor of Nimet Özgüç / Nimet Özgüç'e Armağan*, Ankara, 675–713.

Erlich, A.

2009 *The Art of Hellenistic Palestine* (BAR International Series; 2010), Oxford.

Erskine, A., Llewellyn-Jones, L., and Wallace, S. (eds.)

2017 *The Hellenistic Court. Monarchic Power and Elite Society from Alexander to Cleopatra*, Swansea.

Étienne, R.

2000 La chasse à l'ours, in A. Avram and M. Babeş (eds.), *Civilisation grecque et cultures antiques périphériques. Hommage à Petre Alexandrescu à son 70e anniversaire*, Bucharest, 68–75.

Fabricius, J.

1999 *Die hellenistischen Totenmahlreliefs. Grabrepräsentation und Wertvorstellungen in ostgriechischen Städten* (Studien zur antiken Stadt; 3), Munich.

Facella, M.

2018 Epigramma della "Stele di Xanthos", in «Axon», 2.1, 91–8, published online at https://edizionicafoscari.unive.it/media/pdf/article/axon/2018/1/art-10.14277-2532-6848-2018-001-01_bgamv4r.pdf [16 December 2019].

Fairbanks, A. (ed. and transl.)

1960 *Philostratus. Imagines. Callistratus. Descriptions*, London – Cambridge, MA (Reprint. Original edition: 1931).

Faust, S.

2011 Original und Spolie. Interaktive Strategien im Bildprogramm des Kostantinsbogens, in «Mitteilungen des Deutschen Archäologischen Instituts. Römische Abteilung», 117, 377–408.

Faustoferri, A.

1996 *Il trono di Amyklai e Sparta. Bathykles al servizio del potere* (Aucnus; 2), Naples.

Fauth, W.

1979 Der königliche Gärtner und Jäger im Paradeisos. Beobachtungen zur Rolle des Herrschers in der vorderasiatischen Hortikultur, in «Persica», 8, 1–53.

Fedak, J.

1990 *Monumental Tombs of the Hellenistic Age: a Study of Selected Tombs from the Pre-Classical to the Early Imperial Era* (Phoenix. Supplementary volume = Phoenix. Tome supplémentaire; 27), Toronto – Buffalo – London.

Fehr, B.

1971 *Orientalische und griechische Gelage* (*Abhandlungen* zur Kunst-, Musik- und Literaturwissenschaft; 94), Bonn.

Feldman, M.H.

2006 *Diplomacy by Design. Luxury Arts and an "International Style" in the Ancient Near East, 1400 - 1200 BCE*, Chicago – London.

2014 *Communities of Style. Portable Luxury Arts, Identity, and Collective Memory in the Iron Age Levant*, Chicago – London.

Ferrari, F. (ed., transl. and comm.)

1997 *Senofonte, Ciropedia*, Vol. 1, 2nd ed., Milan.

Ferretti, M.

2007 Minime considerazioni sulla geografia della scultura del Rinascimento in Italia, in L. Gaeta (ed.), *La scultura meridionale in età moderna nei suoi rapporti con la circolazione mediterranea*, Atti del Convegno Internazionale di Studi (Lecce, 2004), Vol. 1, Galatina, 31–40.

Ferretto, C.

1984 *La città dissipatrice. Studi sull'excursus del libro decimo dei Philippika di Teopompo*, Genoa.

Ferri, S. (ed., transl. and comm.)

2000 *Plinio il Vecchio. Storia delle arti antiche*, introduzione di M. Harari, Milan (Reprint. Original edition: C. *Plini Secundi Naturalis historiae quae pertinent ad artes antiquorum / Plinio il Vecchio. Storia delle arti antiche*, Rome, 1946).

Ferron, J.

1993 *Sarcophages de Phénicie. Sarcophages à scènes en relief*, Paris.

FGrH

F. Jacoby, *Die Fragmente der griechischen Historiker*, Berlin – Leiden, 1923–58.

Fischer-Bossert, W.

2003 Zur Löwenjagd des Lykischen Sarkophages aus Sidon, in «Archäologischer Anzeiger», 191–6.

Fleischer, R.

1983 *Der Klagefrauensarkophag aus Sidon* (Istanbuler Forschungen; 34), Tübingen.

1984 Reisenotizen aus Kilikien, in «Archäologischer Anzeiger», 85–104.

Flourentzos, P.

2007 *The Sarcophagus of Palaipafos*, Lefkosia.

Flower, M.A.

1994 *Theopompus of Chios. History and Rhetoric in the Fourth Century B.C.*, Oxford – New York.

Fögen, T. and Thomas, E. (eds.)

2017 *Interactions between Animals and Humans in Graeco-Roman Antiquity*, Berlin – Boston.

Fontan, É.

2007 La sculpture en Phénicie, in É. Fontan and H. Le Meaux (eds.), *La Méditerranée des Phéniciens de Tyr à Carthage* (exhibition catalogue), Paris, 149–58.

Fornasier, J.

2001 *Jagddarstellungen des 6.-4. Jhs. v. Chr. Eine ikonographische und ikonologische Analyse* (EIKON. Beiträge zur antiken Bildersprache; 5), Münster.

Foster, B.R.

2005 *Before the Muses. An Anthology of Akkadian Literature*, 3rd ed., Bethesda, MD.

Francfort, H.-P.

1975 Un cachet achéménide d'Afghanistan, in «Journal Asiatique», 219–22.

Frangipane, M.

2004 Il sito di Arslantepe. Storia di una ricerca archeologica, dal frammento alla storia, in M. Frangipane (ed.), *Alle origini del potere. Arslantepe, la collina dei leoni*, Milan, 13–6.

Frangipane, M. and Liverani, M.

2013 Neo-Hittite Melid: Continuity or Discontinuity?, in K.A. Yener (ed.), *Across the Border: Late Bronze-Iron Age Relations Between Syria and Anatolia*, Proceedings of a Symposium (Istanbul, 2010) (Ancient Near Eastern Studies. Suppl.; 42), Leuven – Paris – Walpole, MA, 349–71.

Frankfort, H.

1996 *The Art and Architecture of the Ancient Orient*, ed. by M. Roaf and D. Matthews, New Haven – London.

Franks, H.M.

2009 Hunting the *Eschata*: an Imagined Persian Empire on the Lekythos of Xenophantos, in «Hesperia», 78, 455–80.

2012 *Hunters, Heroes, Kings. The Frieze of Tomb II at Vergina*, Princeton.

Freccero, A.

2015 Marble Trade in Antiquity: Looking at Labraunda, in «Anatolia Antiqua», 23, published online at http://journals.openedition.org/anatoliaantiqua/344 [28 September 2019].

Frel, J.

1971 The Rhodian Workmanship of the Alexander Sarcophagus, in «Istanbuler Mitteilungen», 21, 121–4.

Friedrich, J.

1957–8 Ein kilikischer Mannesname, in «Archiv für Orientforschung», 18, 61.

Frisone, F. and Lombardo, M.

2007 Periferie? Sicilia, Magna Grecia, Asia Minore, in M. Giangiulio (ed.), *Storia d'Europa e del Mediterraneo*, Vol. 3, Rome, 177–225.

Frost, F.J.

1980 *Plutarch's Themistocles. A Historical Commentary*, Princeton, NJ.

Furtwängler, A.

1900 *Die antiken Gemmen. Geschichte der Steinschneidekunst im klassischen Altertum*, 3 vols, Leipzig – Berlin.

Gabelmann, H.

1979 Zur Chronologie der Königsnekropole von Sidon, in «Archäologischer Anzeiger», 163–77.

Gabrielli, M.

2006 *Le cheval dans l'empire achéménide / Horse in the Achaemenid Empire* (Studia ad Orientem Antiquum Pertinentia; 1), Istanbul.

Galik, A., Forstenpointner, G. and Weissengruber, G.

2012 Archäozoologische Befunde zur Jagd und Viehwirtschaft in Limyra, in M. Seyer (ed.), *40 Jahre Grabung Limyra*, Akten des internationalen Symposions (Wien, 2009) (Forschungen in Limyra; 6), Vienna, 163–8.

Garrison, M.B.

1991 Seals and the Elite at Persepolis: Some Observations on Early Achaemenid Persian Art, in «Ars Orientalis», 21, 1–29.

2002 The "Late Neo-Elamite" Glyptic Style: A Perspective from Fars, in «Bulletin of the Asia Institute», 16, 65–102.

2011 The Seal of "Kuraš the Anzanite, Son of Šešpeš" (Teispes), PFS 93*: Susa – Anšan – Persepolis, in J. Álvarez-Mon and M.B. Garrison (eds.), *Elam and Persia*, Winona Lake, Ind., 375–405.

2014 The Royal-Name Seals of Darius I, in M. Kozuh *et al.* (eds.), *Extraction & Control: Studies in Honor of Matthew W. Stolper* (Studies in Ancient Oriental Civilization; 68), Chicago, 67–104.

2017 Sealing Practice in Achaemenid Times, in B. Jacobs, W.F.M. Henkelman and M.W. Stolper (eds.), *Die Verwaltung im Achämenidenreich. Imperiale Muster und Strukturen / Administration in the Achaemenid Empire. Tracing the Imperial Signature*. Akten Kolloquiums (Landgut Castelen bei Basel, 2013), Wiesbaden, 517–80.

Garstang, J.

1929 *The Hittite Empire. Being a Survey of the History, Geography and Monuments of Hittite Asia Minor and Syria*, London.

Gates, C.

2005 The Place of the Achaemenid Persian Period in Archaeological Research in Cilicia and Hatay (Turkey), in P. Briant and R. Boucharlat (eds.), *L'archéologie de l'empire achéménide: nouvelles recherches* (Persika; 6), Paris, 49–69.

Gates, J.E.

2002 The Ethnicity Name Game: What Lies Behind "Graeco-Persian"?, in «Ars Orientalis», 32, 105–32.

Gentili, B. *et al.* (ed., transl. and comm.)

1995 *Pindaro. Le Pitiche*, Milan.

Geppert, K.

1998 Das reliefverzierte Pfeilergrab in Tüse, in F. Kolb (ed.), *Lykische Studien 4. Feldforschungen auf dem Gebiet von Kyaneai (Yavu-Bergland). Ergebnisse der Kampagnen 1993/94* (Asia Minor Studien; 29), Bonn, 215–24.

Gibson, J.C.L.

1975 *Textbook of Syrian Semitic Inscriptions*, Vol. 2. *Aramaic Inscriptions, Including Inscriptions in the Dialect of Zenjirli*, Oxford.

Gilibert, A.

2011 *Syro-Hittite Monumental Art and the Archaeology of Performance. The Stone Reliefs at Carchemisch and Zincirli in the Earlier First Millennium BCE* (Topoi. Berlin Studies of the Ancient World; 2). Berlin – New York.

Giusfredi, F.

2010 *Sources for a Socio-Economic History of the Neo-Hittite States* (Texte der Hethiter; 28), Heidelberg.

Glatz, C. and Plourde, A.M.

2011 Landscape Monuments and Political Competition in Late Bronze Age Anatolia: an Investigation of Costly Signaling Theory, in «Bulletin of the American Schools of Oriental Research», 361, 33–66.

Godley, A.D. (ed. and transl.)

1966 *Herodotus*, Vol. 1. *Books I and II*, London – Cambridge, MA (Reprint. Original edition: 1920).

1971 *Herodotus*, Vol. 2. *Books III and IV*, London – Cambridge, MA (Reprint. Original edition: 1920).

Gomme, A.W.

1945 *A Historical Commentary on Thucydides*, Vol. 1. *Introduction and Commentary on Book I*, Oxford.

Gorbachov, Y.

2008 Nine Observations on the Old Phrygian Inscription from Vezirhan, in «Kadmos», 47, 91–108.

Götter, Heroen, Herrscher

1990 *Götter, Heroen, Herrscher in Lykien* (exhibition catalogue), Vienna – Munich.

Grayson, A.K.

1991 *Assyrian Rulers of the Early First Millennium BC*, Vol. 1. *(1114–859 BC)* (The Royal Inscriptions of Mesopotamia. Assyrian periods; 2), Toronto – Buffalo – London.

Greaves, A.M.

2007 Trans-Anatolia: Examining Turkey as a Bridge between East and West, in *Transanatolia: Bridging the Gap between East and West in the Archaeology of Ancient Anatolia*, in «Anatolian Studies», 57, 1–15.

Groenewegen-Frankfort, H.A.

1978 *Arrest and Movement. An Essay on Space and Time in the Representational Art of the Ancient Near East*, New York (Reprint. Original edition: London, 1951).

Gschwantler, K.

1993 Bäume, Säulen, Mauern. Zum Fugenschluss der Reliefs von Gölbaşı-Trysa, in J. Borchhardt and G. Dobesch (eds.), *Akten des II. Internationalen Lykien-Symposions* (Wien, 1990), Vol. 2, Vienna, 77–85.

Gubel, É.

2002 *Art phénicien. La sculpture de tradition phénicienne*, Paris.

Guidorizzi, G., Avezzù, G. and Cerri, G. (ed., transl. and comm.)

2008 *Sofocle. Edipo a Colono*, Milan.

Guimier-Sorbets, A.-M.

2008 Architecture et décor des tombes monumentales à l'époque hellénistique: quelques modèles communs (Macédoine, Thrace, Egypte, Asie Mineure, Chypre), in O. Özbek (ed.), *Funeral Rites, Rituals and Ceremonies from Prehistory to Antiquity*, Proceedings of the International Workshop (Çanakkale and Ören, 2006), Istanbul, 27–43.

Gunter, A.C.

2009 *Greek Art and the Orient*, Cambridge – New York.

Guralnick, E.

1976 Composition of Some Narrative Reliefs from Khorsabad, in «Assur», 1.5, 1–9.

Güterbock, H.G.

1942 *Siegel aus Boğazköy, 2. Die Königssiegel von 1939 und die übrigen Hieroglyphensiegel* (Archiv für Orientforschung. Beiheft; 7), Berlin.

1956 Notes on Some Hittite Monuments, in «Anatolian Studies», 6, 53–56.

1957 Narration in Anatolian, Syrian, and Assyrian Art, in «American Journal of Archaeology», 61, 62–71.

1989 Hittite *Kursa* "Hunting Bag", in A. Leonard, Jr. and B.B. Williams (eds.), *Essays in Ancient Civilization Presented to Helene J. Kantor* (Studies in Ancient Oriental Civilization; 47), Chicago, 113–23.

Haerinck, E. and Overlaet, B.

1998 *Luristan Excavation Documents*, Vol. 2. *Chamahzi Mumah: an Iron Age III Graveyard* (Acta Iranica; 33), Leuven.

Hall, J.M.

2014 *Artifact & Artifice. Classical Archaeology and the Ancient Historian*. Chicago – London.

Hallock, R.T.

1969 *Persepolis Fortification Tablets* (The University of Chicago. Oriental Institute Publications; 92), Chicago.

Hämmig, A.E.

2013 *Nevotan niptiyan:* die Fluchformel der Stele von Vezirhan, in «Indogermanische Forschungen», 118, 125–54.

Hanfmann, G.M.A.

1957 Narration in Greek Art, in «American Journal of Archaeology», 61, 71–8.

Harmanşah, Ö.

2008 Rev. Feldman 2006, in «The Art Bulletin», 90, 123–6.

Harper, P.O. *et al.* (eds.)

1995 *Assyrian Origins. Discoveries at Ashur on the Tigris. Antiquities in the Vorderasiatisches Museum, Berlin* (exhibition catalogue), New York.

Hatzopoulos, M.B.

1982 A Reconsideration of the Pixodaros Affair, in B. Barr-Sharrar and E.N. Borza (eds.), *Macedonia and Greece in Late Classical and Early Hellenistic Times* (Studies in the History of Art; 10), Washington, 59–66.

Hauben, H.

1973 The Chief Commanders of the Persian Fleet in 480 B.C., in «Ancient Society», 4, 23–37.

Hawkins, J.D.

1993 A Bowl Epigraph of the Official Taprammi, in M.J. Mellink, E. Porada and T. Özgüç (eds.), *Aspects of Art and Iconography: Anatolia and its Neighbors. Studies in Honor of Nimet Özgüç / Nimet Özgüç'e Armağan*, Ankara, 715–7.

2006 Tudḫaliya the Hunter, in Th.P J. van den Hout (ed.), *The Life and Times of Ḫattušili III and Tutḫaliya IV*, Proceedings of a symposium (Leiden, 2003), Leiden, 49–76.

Heckel, W.

2006 Mazaeus, Callisthenes and the Alexander Sarcophagus, in «Historia», 55, 385–96.

2009 *Who's Who in the Age of Alexander the Great. Prosopography of Alexander's Empire*, Malden, MA – Oxford – Chichester.

Heilmeyer, W.-D.

2009 Arte e artigianato: l'importanza della "produzione in serie" per l'arte antica, in «Annali della Scuola Normale Superiore di Pisa. Classe di Lettere e Filosofia», s. V, 1, 649–64.

Held, W.

2008–9 Rev. Jacobson 2007, in «Berytus», 51/52, 226–9.

Held, W. and Kaplan, D.

2015 The Residence of a Persian Satrap in Meydancıkkale, Cilicia, in R. Rollinger and E. van Dongen (eds.), *Mesopotamia in the Ancient World. Impact, Continuities, Parallels*, Proceedings of the Symposium (Obergurgl, 2013), Münster, 175–91.

Hellmann, M.-C.

2002 *L'architecture grecque*, Vol. 1, Paris.

Henig, M.

1994 *Classical Gems. Ancient and Modern Intaglios and Cameos in the Fitzwilliam Museum, Cambridge*, With Major Contributions by Diana Scarisbrick and Mary Whiting, Cambridge – New York.

Henkelman, W.F.M.

2008 *The Other Gods Who Are. Studies in Elamite-Iranian Acculturation Based on the Persepolis Fortification Texts* (Achaemenid History; 14), Leiden.

2010 "Consumed Before the King". The Table of Darius, that of Irdabama and Irtaštuna, and that of his Satrap, Karkiš, in B. Jacobs and R. Rollinger (eds.), *Der Achämenidenhof / The Achaemenid Court*. Akten des Kolloquiums (Landgut Castelen bei Basel, 2007) (Classica et Orientalia; 2), Wiesbaden, 667–775.

Henry, O. (ed.)

2013 *4th century Karia. Defining a Karian identity under the Hekatomnids* (Varia Anatolica; 28), Istanbul – Paris.

Henry, O.

2009 *Tombes de Carie. Architecture funéraire et culture carienne, VIe-IIe s. av. J.-C.* (Archéologie & Culture), Rennes.

2010 Hekatomnos, Persian Satrap or Greek Dynast? The Tomb at Berber İni, in R. van Bremen and J.-M. Carbon (eds.), *Hellenistic Karia*, Proceedings of the Conference (Oxford, 2006) (Études; 28), Bordeaux, 103–121

2014 Then Whose Tomb is That?, in L. Karlsson, S. Carlsson and J. Blid Kullberg (eds.), *ΛΑΒΡΥΣ. Studies Presented to Pontus Hellström* (Boreas; 35), Uppsala, 71–85.

Hermary, A.

1992 Quelques remarques sur les origines proche-orientales de l'iconographie d'Héraclès, in C. Bonnet and C. Jourdain-Annequin (eds.), *Héraclès: d'une rive à l'autre de la Méditerranée. Bilan et perspectives*, Actes de la table ronde (Rome, 1989), Brussels – Rome, 129–43.

Hermary, A. and Mertens, J.R.

2014 *The Cesnola Collection of Cypriot Art: Stone Sculpture*, New York – New Haven – London.

Herrmann, G. and Laidlaw, S.

2008 *Ivories from the North West Palace (1845-1992)* (Ivories from Nimrud; 6), London.

Higgs, P.

2006 Late Classical Asia Minor: Dynasts and their Tombs, in O. Palagia (ed.), *Greek Sculpture. Function, Materials and Techniques in the Archaic and Classical Periods*, Cambridge – New York, 163–207.

Hill, G.

1940 *A History of Cyprus*, Vol. 1. *To the Conquest by Richard Lion Heart*, Cambridge.

Hiller, F.

1960 Zu den Sockelfriesen des Klagefrauensarkophags in Istanbul, in «Marburger Winckelmann-Programm», 1–12.

1961 Zu den Sarkophagreliefs des späten 4. Jh. v. Chr., in «Marburger Winckelmann-Programm», 29–41.

Hitzl, I.

1991 *Die griechischen Sarkophage der archaischen und klassischen Zeit*, Jonsered.

Hoddinott, R.F.

1975 *Bulgaria in Antiquity*. An Archaeological Introduction, London – Tonbridge.

Hoepfner, W.

2013 *Halikarnassos und das Maussolleion. Die modernste Stadtanlage und der als Weltwunder gefeierte Grabtempel des karischen Königs Maussollos*, Darmstadt – Mainz.

Hoff, C.

2017 *Identität und Politik. Kollektive kulturelle und politische Identität der Lykier bis zur Mitte des 4. Jahrhunderts v. Chr.* (Amaltheia; 1), Wiesbaden.

Hoffmann, H.

1962 *Attic Red-Figured Rhyta*, Mainz.

Hölscher, F.

1972 *Die Bedeutung archaischer Tierkampfbilder*, Würzburg.

Hölscher, T.

1973 *Griechische Historienbilder des 5. und 4. Jahrhunderts v. Chr.* (Beiträge zur Archäologie; 6), Würzburg.

2007 *The Language of Images in Roman Art*, transl. by A. Snodgrass and A. Künzl-Snodgrass, Foreword by J. Elsner, Cambridge – New York (Reprint. Original edition: 2004) (Transl. of: *Römische Bildsprache als semantisches System*, Heidelberg, 1987).

Horden, P. and Purcell, N.

2000 *The Corrupting Sea. A Study of Mediterranean History*, Oxford – Malden, MA.

Hornblower, S.

1982 *Mausolus*, Oxford – New York.

1990 The Great Satraps' Revolt, rev. Weiskopf 1989, in «The Classical Review» 40.2, 363–5.

1991 *A Commentary on Thucydides*, Vol. 1. *Books I–III*, Oxford.

Houser, C.

1998 The Alexander Sarcophagus of Abdalonymos. A Hellenistic Monument from Sidon, in O. Palagia and W. Coulson (eds.), *Regional Schools in Hellenistic Sculpture*, Proceedings of an International Conference (Athens, 1996), Oxford, 281–91.

Hull, D.B.

1964 *Hounds and Hunting in Ancient Greece*, Chicago.

Hunter, R. and Rutherford, I. (eds.)

2009 *Wandering Poets in Ancient Greek Culture. Travel, Locality and Pan-Hellenism*, Cambridge – New York.

IG

Inscriptiones Graecae, Berlin, 1873– .

Israel, J.

2016 *Mehrgeschossige Podiumsgrabbauten (550-330 v. Chr.): Ausprägung und Rezeption einer kleinasiatischen Grabform zwischen Pasargadai und Athen* (Asia Minor Studien; 81), Bonn.

Işık, C.

2019 *Die Wandmalereien in der Grabkammer des Hekatomneions. Beobachtungen zu Figurentypen, zur Komposition, Ikonographie und zum Stil* (Asia Minor Studien; 91), Bonn.

Jacobs, B.

1987 *Griechische und persische Elemente in der Grabkunst Lykiens zur Zeit der Achämenidenherrschaft* (Studies in Mediterranean Archaeology; 78), Jonsered.

2002 Achämenidische Kunst – Kunst im Achämenidenreich. Zur Rolle der achämenidischen Großplastik als Mittel der herrscherlichen Selbstdarstellung und der Verbreitung politischer Botschaften im Reich, in «Archäologische Mitteilungen aus Iran und Turan», 34, 345–95.

2014 Bildkunst als Zeugnis für Orientierung und Konsens innerhalb der Eliten des westlischen Achämenidenreichs, in R. Rollinger and K. Schnegg (eds.), *Kulturkontakte in antiken Welten: vom Denkmodell zum Fallbeispiel*, Proceedings des internationalen Kolloquiums (Innsbruck, 2009), Leuven – Paris – Walpole, MA, 343–38.

Jacobs, B., Henkelman, W.F.M. and Stolper, M.W. (eds.)

2017 *Die Verwaltung im Achämenidenreich. Imperiale Muster und Strukturen / Administration in the Achaemenid Empire. Tracing the Imperial Signature.* Akten des Kolloquiums (Landgut Castelen bei Basel, 2013), Wiesbaden.

Jacobs, B. and Rollinger, R. (eds.)

2010 *Der Achämenidenhof / The Achaemenid Court.* Akten des Kolloquiums (Landgut Castelen bei Basel, 2007) (Classica et Orientalia; 2), Wiesbaden.

Jacobson, D.M.

2007 *The Hellenistic Paintings of Marisa. Including a Facsimile Reprint of "Painted Tombs in the Necropolis of Marissa (Marêshah)" by John P. Peters and Hermann Thiersch. Edited by Stanley A. Cook (1905)* (The Palestine Exploration Fund Annual; 7), Leeds.

Jaeger, W.

1986 *Paideia: the Ideals of Greek Culture*, Vol. 3. *The Conflict of Cultural Ideals in the Age of Plato*, New York – Oxford (Reprint. Original edition: 1944).

Jakob, S.

2017a The Middle Assyrian Period (14th to 11th Century BCE), in E. Frahm (ed.), *A Companion to Assyria*, New Haven, US, 117–42.

2017b Economy, Society, and Daily Life in the Middle Assyrian Period, in E. Frahm (ed.), *A Companion to Assyria*, New Haven, US, 143–60.

Jenkins, I.

2006 *Greek Architecture and its Sculpture*, Cambridge, MA.

Jensen, H.

1958 *Die Schrift in Vergangenheit und Gegenwart*, 2nd ed., Berlin.

Jeppesen, K.

1958 *Paradeigmata. Three Mid-Fourth Century Main Works of Hellenic Architecture Reconsidered* (Jutland Archaeological Society Publications; 4), Aarhus.

1992 Tot operum opus. Ergebnisse der dänischen Forschungen zum Maussolleion von Halikarnass seit 1966, in «Jahrbuch des Deutschen Archäologischen Instituts», 107, 59–102.

2000 *The Maussolleion at Halikarnassos. Reports of the Danish Archaeological Expedition to Bodrum*, Vol. 4. *The Quadrangle. The Foundations of the Maussolleion and its Sepulchral Compartments* (Jutland Archaeological Society Publications; 15.4), Aarhus.

2002 *The Maussolleion at Halikarnassos. Reports of the Danish Archaeological Expedition to Bodrum*, Vol. 5. *The Superstructure. A Comparative Analysis of the Architectural, Sculptural, and Literary Evidence* (Jutland Archaeological Society Publications; 15.5), Højbjerg.

Jeppesen, K., Højlund, F. and Aaris-Sørensen, K.

1981 *The Maussolleion at Halikarnassos. Reports of the Danish Archaeological Expedition to Bodrum*, Vol. 1. The Sacrificial Deposit (Jutland Archaeological Society Publications; 15.1), Copenhagen.

Jex-Blake, K. and Sellers, E. (ed., transl. and comm.)

1982 *The Elder Pliny's Chapters on the History of Art*, with Prefaces to the First and Second American Editions and Select Bibliography by R.V. Schoder, Chicago (Reprint. Original edition: London – New York, 1896).

Jones, H.L. (ed. and transl.)

1961 *The Geography of Strabo*, Vol. 7, Cambridge, MA – London (Reprint. Original edition: 1930).

Kalof, L. (ed.)

2007 *A Cultural History of Animals in Antiquity*, Oxford – New York.

Kaptan, D.B.

1996 Some Remarks About the Hunting Scenes on the Seal Impressions of Daskyleion, in M.-F. Boussac and A. Invernizzi (eds.), *Archives et sceaux du monde hellénistique / Archivi e sigilli nel mondo ellenistico* (Torino, 1993) (Bulletin de Correspondance Hellénique. Suppléments; 29), Athens – Paris, 85–100.

Karageorghis, V.

1981 A Decorated Bronze Bowl from Armou, in «Report of the Department of Antiquities, Cyprus», 142–6.

2000 *Ancient Art from Cyprus. The Cesnola Collection in the Metropolitan Museum of Art*, in Collaboration with J.R. Mertens and M.E. Rose, New York.

2002 *Early Cyprus. Crossroads of the Mediterranean*, Los Angeles.

2005 Kypriaka XVI, in «Report of the Department of Antiquities, Cyprus», 109–15.

Karagöz, Ş.

2013 *Kleinasiatisch-gräko-persische Kunstwerke im Archäologischen Museum von Istanbul* (Istanbuler Forschungen; 54), Tübingen.

Karlsson, L., Blid, J. and Henry, O.

2012 Labraunda 2011. A Preliminary Report on the Swedish Excavations with an Appendix by Ragnar Hedlund, in «Opuscula», 5, 49–87.

Keen, A.G.

1992 The Dynastic Tombs of Xanthos: Who Was Buried Where?, in «Anatolian Studies», 42, 53–63.

1998 *Dynastic Lycia. A Political History of the Lycians and their Relations with Foreign Powers, C. 545-362 B.C.*, Leiden – Boston – Cologne.

2002 The "Kings" of Lycia in the Achaemenid Period, in R. Brock and S. Hodkinson (eds.), *Alternatives to Athens. Varieties of Political Organization and Community in Ancient Greece*, Oxford – New York, 269–79.

Khatchadourian, L.

2012 The Achaemenid Provinces in Archaeological Perspective, in D.T. Potts (ed.), *A Companion to the Archaeology of the Ancient Near East*, Vol. 2, Chichester, 963–83.

Kitov, G.

2001 A Newly Found Thracian Tomb with Frescoes, in «Archaeologia Bulgarica», 5, 15–29.

2005 New Discoveries in the Thracian Tomb with Frescoes by Alexandrovo, in «Archaeologia Bulgarica», 9, 15–28.

Kleemann, I.

1958 *Der Satrapen-Sarkophag aus Sidon* (Istanbuler Forschungen; 20), Berlin.

Klengel, H.

2007 Studien zur hethitischen Wirtschaft, 3: Tierwirtschaft und Jagd, in «Altorientalische Forschungen», 34, 154–73.

Klinkott, H.

2005 *Der Satrap: ein achaimenidischer Amtsträger und seine Handlungsspielräume* (Oikumene: Studien zur antiken Weltgeschichte; 1), Frankfurt am Main.

Knauss, F.S. and Franke, P.R.

2001 "Barbar" und Hoplit. Das Siegel eines lykischen Herrschers?, in «Münchner Jahrbuch der bildenden Kunst», 52, 7-16.

Koch, H.

1992 *Es kündet Dareios der König. Vom Leben im persischen Grossreich* (Kulturgeschichte der antiken Welt; 55), Mainz.

Kolb, F.

2018 *Lykien. Geschichte einer antiken Landschaft*, Darmstadt.

Konuk, K.

2013 Coinage and Identities under the Hekatomnids, in O. Henry (ed.), *4th century Karia. Defining a Karian identity under the Hekatomnids* (Varia Anatolica; 28), Istanbul – Paris, 101–21.

Kubala, A.

2000 Remarks on So-Called Graeco-Persian Art from the Area of Cilicia, in K.M. Ciałowicz and J.A. Ostrowski (eds.), *Les civilisations du bassin méditerranéen. Hommages à Joachim Śliwa*, Cracow, 249–59.

2003 Funerary Steles from Daskyleion. Remarks on the So-Called Greek-Persian Style in Anatolia, in F.M. Stępniowski (ed.), *The Orient and the Aegean*, Symposium (Warsaw, 1999), Warsaw, 103–22.

Kuhrt, A.

2007 *The Persian Empire. A Corpus of Sources from the Achaemenid Period*, 2 vols, London – New York.

Landskron, A.

2008 Mythos und Lebensbild: Das Heroon von Trysa, in «Jahrbuch des Kunsthistorischen Museums Wien», 10, 116–27.

2011 Zur Komposition der Friese auf der Nord- und Ostseite des Heroons von Trysa, in «Adalya», 14, 31–56.

2015 *Das Heroon von Trysa. Ein Denkmal in Lykien zwischen Ost und West. Untersuchungen zu Bildschmuck, Bauform und Grabinhaber* (Schriften des Kunsthistorischen Museums; 13 A-B), 2 vols, Vienna.

2017 Greek Images and Local Identities in Lycia: The Case of the Heroon of Trysa, in D. Rodríguez Pérez (ed.), *Greek Art in Context. Archaeological and Art Historical Perspectives*, London – New York, 211–222.

Langer-Karrenbrock, M.-T.

2000 *Der Lykische Sarkophag aus der Königsnekropole von Sidon* (Charybdis; 3), Münster – Hamburg – London.

Laroche, E. and Davesne, A.

1981 Les fouilles de Meydandjık près de Gülnar (Turquie) et le trésor monétaire hellénistique, in «Comptes rendus des séances de l'Académie des Inscriptions et Belles-Lettres», 356–70.

Lausberg, H.

1998 *Handbook of Literary Rhetoric. A Foundation for Literary Study*, edited by D.E. Orton and R.D. Anderson, Leiden – London – Cologne (Transl. of: *Handbuch der literarischen Rhetorik. Eine Grundlegung der Literaturwissenschaft*, 2nd ed., Munich, 1973).

Lazzarini, L. and Marconi, C.

2014 A New Analysis of Major Greek Sculptures in the Metropolitan Museum: Petrological and Stylistic, in «Metropolitan Museum Journal», 49, 117–40.

Lehmann, R.G.

2005 *Die Inschrift(en) des Aḥīrōm-Sarkophags und die Schachtinschrift des Grabes V in Jbeil (Byblos)*, in *Dynastensarkophage mit szenischen Reliefs aus Byblos und Zypern*, Vol. 1.2, Mainz.

Leick, G.

2013 *Tombs of the Great Leaders. A Contemporary Guide*, London.

Lemaire, A.

1991 Recherches d'épigraphie araméenne en Asie Mineure et en Égypte et le problème de l'acculturation, in H. Sancisi-Weerdenburg and A. Kuhrt (eds.), *Asia Minor and Egypt. Old Cultures in a New Empire*, Proceedings of the Workshop (Achaemenid History; 6), Leiden, 199–206.

2000a *Textes araméens d'Anatolie d'époque perse*, 5. *Inscriptions de Cilicie*, 3. *Saraïdin*, published online at http://www.achemenet.com/pdf/aramaic/cilicie03.pdf [15 July 2019].

2000b *Textes araméens d'Anatolie d'époque perse*, 5. *Inscriptions de Cilicie*, 6. *Hemite*, published online at http://www.achemenet.com/pdf/aramaic/cilicie06.pdf [15 July 2019].

2014 *Outlook: Aramaeans Outside of Syria*, 3. *Anatolia*, in H. Niehr (ed.), *The Aramaeans in Ancient Syria* (Handbook of Oriental Studies / Handbuch der Orientalistik. Section 1, Ancient Near East; 106), Leiden – Boston, 319–28.

Lemaire, A. and Lozachmeur, H.

1990 La Cilicie à l'époque perse, recherches sur les pouvoirs locaux et l'organisation du territoire, in «Transeuphratène», 3, 143–55.

1996 Remarques sur le plurilinguisme en Asie Mineure à l'époque perse, in F. Briquel-Chatonnet (ed.), *Mosaïque de langues. Mosaïque culturelle. Le bilinguisme dans le Proche-Orient ancien*, Actes de la table-ronde (Paris, 1995) (Antiquités Sémitiques; 1), Paris, 91–123.

Lembke, K.

2001 *Phönizische anthropoide Sarkophage* (Damaszener Forschungen; 10), Mainz.

Lendle, O.

1995 *Kommentar zu Xenophons Anabasis (Bücher 1-7)*, Darmstadt.

Lenfant, D. (ed.)

2004 *Ctésias de Cnide, La Perse. L'Inde. Autres fragments*, Paris.

2009 *Les Histoires perses de Dinon et d'Héraclide. Fragments édités, traduits et commentés* (Persika; 13), Paris.

2011 *Les Perses vus par les Grecs: Lire les sources classiques sur l'empire achéménide*, Paris.

Le Roux, P.

2009 L'empereur romain et la chasse, in J. Trinquier and C. Vendries (eds.), *Chasses antiques. Pratiques et représentations dans le monde gréco-romain (IIIe s. av.-IVe s. apr. J.-C.)*, Actes du colloque (Rennes, 2007), Rennes, 23–35.

Le Roy, C.

1996 À propos de Mausole, in P. Carlier (ed.), *Le IVe siècle av. J.-C. Approches historiographiques* (Études anciennes; 15), Nancy, 351–5.

Leroy, P.-O. (ed., transl. and comm.)

2016 *Strabon. Géographie*, Vol. 12. *Livre XV: l'Inde, l'Ariane et la Perse*, Paris.

Letta, C.

2013 Dalla "Tabula Lugdunensis" alla Tomba François: la tradizione etrusca su Servio Tullio, in «Studi Classici e Orientali», 59, 91–115.

Lewis, D.M.

1977 *Sparta and Persia*, Leiden.

Lidov, J.

2016 Songs for Sailors and Lovers, in A. Bierl and A. Lardinois (eds.), *The Newest Sappho: P. Sapph. Obbink and P. GC inv. 105, Frs. 1–4. Studies in Archaic and Classical Greek Song*, Vol. 2 (Mnemosyne. Suppl.; 392), Leiden – Boston, 55–109.

LIMC

Lexicon Iconographicum Mythologiae Classicae, 8 vols, Zurich – Munich – Düsseldorf, 1981–97.

Lincoln, B.

2003 À la recherche du paradis perdu, in «History of Religions», 43, 139–54.

Lippolis, E. and Caliò, L.

2016 Rev. Hoepfner 2013, in «Gnomon», 88, 145–52.

Liverani, M.

2006 *Uruk. The First City*, edited and translated by Z. Bahrani and M. Van De Mieroop, London – Oakville.

2011 *Antico Oriente. Storia, società, economia*, n. ed., Rome – Bari.

Llewellyn-Jones, L.

2013 *King and Court in Ancient Persia 559 to 331 BCE*, Edinburgh.

Llewellyn-Jones, L. and Robson, J.

2010 *Ctesias' History of Persia. Tales of the Orient*, London – New York.

Lockwood, S.

2016 Family Matters: the Interpretation of Lycian "Funerary Banquet" Reliefs, in C.M. Draycott and M. Stamatopoulou (eds.), *Dining and Death: Interdisciplinary Perspectives on the "Funerary Banquet" in Ancient Art, Burial and Belief* (Colloquia Antiqua; 16), Leuven – Paris – Bristol, CT, 299–327.

Longo, O.

1987 Le regole della caccia nel mondo greco-romano, in «Aufidus», 1, 59–91.

Lucchese, C.

2009 *Il Mausoleo di Alicarnasso e i suoi maestri* (Maestri dell'arte classica; 1), Rome.

Luckenbill, D.D.

1989 *Ancient Records of Assyria and Babylonia*, Vol. 1. *Historical Records of Assyria from the Earliest Times to Sargon*, London (Reprint. Original edition: Chicago, 1926).

Ma, J.

2008 Mysians on the Çan Sarcophagus? Ethnicity and Domination in Achaimenid Military Art, in «Historia», 57, 243–54.

Macridy, Th.

1908 La porte des sphinx à Euyuk. Fouilles du Musée Impérial Ottoman (Mitteilungen der Vorderasiatischen Gesellschaft; 13.3), Berlin.

Maddoli, G.

2006 Pixodaros di Hekatòmnos e la datazione della Trilingue del Letôon, in «Athenaeum», 94, 601–8.

Maggiani, A. (ed.)

1985 *Artigianato artistico. L'Etruria settentrionale interna in età ellenistica* (exhibition catalogue), Milan.

Mairs, R.

2013 Bilingualism, in R.S. Bagnall *et al.* (eds.), *The Encyclopedia of Ancient History*, Vol. 3, Chichester, 1115–7.

Majidzadeh, Y.

1992 The Arjan Bowl, in «Iran», 30, 131–44.

Manassero, N.

2008 *Rhyta e corni potori dall'Età del Ferro all'epoca sasanide. Libagioni pure e misticismo tra la Grecia e il mondo iranico* (BAR International Series; 1750), Oxford.

Manfredini, M., Orsi, D.P. and Antelami, V. (ed., transl. and comm.)

1987 *Le Vite di Arato e Artaserse*, Milan.

Marangou, A. and Petit, Th.

1992 Le palais, in *Rapport sur les travaux de l'École Française à Amathonte de Chypre en 1991*, in «Bulletin de Correspondance Hellénique», 116, 760–2.

Marchant, E.C. (ed. and transl.)

1971 *Scripta Minora*, in E.C. Marchant and G.W. Bowersock (eds.), *Xenophon*, Vol. 7. *Scripta Minora / Pseudo-Xenophon. Constitution of the Athenians*, London – Cambridge, MA, 1–457 (Reprint. Original edition: 1925).

Marconi, C.

1997 Storie di caccia in Sicilia occidentale, in *Seconde giornate internazionali di studi sull'area elima*, Atti (Gibellina, 1994), Vol. 2, Pisa – Gibellina, 1071–120.

2007 *Temple Decoration and Cultural Identity in the Archaic Greek World. The Metopes of Selinus*, Cambridge – New York.

2009 The Parthenon Frieze. Degrees of Visibility, in «RES», 55/56, 157–73

2010 Orgoglio e pregiudizio. La "connoisseurship" della scultura in marmo dell'Italia meridionale e della Sicilia, in G. Adornato (ed.), *Scolpire il marmo. Importazioni, artisti itineranti, scuole artistiche nel Mediterraneo antico*, Atti del Convegno (Pisa, 2009), Milan, 339–59.

Marek, Chr.

2015 Zum Charakter der Hekatomnidenherrschaft im Kleinasien des 4. Jh. v. Chr., in E. Winter and K. Zimmermann (eds.), *Zwischen Satrapen und Dynasten. Kleinasien im 4. Jahrhundert v. Chr.* (Asia Minor Studien; 76), Bonn, 1–20.

2016 *In the Land of a Thousand Gods: A History of Asia Minor in the Ancient World*, in collaboration with Peter Frei. Translated by Steven Rendall, Princeton (Transl. of: *Geschichte Kleinasiens in der Antike*, unter Mitarbeit von Peter Frei, Munich, 2010).

Marek, Chr. and Zingg, E.

2018 *Die Versinschrift des Hyssaldomos und die Inschriften von Uzunyuva (Milas / Mylasa)* (Asia Minor Studien; 90), Bonn.

Markoe, G.

1985 *Phoenician Bronze and Silver Bowls from Cyprus and the Mediterranean* (University of California Publications: Classical Studies; 26), Berkeley – Los Angeles – London.

2000 *Phoenicians: Peoples of the Past*, London.

Marksteiner, T.

2002 *Trysa – eine Zentrallykische Niederlassung im Wandel der Zeit. Siedlungs-, architektur- und kunstgeschichtliche Studien zur Kulturlandschaft Lykien* (Wiener Forschungen zur Archäologie; 5), Vienna.

2010 *Lykien. Ein archäologischer Führer*, Vienna.

Martelli, M.

1975 Un aspetto del commercio di manufatti artistici nel IV sec. a.C.: i sarcofagi in marmo, in «Prospettiva», 3, 9–17.

Martin, S.R.

2017 *The Art of Contact. Comparative Approaches to Greek and Phoenician Art*, Philadelphia.

Martini, W. and Schernig, E.

2000 Das Jagdmotiv in der imperialen Kunst hadrianischer Zeit, in W. Martini (ed.), *Die Jagd der Eliten in den Erinnerungskulturen von der Antike bis in die Frühe Neuzeit* (Formen der Erinnerung; 3), Göttingen, 129–55.

Masaracchia, A. (ed., transl. and comm.)

1978 *Erodoto. La sconfitta dei Persiani. Libro IX delle Storie*, Milan.

Matthäus, H.

1985 *Metallgefäße und Gefäßuntersätze der Bronzezeit, der geometrischen und archaischen Periode auf Cypern, Mit einem Anhang der bronzezeitlichen Schwertfunde auf Cypern* (Prähistorische Bronzefunde; 2.8), Munich.

2009 Phoenician Metal-Work up to Date. Phoenician Metal Bowls with Figural Decoration in the Eastern Mediterranean, Near and Middle East and North Africa, in F. Husseini and A.-M. Maïla-Afeiche (eds.), *Interconnections in the Eastern Mediterranean. Lebanon in the Bronze and Iron Ages*, Proceedings of the International Symposium (Beirut, 2008) (Bulletin d'Archéologie et d'Architecture Libanaises. Hors-Série; 6), Beirut, 439–52.

Matthews, D.M.

1990 *Principles of Composition in Near Eastern Glyptic of the Later Second Millennium B.C.* (Orbis Biblicus et Orientalis. Series Archaeologica; 8), Freiburg – Göttingen.

Matthews, K.J.

2005 Scientific Appendix. Report on the Stable Isotope Analysis of Fragments from the Friezes of the Mausoleum at Halicarnassus, in B.F. Cook, *Relief Sculpture of the Mausoleum at Halicarnassus*, with contributions by B. Ashmole and D. Strong (Oxford Monographs on Classical Archaeology), Oxford, 37–40.

Matthiae, P.

1963 *Studi sui rilievi di Karatepe* (Studi Semitici; 9), Rome.

1996 *L'arte degli Assiri. Cultura e forma del rilievo storico*, Rome – Bari.

1997 *La storia dell'arte dell'Oriente Antico. I primi imperi e i primi principati del Ferro. 1600-700 a.C.*, Milan.

1998 *Ninive*, Milan.

Maximova, M.E.

1928 Griechish-persische Kleinkunst in Kleinasien nach den Perserkriegen, in «Archäologischer Anzeiger», 648–77.

May, G. and Metzger, B.M. (eds.)

1962 *The Holy Bible. The Oxford Annotated Bible. Revised Standard Version Containing the Old and New Testaments*, New York.

Mazzoni, S.

1992 Significato e ruolo del paesaggio nei rilievi di Sennacherib, in «Contributi e Materiali di Archeologia Orientale», 4, 151–66.

1997 The Gate and the City: Change and Continuity in Syro-Hittite Urban Ideology, in G. Wilhelm (ed.), *Die orientalische Stadt: Kontinuität, Wandel, Bruch. 1. Internationales Colloquium der Deutschen Orient-Gesellschaft* (Halle / Saale, 1996), Saarbrücken, 307–38.

2005 Narrare il trionfo nell'arte siro-ittita, in F. Pecchioli Daddi and M.C. Guidotti (eds.), *Narrare gli eventi*, Atti del Convegno (Studia Asiana; 3), Rome, 233–43.

McMahon, A.

2009 The Lion, the King and the Cage: Late Chalcolithic Iconography and Ideology in Northern Mesopotamia, in «Iraq», 71, 115–24.

Meadows, A.R.

2005 The Administration of the Achaemenid Empire, in J.E. Curtis and N. Tallis (eds.), *Forgotten Empire. The World of Ancient Persia* (exhibition catalogue), London, 181–209.

Meissner, B. and Opitz, D.

1940 *Studien zum Bît Hilâni im Nordpalast Assurbanaplis zu Ninive* (Abhandlungen der Preußischen Akademie der Wissenschaften. Philosophisch-historische Klasse; Jahrgang 1939; 18), Berlin.

Mellink, M.J.

1970 Observations on the Sculptures of Alaca Höyük, in «Anadolu», 14, 15–27.

1971 Excavations at Karataş-Semayük and Elmalı, Lycia, 1970, in «American Journal of Archaeology», 75, 245–55.

1972 Excavations at Karataş-Semayük and Elmalı, Lycia, 1971, in «American Journal of Archaeology», 76, 257–69.

1974 Hittite Friezes and Gate Sculptures, in K. Bittel *et al.* (eds.), *Anatolian Studies Presented to Hans Gustav Güterbock on the Occasion of his 65th Birthday*, Istanbul, 201–14.

1998 *Kızılbel: an Archaic Painted Tomb Chamber in Northern Lycia*, Philadelphia.

Mendel, G.

1912 *Catalogue des sculptures grecques, romaines et byzantines*, Vol. 1, Costantinople.

Merlotti, A. (ed.)

2017 *Le cacce reali nell'Europa dei principi* (Centro Studi della Reggia di Venaria. La civiltà delle corti; 1), Florence.

Messerschmidt, W.

1989 Historische und ikonographische Untersuchungen zum Alexandersarkophag, in «Boreas», 12, 64–92.

Metzger, H. *et al.*

1979 *La stèle trilingue du Létôon* (Fouilles de Xanthos; 6), Paris.

Meuszyński, J.

1981 *Die Rekonstruktion der Reliefdarstellungen und ihrer Anordnung im Nordwestpalast von Kalḫu (Nimrūd)* (Baghdader Forschungen; 2), Mainz.

Middleton, J.H.

1891 *The Engraved Gems of Classical Times with a Catalogue of the Gems in the Fitzwilliam Museum*, Cambridge.

Mildenberg, L.

1993 Über das Münzwesen im Reich der Achämeniden, in «Archäologische Mitteilungen aus Iran», 26, 55–79.

2000 On the So-Called Satrapal Coinage, in O. Casabonne (ed.), *Mécanismes et innovations monétaires dans l'Anatolie achéménide. Numismatique et histoire*, Actes de la table ronde internationale (Istanbul, 1997) (Varia Anatolica; 12), Istanbul – Paris, 9–20.

Miller, M.C.

1997 *Athens and Persia in the Fifth Century BC. A Study in Cultural Receptivity*, Cambridge.

2003 Art, Myth and Reality: Xenophantos' Lekythos Re-Examined, in E. Csapo and M.C. Miller (eds.), *Poetry, Theory, Praxis. The Social Life of Myth, Word and Image in Ancient Greece. Essays in Honour of William J. Slater*, Oxford, 19–47.

2007 The Poetics of Emulation in the Achaemenid World: the Figured Bowls of the "Lydian Treasure", in «Ancient West and East», 6, 43–72.

2011 Town and Country in the Satrapies of Western Anatolia: The Archaeology of Empire, in L. Summerer, A. Ivantchik and A. von Kienlin (eds.), *Kelainai – Apameia Kibotos: Développement urbain dans le contexte anatolien / Stadtentwicklung im anatolischen Kontext*, Actes du colloque international / Akten des internationalen Kolloquiums (Munich, 2009) (Kelainai; 1), Bordeaux, 319–44.

Miller, S.G.

2014 Hellenistic Painting in the Eastern Mediterranean, Mid-Fourth to Mid-First Century B.C., in J.J. Pollitt (ed.), *The Cambridge History of Painting in the Classical World*, New York, 170–237.

Miller, W. (ed. and transl.)

1968 *Xenophon*, Vol. 5. *Cyropaedia*, 2 vols, London – Cambridge, MA (Reprint. Original edition: 1914).

Minunno, G.

2008 Pratiche di mutilazione dei nemici caduti nel Vicino Oriente Antico, in «Mesopotamia», 43, 9–29.

Moggi, M. and Osanna, M. (ed., transl. and comm.)

2000 *Pausania. Guida della Grecia. Libro VII. L'Acaia*, Milan.

Momigliano, A.

1993a *The Development of Greek Biography*, exp. ed., Cambridge, MA – London (Reprint with additions. Original edition: 1971).

1993b *Alien Wisdom. The Limits of Hellenization*, Cambridge – New York (Reprint. Original edition: 1975).

Montiglio, S.

2005 *Wandering in Ancient Greek Culture*, Chicago – London.

Moreno, P.

1979 Arti figurative: recenti scoperte, in *La crisi della polis. Arte, religione, musica* (Storia e civiltà dei Greci; 6), Milan, 695–721.

Moretti Sgubini, A.M. (ed.)

2004 *Eroi etruschi e miti greci: gli affreschi della Tomba François tornano a Vulci* (exhibition catalogue), Rome.

Morgan, J.

2016 *Greek Perspectives on the Achaemenid Empire: Persia Through the Looking Glass*, Edinburgh.

Mørkholm, O. and Zahle, J.

1976 The Coinages of the Lycian Dynasts Kheriga, Kherêi and Erbbina. A Numismatic and Archaeological Study, in «Acta Archaeologica», 47, 47–90.

Morris, I.

1996 *Death-Ritual and Social Structure in Classical Antiquity*, Cambridge (Reprint. Original edition: 1992).

Moysey, R.A.

1992 Plutarch, Nepos and the Satrapal Revolt of 362/1 B.C., in «Historia», 41, 158–68.

Mullen, A. and James, P. (eds.)

2012 *Multilingualism in the Graeco-Roman Worlds*, Cambridge – New York.

Müller, S. *et al.* (eds.)

2017 *The History of the Argeads. New Perspectives* (Classica et Orientalia; 19), Wiesbaden.

Munn-Rankin, J.M.

1959 Ancient Near Eastern Seals in the Fitzwilliam Museum, Cambridge, in «Iraq», 21, 20–37.

Muscarella, O.W. (ed.)

1974 *Ancient Art. The Norbert Schimmel Collection*, Mainz.

Müseler, W. and Schürr, D.

2018 Zur Chronologie in den Inschriften auf dem Agora-Pfeiler von Xanthos (TL 44), den betroffenen Dynasten und ihren Münzen, in «Klio», 100, 381–406.

Musti, D. and Torelli, M. (ed., transl. and comm.)

1991 *Pausania. Guida della Grecia. Libro III. La Laconia*, Milan.

Nadali, D.

2006 *Percezione dello spazio e scansione del tempo. Studio della composizione narrativa del rilievo assiro di VII secolo a.C.* (Contributi e Materiali di Archeologia Orientale; 12), Rome.

Neils, J.

2001 *The Parthenon Frieze*, Cambridge.

Niehr, H.

2014 Religion, in H. Niehr (ed.), *The Aramaeans in Ancient Syria* (Handbook of Oriental Studies / Handbuch der Orientalistik. Section 1, Ancient Near East; 106), Leiden – Boston, 127–203.

Nieswandt, H.-H.

1995 Zur Herrschaftsrepräsentation am Nereiden-Monument von Xanthos anhand des Jagd-, Opfer- und Gelagefrieses, in «Lykia», 2, 115–44.

2011 *Ikonographische und ikonologische Untersuchungen zur Herrschaftsrepräsentation xanthischer Dynastengräber* (Diss. 1995), Münster.

Nikoulina, N.M.

1971 La glyptique "grecque orientale" et "gréco-perse", in «Antike Kunst», 14, 90–106.

Nimmo, M. and Olivetti, C.

1985–6 Sulle tecniche di trasposizione dell'immagine in epoca medioevale, in «Rivista dell'Istituto Nazionale d'Archeologia e Storia dell'Arte», s. III, 8/9, 399–411.

Nisbet, R.G.M. and Rudd, N.

2004 *A Commentary on Horace: Odes. Book III*, Oxford – New York.

Nollé, J.

2001 *Die Abwehr der wilden Schweine. Schwarzwildjagden im antiken Lykien*, Munich.

Nollé, M.

1992 *Denkmäler vom Satrapensitz Daskyleion. Studien zur graeco-persischen Kunst* (Antike in der Moderne), Berlin.

Norlin, G. (ed. and transl.)

1966 *Isocrates*, with an English Translation by George Norlin, Vol. 1, London – Cambridge, MA (Reprint. Original edition: 1928).

Novák, M.

2019 Histoire des principautés néo-hittites (louvito-araméennes), in V. Blanchard (ed.), *Royaumes oubliés. De l'Empire Hittite aux Araméens* (exhibition catalogue), Paris, 105–13.

Nuzzo, G. (ed.)

2012 *Publio Papinio Stazio. Achilleide*, Palermo.

Oberleitner, W.

1994 *Das Heroon von Trysa. Ein lykisches Fürstengrab des 4. Jahrhunderts v. Chr.* (Zaberns Bildbände zur Archäologie; 18), Mainz.

Oggiano, I. and Pedrazzi, T.

2013 *La Fenicia in età persiana. Un ponte tra il mondo iranico e il Mediterraneo*, Pisa – Rome.

Oggiano, I. and Xella, P.

2009 Sidone e il suo territorio in età persiana. Epigrafia e archeologia, in S. Helas and D. Marzoli (eds.), *Phönizisches und Punisches Städtewesen*, Akten der internationalen Tagung (Rom, 2007) (Iberia Archaeologica; 13), Mainz, 69–81.

Oldfather, C.H. (ed. and transl.)

1954 *Diodorus of Sicily*, Vol. 6. *Books XIV - XV,19*, Cambridge, MA – London.

Olson, S.D. (ed. and transl.)

2010 *Athenaeus. The Learned Banqueters*, Vol. 6. *Books 12 - 13.594b*, Cambridge, MA – London.

Oppermann, M.

1991 Bemerkungen zu einem Jagddenkmal des Kaisers Hadrian, in «Nikephoros», 4, 211–7.

Orthmann, W.

1971 *Untersuchungen zur späthethitischen Kunst*, Bonn.

Osborne, R.

2012 Cultures as Languages and Languages as Cultures, in A. Mullen and P. James (eds.), *Multilingualism in the Graeco-Roman Worlds*, Cambridge – New York, 317–34.

Osman Hamdy Bey and Reinach, T.

1892 *Une nécropole royale à Sidon: Fouilles de Hamdy Bey*, Paris.

Ottone, G.

2009 Agli estremi della tradizione: Questioni di cronologia teopompea, in F. Gazzano, G. Ottone and L. Santi Amantini (eds.), *Ingenia Asiatica: fortuna e tradizione di storici d'Asia Minore*, Atti della Giornata di Studio (Genova, 2007), Tivoli, 123–53.

2010 Entre biographie et anecdote: les "mauvaises" mises en forme des notices biographiques dans les "vies" de Théopompe chez Photios et dans la Souda, in M.-R. Guelfucci (ed.), *Jeux et enjeux de la mise en forme de l'histoire: recherches sur le genre historique en Grèce et à Rome*, Vol. 1 (Dialogues d'histoire ancienne. Supplément; 4.1), Besançon, 115–39.

Özgüç, T.

1971 *Demir Devrinde Kültepe ve Civarı / Kültepe and its Vicinity in the Iron Age* (Türk Tarih Kurumu Yayınlarından. V. Seri; 29), Ankara.

Özhanlı, M.

2001–2 İsinda Dikme Anıtı, in «Adalya», 5, 73–106.

Özyar, A.

1992 *Architectural Relief Sculpture at Karkamish, Malatya, and Tell Halaf: A Technical and Iconographic Study* (Diss. 1991), Ann Arbor, MI.

2008 Untersuchungen zu den kleinen Orthostaten aus Tell Halaf. Späthethitische Kunst, aramäische Bildwerke oder hurritisches Erbe?, in G. Wilhelm (ed.), *Ḫattuša-Boğazköy. Das Hethiterreich im Spannungsfeld des Alten Orients*, Internationales Colloquium (Würzburg, 2006), Wiesbaden, 397–420.

Palagia, O.

2000 Hephaestion's Pyre and the Royal Hunt of Alexander, in A.B. Bosworth and E.J. Baynham (eds.), *Alexander the Great in Fact and Fiction*, Oxford – New York, 167–206.

2017 The Argeads: Archaeological Evidence, in S. Müller *et al.* (eds.), *The History of the Argeads. New Perspectives* (Classica et Orientalia; 19), Wiesbaden, 151–61.

Paley, S.M. and Sobolewski, R.P.

1987 *The Reconstruction of the Relief Representations and their Positions in the Northwest-Palace at Kalḫu (Nimrūd)*, Vol. 2 (Baghdader Forschungen; 10), Mainz.

Paltineri, S.

2012 I segni della discordia. Annotazioni sui "sodales" della Tomba François, in M. Harari and S. Paltineri (eds.), *Segni e colore. Dialoghi sulla pittura tardoclassica ed ellenistica*, Atti del Convegno (Pavia, 2012), Rome, 115–22.

Papini, M.

2012 Rev. Lucchese 2009, in «Gnomon», 84, 44–50.

Para

1971 J.D. Beazley, *Paralipomena. Additions to Attic Black-Figure Vase-Painters and to Attic Red-Figure Vase-Painters*, 2nd ed., Oxford.

Parrot, A.

1951 Cylindre hittite nouvellement acquis (AO 20138), in «Syria», 28, 180–90.

1961 *Gli Assiri*, Milan (Transl. of: *Assur*, Paris, 1961).

Pastoureau, M.

2008 *L'orso. Storia di un re decaduto*, Turin (Transl. of: *L'ours. Histoire d'un roi déchu*, Paris, 2007).

Pecorella, P.E.

2004 Arslantepe ittita: architettura pubblica e iconografia del potere, in M. Frangipane (ed.), *Alle origini del potere. Arslantepe, la collina dei leoni*, Milan, 167–71.

Pedersen, P.

1991 *The Maussolleion at Halikarnassos*, Vol. 3. *The Maussolleion Terrace and Accessory Structures* (Jutland Archaeological Society Publications; 15.3:1–2), 2 vols, Aarhus.

2009 *The Palace of Maussollos in Halikarnassos and Some Thoughts on Its Karian and International Context*, in F. Rumscheid (ed.), *Die Karer und die Anderen*, Internationales Kolloquium (Berlin, 2005), Bonn, 315–48.

2013 *Architectural Relations between Karia and Lykia at the time of the Ionian Renaissance*, in P. Brun *et al.* (eds.), *Euploia. La Lycie et la Carie antiques. Dynamiques des territoires, échanges et identités*, Actes du colloque (Bordeaux, 2009) (Mémoires; 34), Bordeaux, 127–41.

Pekridou-Gorecki, A.

2012 Ikonographische Analysen mit hermeneutischen Anmerkungen, in J. Borchhardt and A. Pekridou-Gorecki (eds.), *Limyra. Studien zu Kunst und Epigraphik in den Nekropolen der Antike* (Forschungen in Limyra; 5), Vienna, 37–157.

Perrin, B. (ed. and transl.)

1962 *Plutarch's Lives*, Vol. 11. *Aratus, Artaxerxes, Galba and Otho*, London – Cambridge, MA (Reprint. Original edition: 1926).

Peters, J.P. and Thiersch, H.

1905 *Painted Tombs in the Necropolis of Marissa (Marêshah)*, ed. by S.A. Cook, London (repr. in Jacobson 2007).

Petit, Th.

1990 *Satrapes et satrapies dans l'empire achéménide de Cyrus le Grand à Xerxès Ier* (Bibliothèque de la Faculté de Philosophie et Lettres de l'Universitè de Liège; 254), Paris.

1996 La céramique grecque du palais d'Amathonte. Description et interprétation, in *Bulletin de la S.F.A.C.* (28, 1994–5), in «Revue Archéologique», 211–23.

2007 Aspects de l'hellénisme chez les dynastes orientaux (Asie Mineure, Phénicie et Chypre) à l'époque classique, in A. Laronde and J. Leclant (eds.), *La Méditerranée d'une rive à l'autre: culture classique et cultures périphériques*, Paris, 9–32.

Petrovic, A.

2009 Epigrammatic Contests, "Poeti Vaganti" and Local History, in R. Hunter and I. Rutherford (eds.), *Wandering Poets in Ancient Greek Culture. Travel, Locality and Pan-Hellenism*, Cambridge – New York, 195–216.

Pfrommer, M.

1998 *Untersuchungen zur Chronologie und Komposition des Alexandermosaiks auf antiquarischer Grundlage* (Aegyptiaca Treverensia; 8), Mainz.

Pfuhl, E. and Möbius, H.

1977 *Die ostgriechischen Grabreliefs*, Vol. 1, Mainz.

Pirson, F.

2006 Das vielfältige Bild des Krieges: Kampf und Gewalt in der lykischen Reliefkunst des späten 5. und des 4. Jhs. v. Chr., in K. Dörtlük *et al.* (eds.), *III. Uluslararası Likya Sempozyumu*, Sempozyum Bildirileri / *The IIIrd International Symposium on Lycia*, Symposium Proceedings (Antalya, 2005), Vol. 2, Antalya, 639–646.

2014 *Ansichten des Krieges. Kampfreliefs klassischer und hellenistischer Zeit im Kulturvergleich* (Archäologische Forschungen; 31), Wiesbaden.

Pittman, H.

1996 The White Obelisk and the Problem of Historical Narrative in the Art of Assyria, in «The Art Bulletin», 78, 334–55.

Podda, M.

2012 All'ombra delle palme. Fenice, Nestore, le palme della Tomba François e altri elementi vegetali, in M. Harari and S. Paltineri (eds.), *Segni e colore. Dialoghi sulla pittura tardoclassica ed ellenistica*, Atti del Convegno (Pavia, 2012), Rome, 123–8.

Poggio, A.

2007 Il fregio della mnesterofonia a Trysa, in F. de Angelis (ed.), *Lo sguardo archeologico. I normalisti per Paul Zanker*, Pisa, 63–76.

2010 Modelli di diffusione della scultura in marmo tra VI e V sec. a.C.: la Licia, in G. Adornato (ed.), *Scolpire il marmo. Importazioni, artisti itineranti, scuole artistiche nel Mediterraneo antico*, Atti del Convegno (Pisa, 2009), Milan, 235–49.

2011 Incidents in Dynastic Hunts in Lycia and Phoenicia, in K. Duistermaat and I. Regulski (eds.), *Intercultural Contacts in the Ancient Mediterranean*, Proceedings of the Conference (Cairo, 2008) (Orientalia Lovaniensia Analecta; 202), Leuven – Paris – Walpole, MA, 479–43.

2012 Immagini venatorie e monumenti dinastici: l'Impero Persiano tra centro e periferia, in M. Castiglione and A. Poggio (eds.), *Arte-Potere. Forme artistiche, istituzioni, paradigmi interpretativi*, Atti del convegno (Pisa, 2010), Milan, 227–41.

2015 Between Myth and History: Mediterranean Funerary Monuments in the 4th century BC, in P.M. Militello and H. Öniz (eds.), *SOMA 2011*, Proceedings of the Symposium (Catania, 2011) (BAR Publishing International Series; 2695), Vol. 2, Oxford, 2015, 657–9.

2016a Impressions of Power: "Greco-Persian" Seals in perspective, in E. Foietta *et al.* (eds.), *Cultural and Material Contacts in the Ancient Near East*, Proceedings of the International Workshop (Turin, 2014), Sesto Fiorentino, 157–63.

2016b Which Language for the Dynastic Message? The Role of the Hellenic Culture in 4th-Century Lycia, in R.A. Stucky, O. Kaelin and H.-P. Mathys (eds.), *Proceedings of the 9th International Congress on the Archaeology of the Ancient Near East* (Basel, 2014), Vol. 2, Wiesbaden, 209–20.

2017a Versatilità delle immagini del mito. L'impiego di schemi iconografici nella Licia di IV sec. a.C., in «La Rivista di Engramma (online)» published online at http://www.engramma.it/eOS/index.php?id_articolo=3288 [15 December 2019].

2017b Banqueting in Western Anatolia: Dynastic Lifestyle under the Persian Rule, in L. Thys-Şenocak (ed.), *Of Vines and Wines: The Production and Consumption of Wine in Anatolian Civilizations through the Ages* (Ancient Near Eastern Studies. Suppl.; 51), Leuven – Paris – Bristol, CT, 61–82.

2018a Exerting Patronage at Home and Beyond: Art and Power in Asia Minor in the Sixth and Fourth Centuries BC, in B. Horejs *et al.* (eds.), *Proceedings of the 10th International Congress on the Archaeology of the Ancient Near East* (Vienna, 2016), Vol. 1, Wiesbaden, 497–507.

2018b Tra ellenocentrismo e iranocentrismo. Riflessioni sullo studio dell'Anatolia occidentale nel IV sec. a.C., in M. Betrò *et al.* (eds.), *Egitto e Vicino Oriente antichi: tra passato e futuro. Studi e ricerche sull'Egitto e Vicino Oriente in Italia*, I Convegno Nazionale (Pisa, 2017), Pisa, 229–38.

2018c White Marble for Lycian Monuments: the Fifth-Century BC *Peplophoroi* from Xanthos, in «Marmora», 14, 37–52.

2019a Innovazione e circolazione. La caccia al cinghiale calidonio nel IV secolo a.C., tra Anatolia e Grecia, in «Annali della Scuola Normale Superiore di Pisa. Classe di Lettere e Filosofia», s. V, 11, 137–57, 371–2.

2019b A Multi-Horizon Perspective. Western Anatolian Material Evidence in the Persian Period, in B. Genito and G. Maresca (eds.), *Ceramics and the Archaeological Achaemenid Horizon. Near East, Iran and Central Asia* (Università degli Studi di Napoli "L'Orientale", Dipartimento Asia, Africa e Mediterraneo: Series Minor; 86. ISMEO - Associazione Internazionale di Studi sul Mediterraneo e l'Oriente: Serie Orientale Roma; 14 – Orientalia Romana; 1), Naples – Rome, 21–36.

forthcoming Un programma per il dinasta. Architettura e decorazione nell'Heroon di Trysa, in A. Gottsmann and G. Plattner (eds.), *Das Heroon von Trysa*, Vienna – Cologne – Weimar.

Polat, G.

1994 Eine Neuerwerbung des Uşak Museums. Eine anatolisch-persische Grabstele, in «Arkeoloji Dergisi», 2, 61–6.

Poliakoff, M.B.

2001 Competition, in D. Papenfuß and V.M. Strocka (eds.), *Gab es das Griechische Wunder? Griechenland zwischen dem Ende des 6. und der Mitte des 5. Jahrhunderts v. Chr.*, Tagungsbeiträge (Freiburg im Breisgau, 1999). Mainz, 51–64.

Pongratz-Leisten, B.

2015 *Religion and Ideology in Assyria* (Studies in Ancient Near Eastern Records; 6), Boston – Berlin.

Pottier, E.

1922 *Vases antiques du Louvre. Troisième série. Salle G. Le style attique à figures rouges*, Paris.

Prestianni Giallombardo, A.M.

1991 Recenti testimonianze iconografiche sulla *kausia* in Macedonia e la datazione del fregio della "Caccia" della II tomba reale di Vergina, in «Dialogues d'histoire ancienne», 17, 1, 257–304.

Procopé-Walter, A.

1937 Une intaille à scène de chasse et les cachets prismatiques de l'Asie Mineure, in «Le monde oriental», 31, 23–41.

Prost, F.

2012a *Lycian Dynast, Greek Art: the Two Small Friezes of the Nereid Monument at Xanthos*, in M. Castiglione and A. Poggio (eds.), *Arte-Potere. Forme artistiche, istituzioni, paradigmi interpretativi*, Atti del convegno (Pisa, 2010), Milan, 243–57.

2012b *Un nouveau fragment du sarcophage de Payava*, in K. Konuk (ed.), *Stephanèphoros. De l'économie antique à l'Asie Mineure. Hommages à Raymond Descat* (Mémoires; 28), Bordeaux, 369–75.

2013 Retour au Mausolée et au Monument des Néréides. Identités ethniques et frontières culturelles en Lycie et en Carie, in P. Brun *et al.* (eds.), *Euploia. La Lycie et la Carie antiques. Dynamiques des territoires, échanges et identités*, Actes du colloque (Bordeaux, 2009) (Mémoires; 34), Bordeaux, 175–186.

2015 La tradition de la sculpture parienne en Asie Mineure, in S. Montel (ed.), *La sculpture gréco-romaine en Asie Mineure. Synthèse et recherches récentes*. Colloque international (Besançon, 2014), Besançon, 209–22.

Pucci, M.

2008 *Functional Analysis of Space in Syro-Hittite Architecture* (BAR International Series; 1738), Oxford.

2015 Founding and Planning a New Town: the Southern Town Gate at Zincirli, in P. Ciafardoni and D. Giannessi (eds.), *From the Treasures of Syria. Essays on Art and Archaeology in Honour of Stefania Mazzoni*, Leiden, 35–74.

Queyrel, F.

2011 L'invention de l'histoire: réflexions sur le "sarcophage d'Alexandre" de la nécropole royale de Sidon, in «Mare Internum», 3, 35–45.

Quinn, J.

2018 *In Search of the Phoenicians*, Princeton – Oxford.

Radt, W.

1983 Eine gräko-persische Grabstele im Museum Bergama, in «Istanbuler Mitteilungen», 33, 53–68.

Raeck, W.

1981 *Zum Barbarenbild in der Kunst Athens im 6. und 5. Jahrhundert v. Chr.* (Habelts Dissertationsdrucke. Reihe klassische Archäologie; 14), Bonn.

Rashad, M.

1996 Die Bedeutung der Jagd für die Herrscherdarstellungen bei den Achämeniden, Parthern und Sasaniden, in U. Magen and M. Rashad (eds.), *Vom Halys zum Euphrat. Thomas Beran zu Ehren* (Altertumskunde des Vorderen Orients; 7), Münster, 241–55.

RAVA

Reallexikon der Assyriologie und vorderasiatischen Archäologie, ed. by E. Ebeling *et al.*, Berlin – New York, 1928– .

RE

Paulys Real-Encyclopädie der classischen Altertumswissenschaft. Neue Bearbeitung, ed. by G. Wissowa *et al.*, Stuttgart – Munich, 1893–1980.

Reade, J.E.

1994 Les relations anglo-françaises en Assyrie, in É. Fontan (ed.), *De Khorsabad à Paris. La découverte des Assyriens* (Notes et Documents des Musées de France; 26), Paris, 116–35.

2001 More about Adiabene, in «Iraq», 63, 187–99.

2018 The Assyrian Royal Hunt, in G. Brereton (ed.), *I am Ashurbanipal: King of the World, King of Assyria* (exhibition catalogue), London, 52–79.

Rehm, E.

2004 *Der Ahiram-Sarkophag*, in *Dynastensarkophage mit szenischen Reliefs aus Byblos und Zypern*, Vol. 1.1, Mainz.

Reinhardt, C.

2018 *Akroter und Architektur. Figürliche Skulptur auf Dächern griechischer Bauten vom 6. bis zum 4. Jahrhundert v. Chr.* (Image & Context; 18), Berlin – Boston.

Renberg, G.H.

2014 Unexplored Aspects of the Lycian "Twelve Gods Reliefs", in «Epigraphica Anatolica», 47, 107–32.

Richter, G.M.A.

1946 Greeks in Persia, in «American Journal of Archaeology», 50, 15–30.

1949 The Late "Achaemenian" or "Graeco-Persian" Gems, in *Commemorative Studies in Honor of Theodore Leslie Shear* (Hesperia. Supplements; 8), 291–8.

2006 *Catalogue of Engraved Gems. Greek, Etruscan and Roman, The Metropolitan Museum of Art, New York*, Rome (Reprint with colour illustrations. Original edition: 1956).

Ridgway, B.S.

1997 *Fourth-Century Styles in Greek Sculpture*, Madison.

Robert, L.

1960 *Hellenica. Recueil d'épigraphie, de numismatique et d'antiquités grecques*, XI-XII, Paris.

1975 Une nouvelle inscription grecque de Sardes: règlement de l'autorité perse relatif à un culte de Zeus, in «Comptes rendus des séances de l'Académie des Inscriptions et Belles-Lettres», 306–30.

1978 Les conquêtes du dynaste lycien Arbinas, in «Journal des Savants», 3–48.

Robinson, T.

1995 The Nereid Monument at Xanthos or the Eliyãna Monument at Arñna? in «Oxford Journal of Archaeology», 14, 355–9.

Rollinger, R.

2018 Herodotus and the Transformation of Ancient Near Eastern Motifs. Darius I, Oebares, and the Neighing Horse, in T. Harrison and E. Irwin (eds.), *Interpreting Herodotus*, Oxford – New York, 125–48.

Rondholz, A.

2020 Something to do with Sarpedon? Eine Neuinterpretation des Harpyienmonuments in Xanthos, in M. Zimmermann (ed.), *Das Xanthostal Lykiens in archaisch-klassischer Zeit. Eine archäologisch-historische Bestandsaufnahme* (Die hellenistische Polis als Lebensform; 7), Göttingen, 119–40.

Roosevelt, C.H.

2009 *The Archaeology of Lydia, from Gyges to Alexander*, New York.

Root, M.C.

1979 *The King and Kingship in Achaemenid Art. Essays on the Creation of an Iconography of Empire* (Acta Iranica; 19), Leiden.

1991 From the Heart: Powerful Persianisms in the Art of the Western Empire, in H. Sancisi-Weerdenburg and A. Kuhrt (eds.), *Asia Minor and Egypt: Old Cultures in a New Empire*, Proceedings of the Workshop (Achaemenid History; 6), Leiden, 1–29.

Rose, C.B.

2007 The Tombs of the Granicus River Valley, in İ. Delemen (ed.), *The Achaemenid Impact on Local Populations and Cultures in Anatolia (Sixth-Fourth Centuries B.C.)*, International Workshop (Istanbul, 2005), Istanbul, 247–64.

2014 *The Archaeology of Greek and Roman Troy*, Cambridge – New York.

Roux, G.

1975 Un chef-d'oeuvre d'architecture gréco-lycienne. Le "Monument des Néréides" à Xanthos, in «Revue des Études Grecques», 88, 182–9.

Rudolph, C.

2003 *Das "Harpyien-Monument" von Xanthos: seine Bedeutung innerhalb der spätarchaischen Plastik* (BAR International Series; 1108), Oxford.

Rumscheid, F.

2010 Maussollos and the "Uzun Yuva" in Mylasa: an Unfinished Proto-Maussolleion at the Heart of a New Urban Centre?, in R. van Bremen and J.-M. Carbon (eds.), *Hellenistic Karia*, Proceedings of the Conference (Oxford, 2006) (Études; 28), 69–102.

Russell, J.M.

1998 The Program of the Palace of Assurnasirpal II at Nimrud: Issues in the Research and Presentation of Assyrian Art, in «American Journal of Archaeology», 102, 655–715.

2017 Assyrian Art, in E. Frahm (ed.), *A Companion to Assyria*, New Haven, US, 453–510.

Rutherford, I.

2002 Interference or Translationese? Some Patterns in Lycian-Greek Bilingualism, in J.N. Adams, M. Janse and S. Swain (eds.), *Bilingualism in Ancient Society: Language Contact and the Written Text*, Oxford – New York, 197–219.

Ruzicka, S.

1992 *Politics of a Persian Dynasty. The Hecatomnids in the Fourth Century B.C.*, Norman – London.

Ryle, G.

1966 *Plato's Progress*, Cambridge.

Saatsoglou-Paliadeli, Ch.

2004 *Βεργίνα. Ο τάφος του Φιλίππου, η τοιχογραφία με το κυνήγι*, Athens.

2007 La peinture de la Chasse de Vergina, in S. Descamps-Lequine (ed.), *Peinture et couleur dans le monde grec antique*, Actes de colloque (Paris, 2004), Milan – Paris, 47–55.

Sachs, G.

2012 *Die Jagd im antiken Griechenland. Mythos und Wirklichkeit* (Antiquitates. Archäologische Forschungsergebnisse; 56), Hamburg.

Saladino, V.

2017 Il realismo nei ritratti dei governanti, la statua di Seute III e le monete coniate in Asia Minore in epoca achemenide, in D. Boschung and F. Queyrel (eds.), *Bilder der Macht. Das griechische Porträt und seine Verwendung in der antiken Welt* (Morphomata; 34), Paderborn, 121–62.

Salmeri, G.

1994 *I Greci e le lingue indigene d'Asia Minore: il caso del cario*, in M.E. Giannotta (ed.), *La decifrazione del cario*, Atti (Roma, 1993), Rome, 87–99.

2004 *Hellenism on the Periphery: the Case of Cilicia and an Etymology of Soloikismos*, in S. Colvin (ed.), *The Greco-Roman East. Politics, Culture, Society* (Yale Classical Studies; 31), Cambridge, 181–206.

Sancisi-Weerdenburg, H.

1987 Decadence in the Empire or Decadence in the Sources? From Source to Synthesis: Ctesias, in H. Sancisi-Weerdenburg (ed.), *Sources, Structures and Synthesis*, Proceedings of the workshop (Groningen, 1983) (Achaemenid History; 1), Leiden, 33–45.

Santi Amantini, L.

2011 Teopompo di Chio e la figura di Filippo II: qualche annotazione, in F. Gazzano, G. Ottone and L. Santi Amantini (eds.), *Ex fragmentis per fragmenta historiam tradere*. Atti della Giornata di Studio (Genova, 2009), Tivoli, 131–45.

Santillo Frizell, B. (ed.)

2004 *Pecus. Man and Animal in Antiquity*, Proceedings of the Conference (Rome, 2002) (The Swedish Institute in Rome. Projects and seminars; 1), Rome.

Şare, T.

2013 The Sculpture of the Heroon of Perikle at Limyra: the Making of a Lycian King, in «Anatolian Studies», 63, 55–74.

Savalli, I.

1988 L'idéologie dynastique des poèmes grecs de Xanthos, in «L'Antiquité Classique», 57, 103–23.

Schachner, A.

2012 Gedanken zur Datierung, Entwicklung und Funktion der hethitischen Kunst, in «Altorientalische Forschungen», 39, 130–66.

2013 Hitit sanatının gelişimi ve toplumsal işlevlerine dair / On the Development of Hittite Art and its Social Functions, in M. Doğan-Alparslan and M. Alparslan (eds.), *Hititler. Bir Anadolu imparatorluğu / Hittites. An Anatolian Empire*, Istanbul, 534–63.

Schaeffer, C.F.A.

1949 *Ugaritica II. Nouvelles Études Relatives aux Découvertes de Ras Shamra* (Mission de Ras Shamra; 5), Paris.

Schauenburg, K.

1969 *Jagddarstellungen in der griechischen Vasenmalerei* (Die Jagd in der Kunst), Hamburg – Berlin.

Schefold, K.

1968 *Der Alexander-Sarkophag*, Berlin.

Schmidt-Colinet, A.

1996 Zur Ikonographie der hadrianischen Tondi am Konstantinsbogen, in F. Blakolmer *et al.* (eds.), *Fremde Zeiten. Festschrift für Jürgen Borchhardt zum sechzigsten Geburtstag am 25. Februar 1996 dargebracht von Kollegen, Schülern und Freunden*, Vol. 2, Vienna, 261–73.

Schmidt-Colinet, C.

2005 König und Nachfolger: Zu den Löwenjagd-Reliefs aus Raum S des Nordpalasts in Ninive und noch einmal zur Bankettszene Assurbanipals, in «Mesopotamia», 40, 31–79.

Schmidt-Dounas, B.

1985 *Der lykische Sarkophag aus Sidon* (Istanbuler Mitteilungen. Beiheft; 30), Tübingen.

Schmitt, R.

2011 *Darius*, 6. *Achaemenid Princes*, published online at http://www.iranicaonline.org/articles/darius-vi [15 July 2019].

Schmitt Pantel, P.

1992 *La cité au banquet. Histoire des repas publics dans les cités grecques* (Collection de l'École française de Rome; 157), Rome.

Schmitt Pantel, P. and Schnapp, A.

1982 Image et société en Grèce ancienne: les représentations de la chasse et du banquet, in «Revue Archéologique», 57–74.

Schnapp, A.

1979a Images et programme. Les figurations archaïques de la chasse au sanglier, in «Revue Archéologique», 195–218.

1979b Pratiche e immagini di caccia nella Grecia antica, in «Dialoghi di Archeologia», n.s., 1, 36–59.

1997 *Le chasseur et la cité. Chasse et érotique dans la Grèce ancienne*, Paris.

Schollmeyer, P.

2007 *Der Sarkophag aus Golgoi: zur Grabrepräsentation eines zyprischen Stadtkönigs*, in A. Stylianou and P. Schollmeyer, *Dynastensarkophage mit szenischen Reliefs aus Byblos und Zypern*, Vol. 2, Mainz, 189–244.

Schürr, D.

2009 Zum Agora-Pfeiler in Xanthos II: Selbstlob auf Perserart und Ordnung des Raumes, in «Kadmos», 48, 157–76.

2013 Beobachtungen zu den Zwölfgötter-Reliefs in Lykien, in «Adalya», 16, 213–23.

2016 Zum Agora-Pfeiler in Xanthos V: das Nordgedicht auf Cheriga (TL 44c, 32 ff.), in «Kadmos», 55, 147–96.

Schwabacher, W.

1968 Lycian Coin-Portraits, in C.M. Kraay and G.K. Jenkins (eds.), *Essays in Greek Coinage, Presented to Stanley Robinson*, Oxford, 111–24.

Sekunda, N.V.

1988 Some Notes on the Life of Datames, in «Iran», 26, 35–53.

Setari, E.

2007 Osservazioni sulla tecnica esecutiva, in A. Bottini and E. Setari (eds.), *Il Sarcofago delle Amazzoni*, Milan, 62–73.

Settis, S. (ed.)

2015 *Serial / Portable Classic. The Greek Canon and its Mutations* (exhibition catalogue), Milan.

Settis, S.

1970 Qui multas facies pingit cito (Iuven. IX, 146), in «Atene e Roma», 15, 117–21.

2006 Il Papiro di Artemidoro: un libro di bottega e la storia dell'arte antica, in C. Gallazzi and S. Settis (eds.), *Le tre vite del Papiro di Artemidoro. Voci e sguardi dall'Egitto greco-romano* (exhibition catalogue), Milan, 20–65.

2010 *Artisti e committenti fra Quattro e Cinquecento*, postfazione di Antonio Pinelli, Turin.

Sevinç, N. *et al.*

2001 A New Painted Graeco-Persian Sarcophagus from Çan, in «Studia Troica», 11, 383–420.

Seyer, M.

1996 Ein Jagdrelief aus Limyra, in F. Blakolmer *et al.* (eds.), *Fremde Zeiten. Festschrift für Jürgen Borchhardt zum sechzigsten Geburtstag am 25. Februar 1996 dargebracht von Kollegen, Schülern und Freunden*, Vol. 1, Vienna, 111–21.

2007 *Der Herrscher als Jäger. Untersuchungen zur königlichen Jagd im persischen und makedonischen Reich vom 6. – 4. Jahrhundert v. Chr. sowie unter den Diadochen Alexanders des Großen* (Wiener Forschungen zur Archäologie; 11), Vienna.

2016 Zum Löwengrab von Xanthos, in F. Blakolmer, M. Seyer and H.D. Szemethy (eds.), *Angekommen auf Ithaka. Festgabe für Jürgen Borchhardt zum 80. Geburtstag*, Vienna, 67–81.

Seyrig, H.

1940 Antiquités syriennes, in «Syria», 21, 113–22.

1952 Cachets achéménides, in G.C. Miles (ed.), *Archaeologica Orientalia in Memoriam Ernst Herzfeld*, New York, 195–202.

Shahbazi, A.S.

1975 *The Irano-Lycian Monuments. The Principal Antiquities of Xanthos and its Region as Evidence for Iranian Aspects of Achaemenid Lycia* (Institute of Achaemenid Research Publications; 2), Tehran.

Sidéra, I. (ed.)

2006 *La chasse. Pratiques sociales et symboliques*, Paris.

Simon, Z.

2019 Syennesis: Personenname, kein luwischer Herrschertitel, in «Nouvelles Assyriologiques Brèves et Utilitaires», 3, 122–3.

Simpson, S.J.

2005 The Royal Table, in J.E. Curtis and N. Tallis (eds.), *Forgotten Empire. The World of Ancient Persia* (exhibition catalogue), London, 104–31.

Skrzhinskaya, M.V.

2000 Xenophantos, an Artisan of Athens, in «Ancient Civilizations from Scythia to Siberia», 6, 3-4, 281–95.

Small, J.P.

1999 Time in Space: Narrative in Classical Art, in «The Art Bulletin», 81, 562–75.

SNG v. Aulock

O. Mørkholm, *Sylloge Nummorum Graecorum. Deutschland. Sammlung v. Aulock*, 11, Berlin, 1965.

Spawforth, A.J.S. (ed.)

2007a *The Court and Court Society in Ancient Monarchies*, Cambridge – New York.

Spawforth, A.J.S.

2007b The Court of Alexander the Great between Europe and Asia, in A.J.S. Spawforth (ed.), *The Court and Court Society in Ancient Monarchies*, Cambridge – New York, 82–120.

Starr, C.G.

1975 Greeks and Persians in the Fourth Century B.C. A Study in Cultural Contacts before Alexander. Part I, in «Iranica Antiqua», 11, 39–99.

1977 Greeks and Persians in the Fourth Century B.C. A Study in Cultural Contacts before Alexander. Part II. The Meeting of Two Cultures, in «Iranica Antiqua», 12, 49–115.

Stevenson, R.B.

1997 *Persica: Greek Writing about Persia in the Fourth Century BC*, Edinburgh.

Stockwell, S.

2010 Before Athens: Early Popular Government in Phoenician and Greek City States, in «Geopolitics, History, and International Relations», 2, 123–35.

Stronach, D.

1989 The Royal Garden at Pasargadae: Evolution and Legacy, in L. De Meyer and E. Haerinck (eds.), *Archaeologica Iranica et Orientalis: Miscellanea in Honorem Louis Vanden Berghe*, Vol. 1, Leuven, 475–502.

1990 The Garden as a Political Statement: Some Case Studies from the Near East in the First Millennium B.C., in «Bulletin of the Asia Institute», 4, 171–80.

2003 The Tomb at Arjan and the History of Southwestern Iran in the Early Sixth Century BCE, in N.F. Miller and K. Abdi (eds.), *Yeki Bud, Yeki Nabud. Essays on the Archaeology of Iran in Honor of William M. Sumner* (Monograph Series; 48), Los Angeles, 249–59.

2004 Notes on a Fortified Building and a "Yurt" in Adjacent Registers of the Arjan Bowl, in A. Sagona (ed.), *A View from the Highlands. Archaeological Studies in Honour of Charles Burney* (Ancient Near Eastern Studies. Suppl.; 12), Leuven, 711–28.

Strootman, R.

2014 *Courts and Elites in the Hellenistic Empires: The Near East After the Achaemenids, c. 330 to 30 BCE*, Edinburgh.

Stucky, R.A.

1993 Lykien – Karien - Phönizien. Kulturelle Kontakte zwischen Kleinasien und der Levante während der Perserherrschaft, in J. Borchhardt and G. Dobesch (eds.), *Akten des II. Internationalen Lykien-Symposions* (Wien, 1990), Vol. 1, Vienna, 261–8.

2005 *Das Eschmun-Heiligtum von Sidon: Architektur und Inschriften* (Antike Kunst. Beiheft; 19), Basel.

2009 Griechischer Marmor in der Levante. Zur Zeitstellung phönizischer Baureliefs und Architekturelemente aus Marmor, in R. Einicke *et al.* (eds.), *Zurück zum Gegenstand: Festschrift für Andreas E. Furtwängler* (Schriften des Zentrums für Archäologie und Kulturgeschichte des Schwarzmeerraumes; 16), Vol. 1, Langenweißbach, 7–13.

2012 Du marbre grec en Phénicie. Grandeur et décadence de Sidon aux époques perse et hellénistique, in «Comptes rendus des séances de l'Académie des Inscriptions et Belles-Lettres», 1177–203.

2016 Sculptures et éléments d'architecture de Sidon en marbre, in «Bulletin d'Archéologie et d'Architecture Libanaises», 16, 311–28.

Studniczka, F.

1905 Zu den Sarkophagen von Sidon, in «Revue Archéologique», 6, 31–54.

Stylianou, A.

2007 Der Sarkophag aus Amathous: als Beispiel kontaktinduzierten Wandels, in A. Stylianou and P. Schollmeyer, *Dynastensarkophage mit szenischen Reliefs aus Byblos und Zypern*, Vol. 2, Mainz, 1–188.

Summerer, L.

2005 Achämeniden am Schwarzen Meer: Bemerkungen zum spätarchaischen Marmorkopf aus Herakleia Pontike, in «Ancient Near Eastern Studies», 42, 231–52.

Szemethy, H.D.

2005 *Die Erwerbungsgeschichte des Heroons von Trysa. Ein Kapitel österreichisch-türkischer Kulturpolitik* (Wiener Forschungen zur Archäologie; 9), Vienna.

Tallis, N.

2005 Transport and Warfare, in J.E. Curtis and N. Tallis (eds.), *Forgotten Empire. The World of Ancient Persia* (exhibition catalogue), London, 210–35.

TAM

Tituli Asiae Minoris. Conlecti et Editi Auspiciis Caesareae Academiae Litterarum Vindoboniensis, Vienna, 1901– .

Tanner, J.

2013 Figuring out Death: Sculpture and Agency at the Mausoleum of Halicarnassus and the Tomb of the First Emperor of China, in L. Chua and M. Elliott (eds.), *Distributed Objects: Meaning and Mattering after Alfred Gell*, New York – Oxford, 58–87.

Taracha, P.

2011 The Iconographic Program of the Sculptures of Alacahöyük, in «Journal of Ancient Near Eastern Religions», 11, 132–47.

Tatton-Brown, V.

1997 *Ancient Cyprus*, 2nd ed., London.

TGF

A. Nauck (ed.), *Tragicorum Graecorum Fragmenta*, 2nd ed., Leipzig, 1889; Suppl. by B. Snell, Hildesheim, 1964.

Thackeray, H.St.J. (ed. and transl.)

1967 *Josephus*, Vol. 2. *The Jewish War, Books I-III*, London – Cambridge, MA (Reprint. Original edition: 1927).

Thomason, A.K.

2001 Representations of the North Syrian Landscape in Neo-Assyrian Art, in «Bulletin of the American Schools of Oriental Research», 323, 63–96.

2014 The Impact of the "Portable": Integrating "Minor Arts" into the Ancient Near Eastern Canon, in B.A. Brown and M.H. Feldman (eds.), *Critical Approaches to Ancient Near Eastern Art*, Boston – Berlin, 133–57.

Thonemann, P.

2009 Lycia, Athens and Amorges, in J. Ma, N. Papazarkadas and R. Parker (eds.), *Interpreting the Athenian Empire*, London, 167–94.

Todorov, V.

2011 The Thracian Tomb at Alexandrovo, SE Bulgaria: Preliminary Observations on its Painting Technique, in V. Nikolov, K. Bacvarov and H. Popov (eds.), *Interdisziplinäre Forschungen zum Kulturerbe auf der Balkanhalbinsel*, Sofia, 323–34.

Tofi, M.G.

2006 The Banquet Iconography in the Funerary Reliefs of Archaic and Classical Lycia, in K. Dörtlük *et al.* (eds.), *III. Uluslararası Likya Sempozyumu,* Sempozyum Bildirileri / *The IIIrd International Symposium on Lycia*. Symposium Proceedings (Antalya, 2005), Vol. 2, Antalya, 829–46.

Tolini, G.

2013 Les ressources de la Babylonie et la table de Darius le Grand (522-486), in C. Grandjean, C. Hugoniot and B. Lion (eds.), *Le banquet du monarque dans le monde antique*, Rennes – Tours, 145–62.

Tomasi Velli, S.

2007 *Le immagini e il tempo. Narrazione visiva, storia e allegoria tra Cinque e Seicento*, Pisa.

Tombul, M.

2004 Observations on the Çan Sarcophagus, in T. Korkut (ed.), *Anadolu'da Doğdu. 60. Yaşında Fahri Işık'a Armağan / Festschrift für Fahri Işık zum 60. Geburtstag*, Istanbul, 769–75.

Trinquier, J. and Vendries, C. (eds.)

2009 *Chasses antiques. Pratiques et représentations dans le monde gréco-romain (IIIe s. av.-IVe s. apr. J.-C.)*, Actes du colloque (Rennes, 2007), Rennes.

Tripodi, B.

1991 Il fregio della "Caccia" della II tomba reale di Vergina e le Cacce funerarie d'Oriente, in «Dialogues d'histoire ancienne», 17, 1, 143–209 (= Tripodi 1998, 53–97).

1994 Le cacce fatali di Archelao di Macedonia, in «Annali della Scuola Normale Superiore di Pisa. Classe di Lettere e Filosofia», s. III, 24, 491–510 (= Tripodi 1998, 35–52).

1998 *Cacce reali macedoni. Tra Alessandro I e Filippo V* (Pelorias; 3), Messina.

2000 Cacciatori e prede nell'Anabasi di Senofonte (Cacce d'Arabia), in «Annali della Scuola Normale Superiore di Pisa. Classe di Lettere e Filosofia», s. IV, 5, 149–58.

Tuck, S.L.

2005 The Origins of Roman Imperial Hunting Imagery: Domitian and the Redifinition of Virtus under the Principate, in «Greece & Rome», 52, 221–45.

Tuplin, C.

1987 The Administration of the Achaemenid Empire, in I. Carradice (ed.), *Coinage and Administration in the Athenian and Persian Empires*, Symposium (Oxford, 1986) (BAR International Series; 343), Oxford, 109–66.

1996 *Achaemenid Studies* (Historia. Einzelschriften; 99), Stuttgart.

2018 Paradise revisited, in S. Gondet and E. Haerinck (eds.), *L'Orient est son jardin. Hommage à Rémy Boucharlat* (Acta Iranica; 58), Leuven – Paris – Bristol, CT, 477–501

Uccellini, R.

2012 *L'arrivo di Achille a Sciro. Saggio di commento a Stazio Achilleide* 1, 1-396, Pisa.

Umholtz, G.

2002 Architraval Arrogance? Dedicatory Inscriptions in Greek Architecture of the Classical Period, in «Hesperia», 71, 261–93.

Vaag, L.E., Nørskov, V. and Lund, J.

2002 *The Maussolleion at Halikarnassos*, Vol. 7. *The Pottery. Ceramic Material and other Finds from Selected Contexts*, Højbjerg.

Vassileva, M.

2010 Achaemenid Interfaces: Thracian and Anatolian Representations of Elite Status, in «Bollettino di

Archeologia On Line», published online at http://bollettinodiarcheologiaonline.beniculturali.it/edizione-speciale-congresso-di-archeologia-a-i-a-c-2008/ [3 December 2019].

Vidal-Naquet, P.

1968 Le chasseur noir et l'origine de l'éphébie athénienne, in «Annales. Economies, sociétés, civilisations», 23, 947–64.

Vismara, N.

2005 Ritratti umani o teste divine nella monetazione arcaica della Lycia: Manifestazione della potestà d'imperio od espressione del sentimento religioso?, in «Transeuphratène», 30, 173–81.

von Blanckenhagen, P.H.

1957 Narration in Hellenistic and Roman Art, in «American Journal of Archaeology», 61, 78-83.

von den Driesch, A. and Pöllath, N.

2004 *Vor- und frühgeschichtliche Nutztierhaltung und Jagd auf Büyükkaya in Boğazköy-Ḫattuša, Zentralanatolien* (Boğazköy-Berichte; 7), Mainz.

von der Osten-Sacken, E.

1988 Der kleinasiatische Gott der Wildflur, in «Istanbuler Mitteilungen», 38, 63–81.

von Gall, H.

1974 Die Kopfbedeckung des persischen Ornats bei den Achämeniden, in «Archäologische Mitteilungen aus Iran», 7, 145–61.

1989 Zum Bildgehalt der graeco-persischen Grabstelen, in «Anatolia», 22, 143–65.

von Graeve, V.

1970 *Der Alexandersarkophag und seine Werkstatt* (Istanbuler Forschungen; 28), Berlin.

von Oppenheim, M.

1955 *Tell Halaf*, Vol. 3. *Die Bildwerke*, ed. by A. Moortgat, Berlin.

[n.d.] *Tell Halaf. A New Culture in Oldest Mesopotamia*, London – New York (Transl. of: *Der Tell Halaf, eine neue Kultur im ältesten Mesopotamien*, Leipzig, 1931).

Walker, S. and Hughes, M.

2010 Parian Marble in the Dynastic Monuments of Lycia and Caria, in D.U. Schilardi and D. Katsonopoulou (eds.), *Παρία λίθος: λατομεία, μάρμαρο και εργαστήρια γλυπτικής της Πάρου / Paria Lithos: Parian quarries, marble and workshops of sculpture*, Proceedings of the Conference (Paros, 1997), 2nd ed., Athens, 445–52.

Walker, S. and Matthews, K.J.

1997 The Marbles of the Mausoleum, in I. Jenkins and G.B. Waywell (eds.), *Sculptors and Sculpture of Caria and the Dodecanese*, London, 49–59.

Wallace, R.W.

2016 Redating Croesus: Herodotean Chronologies, and the Dates of the Earliest Coinages, in «Journal of Hellenic Studies», 136, 168–81.

Wallace-Hadrill, A.

2008 *Rome's Cultural Revolution*, Cambridge – New York.

Watanabe, C.E.

2018 Reading Ashurbanipal's Palace Reliefs: Methods of Presenting Visual Narratives, in G. Brereton (ed.), *I am Ashurbanipal: King of the World, King of Assyria* (exhibition catalogue), London, 212–33.

Waters, M.W.

2017 *Ctesias' Persica and its Near Eastern Context*, Madison, WI.

Waywell, G.B.

1978 *The Free-Standing Sculptures of the Mausoleum at Halicarnassus in the British Museum. A Catalogue*, London.

1993 The Ada, Zeus, and Idrieus Relief from Tegea in the British Museum, in O. Palagia and W. Coulson (eds.), *Sculpture from Arcadia and Laconia*, Proceedings of an International Conference (Athens, 1992), Oxford, 79–86.

Weber, M.

1947 *The Theory of Social and Economic Organization*, Glencoe, ILL.

Weinberg, J.P.

1976 Bemerkungen zum Problem "Der Vorhellenismus im Vorderen Orient", in «Klio», 58, 5–20.

Weiskopf, M.

1989 *The So-Called "Great Satraps' Revolt", 366-360 B.C. Concerning Local Instability in the Achaemenid Far West* (Historia. Einzelschriften; 63), Stuttgart.

Weller, M.E.

1970 The Procession on the Sarcophagus of the Mourning Women, in «California Studies in Classical Antiquity», 3, 219–27.

Wiegartz, H.

1968 Zu den Columnae Caelatae des jüngeren Artemision, in «Marburger Winckelmann-Programm», 41–73.

Wiesner, I.

1942 Zur orientalisierenden Periode der Mittelmeerkulturen, in «Archäologischer Anzeiger», 57, 391–460.

Williamson, C.

2014 Power of Place: Ruler, Landscape and Ritual Space at the Sanctuaries of Labraunda and Mamurt Kale in Asia Minor, in C. Moser and C. Feldman (eds.), *Locating the Sacred. Theoretical Approaches to the Emplacement of Religion*, Oxford – Oakville, 87–110.

Wilson, N.G. (ed. and transl.)

1997 *Aelian. Historical Miscellany*, Cambridge, MA – London.

Winter, F.

1912 *Der Alexandersarkophag aus Sidon* (Schriften der Wissenschaftlichen Gesellschaft in Straßburg; 15), Strasbourg.

Winter, I.J.

2010a Carved Ivory Furniture Panels from Nimrud: a Coherent Subgroup of the North Syrian Style, in Ead., *On Art in the Ancient Near East*, Vol. 1. *Of the First Millennium B.C.E.* (Culture and History of the Ancient Near East; 34), Leiden – Boston, 225–78 (= in «Metropolitan Museum Journal», 11, 1976, 25–52).

2010b North Syrian Ivories and Tell Halaf Reliefs: the Impact of Luxury Goods upon "Major" Arts, in Ead., *On Art in the Ancient Near East*, Vol. 1. *Of the First Millennium B.C.E.* (Culture and History of the Ancient Near East; 34), Leiden – Boston, 381–403 (= *Essays in Ancient Civilization Presented to Helene J. Kantor*, Chicago, 1989, 321–32).

Wiseman, D.J.

[1960] *Cylinder Seals of Western Asia. Illustrations Selected and Photographed by W. and B. Forman*, London.

Wolf, G.

2016 Vesting Walls, Displaying Structure, Crossing Cultures: Transmedial and Transmaterial Dynamics of Ornament, in G. Necipoğlu and A. Payne (eds.), *Histories of Ornament. From Global to Local*, Princeton – Woodstock, 96–105.

Woolmer, M.

2017 *A Short History of the Phoenicians*, London – New York.

Wroth, W.

1889 *Catalogue of Greek Coins. Pontus, Paphlagonia, Bithynia, and the Kingdom of Bosporus*, London.

Wu, X.

2014 "O young man … make known of what kind you are": Warfare, History, and Elite Ideology of the Achaemenid Persian Empire, in «Iranica Antiqua», 49, 209–99.

Younger, J.G.

1991 Evidence for Planning the Parthenon Frieze, in «American Journal of Archaeology», 95, 295.

Zahle, J.

1979 Lykische Felsgräber mit Reliefs aus dem 4. Jahrhundert v. Chr. Neue und alte Funde, in «Jahrbuch des Deutschen Archäologischen Instituts», 94, 245–346.

Zahle, J. and Kjeldsen, K.

2004 *The Maussolleion at Halikarnassos. Reports of the Danish Archaeological Expedition to Bodrum*, Vol. 6. *Subterranean and Pre-Maussollan Structures on the Site of the Maussolleion. The Finds from the Tomb Chamber of Maussollos* (Jutland Archaeological Society Publications; 15.6), Aarhus.

Zanardi, B.

1999 Projet dessiné et "patrons" dans le chantier de la peinture murale au Moyen Age, in «Revue de l'Art», 124, 43–55.

2002 *Giotto e Pietro Cavallini. La questione di Assisi e il cantiere medievale della pittura a fresco*, Milan.

Zanker, P.

1988 *The Power of Images in the Age of Augustus* (Jerome Lecture; 16), Ann Arbor (Transl. of: *Augustus und die Macht der Bilder*, Munich, 1987).

2002 La tomba come luogo di autorappresentazione, in Id., *Un'arte per l'impero. Funzione e intenzione delle immagini nel mondo romano* (Saggi di archeologia; 7), ed. by E. Polito, Milan, 133–56 (Transl. of: Bürgerliche Selbstdarstellung am Grab im römischen Kaiserreich, in H.-J. Schalles, H. von Hesberg and P. Zanker (eds.), *Die Römische Stadt im 2. Jahrhundert n. Chr. Der Funktionswandel des öffentlichen Raumes*, Cologne – Bonn, 1992, 339–58).

Zazoff, P.

1970 *Jagddarstellungen auf antiken Gemmen* (Die Jagd in der Kunst), Hamburg – Berlin.

Zervoudaki, E.A.

1968 Attische polychrome Reliefkeramik des späten 5. und des 4. Jahrhunderts v. Chr., in «Mitteilungen des Deutschen Archäologischen Instituts. Athenische Abteilung», 83, 1–88.

Zevi, F.

1996 Prigionieri troiani, in M.G. Picozzi and F. Carinci (eds.), *Studi in memoria di Lucia Guerrini. Vicino Oriente, Egeo - Grecia, Roma e mondo romano - Tradizione dell'antico e collezionismo di antichità* (Studi Miscellanei; 30), Rome, 115–27.

Zimmermann, M. (ed.)

2020 Das Xanthostal Lykiens in archaisch-klassischer Zeit. Eine archäologisch-historische Bestandsaufnahme (Die hellenistische Polis als Lebensform; 7), Göttingen.

Zimmermann, M.

2003 Hafen und Hinterland. Wege der Akkulturation an der lykischen Küste. Vorbericht über die Feldforschungen in den zentrallykischen Orten Tyberissos und Timiussa in den Jahren 1999-2001, mit einem Beitrag von Oliver Hülden, in «Istanbuler Mitteilungen», 53, 265–311.

Zupnick, I.L.

1962–3 The "Paratactic" Image in Egyptian Art, in «Art Journal», 22, 96–98.

Index of Passages

Inscriptions

Coins

General Index

As a rule I have used the Latin spelling of Greek names (e.g. Halicarnassus), except in cases where transliteration of the Greek is more common in the scholarly literature (e.g. Xanthos).

Milton Keynes UK
Ingram Content Group UK Ltd.
UKHW051915140124
435933UK00007B/55

9 781407 356389